Karen E[rown's]

Ita[ly]

Charming Bed & Breakfasts

Written by

NICOLE FRANCHINI

Illustrations by Elisabetta Franchini
Cover Painting by Jann Pollard

Karen Brown's Guides, San Mateo, California

Karen Brown Titles

Austria: Charming Inns & Itineraries
California: Charming Inns & Itineraries
England: Charming Bed & Breakfasts
England, Wales & Scotland: Charming Hotels & Itineraries
France: Charming Bed & Breakfasts
France: Charming Inns & Itineraries
Germany: Charming Inns & Itineraries
Ireland: Charming Inns & Itineraries
Italy: Charming Bed & Breakfasts
Italy: Charming Inns & Itineraries
Mexico: Charming Inns & Itineraries
Mid-Atlantic: Charming Inns & Itineraries
New England: Charming Inns & Itineraries
Pacific Northwest: Charming Inns & Itineraries
Portugal: Charming Inns & Itineraries
Spain: Charming Inns & Itineraries
Switzerland: Charming Inns & Itineraries

A Marina per
tutta la sua pazienza e amore

Cover painting: La Fenice, Positano.

Editors: Anthony Brown, Karen Brown, June Eveleigh Brown, Clare Brown, Nicole Franchini, Iris Sandilands, Lorena Aburto Ramirez.

Illustrations: Elisabetta Franchini.

Cover painting: Jann Pollard.

Web designer: Lynn Upthagrove.

Maps: Susanne Lau Alloway, Michael Fiegel.

Technical support: Michael Fiegel.

Distributed by Fodor's Travel Publications, Inc., 280 Park Avenue, New York, NY 10017, USA.

Distributed in Canada by Random House Canada, 2775 Matheson Boulevard. East, Mississanga, Ontario L4W 4P7, Canada, phone: (905) 624 0672, fax: (905) 624 6217.

Distributed in the United Kingdom, Ireland, and Europe by Random House UK, 20 Vauxhall Bridge Road, London, SW1V 2SA, England, phone: 44 20 7840 4000, fax: 44 20 7840 8406.

Distributed in Australia by Random House Australia, 20 Alfred Street, Milsons Point, Sydney NSW 2061, Australia, phone: 61 2 9954 9966, fax: 61 2 9954 4562.

Distributed in New Zealand by Random House New Zealand, 18 Poland Road, Glenfield, Auckland, New Zealand, phone: 64 9 444 7197, fax: 64 9 444 7524.

Distributed in South Africa by Random House South Africa, Endulani, East Wing, 5A Jubilee Road, Parktown 2193, South Africa, phone: 27 11 484 3538, fax: 27 11 484 6180.

A catalog record for this book is available from the British Library.

ISSN 1532-8775

Contents

ITALIAN FARMER'S POEM

Our memories are crouched
in silence within the belly of the earth.
Yet it takes only a day of sunshine,
an impromptu storm in the sky,
the perfume of freshly cut hay,
and immense fields dotted with golden haystacks,
to ignite in us the memories
of certain evenings spent full of gaiety.
It was at sunset when we used to join together
in the barn filled with grain
to celebrate the end of the harvest.
The "gioanassa" musician friend,
pressing the keys of his worn-out accordion,
succeeding in emitting the notes
to a waltz or mazurka, leaving us
drunk with happiness.
One more glass of wine before the night
fades into day.
One more toast to bid farewell
to another summer
that crossed the path of our youth.

Anonymous

Introduction

BED AND BREAKFAST ITALIAN-STYLE—*agriturismo*, as the bed and breakfast activity is called in Italy, has made great strides over the past decade or so. The bed and breakfast concept is relatively new to Italy, which followed suit after France and England originated the trend. Accommodations vary from simple farmhouses to noble country villas, all promising unique and memorable stays. "*Agritourism*" travel offers visitors to Italy the unique opportunity to observe daily life "up close" as a guest in someone's home. It is a superb way to interact directly with Italians, experiencing their way of life as a participant rather than just an observer. It offers a more intimate contact with the country's traditional ways of life than can ever be experienced during hotel stays. It is the alternative vacation for curious visitors who wish to explore the back roads of this fascinating country and depart with a more in-depth understanding of Italians and their lifestyles than they could possibly get from city stays and sightseeing alone. The individual who will benefit most from agritourism will have an open, inquiring mind and a certain amount of flexibility. In return, agritourism rewards the traveler with a feeling of being "at home" while abroad. The warm welcome and the value you'll receive will tempt you back to the agritourism track year after year.

HISTORY: *Agriturismo*, defined as agricultural tourism, was launched in 1965 as part of the Italian government's national agricultural department's plan to make it possible for farmers to supplement their declining income in two ways: through offering accommodation to tourists and through direct sales of their produce.

After World War II, during reconstruction and the subsequent industrial boom, Italians abandoned the countryside in droves in search of employment in urban centers, reducing the rural population from eight to three million people. Consequently, farmhouses, villas, and castles all across the country were neglected and went to ruin. This phenomenon also disrupted the centuries-old tradition of passing customs and property from one generation to the next.

The agritourism concept, with its government funding, proclaimed tax breaks, and an increasing need to escape congested cities, has lured proprietors back to their land and ancestral homes, providing them with the incentive to restore and preserve these historical buildings (with many treasures among them), without spoiling the natural landscape. An additional consequence is an improved distribution of tourism between Italy's overcrowded cities and the countryside, which serves to raise awareness of the many marvelous historical and cultural attractions, from art and architecture to scenery and cuisine, that await tourists off the beaten track.

Each of Italy's 20 regions participates in agritourism, with 9,000 properties offering accommodation and a full 60% of participants concentrated in Tuscany and Trentino-Alto Adige. This edition of *Italy: Charming Bed & Breakfasts* includes selections from 17 of Italy's regions. Unfortunately, this type of accommodation is still very scarce in Italy's southernmost regions such as Calabria, Basilicata, and Campania. We are happy to offer a new selection of bed and breakfasts in Sardinia and Sicily, where the activity is gradually taking hold.

In practical terms, agritourism was developed to stimulate the local economy in rural areas by encouraging the creation of accommodations (rooms, apartments, and campgrounds) in places where they had never before been available. In a more long-term and idealistic sense, it was hoped that the promotion and development of tourism in rural Italy would also bring about greater environmental awareness as well as rescue traditional folklore and customs, such as regional cuisine and handicrafts, from oblivion.

For Italians, agritourism facilitates an exchange of views between farmers and urbanites who come in search of a peaceful vacation surrounded by natural beauty. In fact, agritourism and the rich culture of the farmer represent for many an affirmation and validation of their heritage. Lamentably, some Italians still have a misconception of agritourism because it was originally organized as an exchange of very basic room and board for work in the fields. A wave of positive press in recent years and higher quality standards have helped enormously to change this outdated image.

Controversy also surrounds the fact that there are few established regulations governing this type of activity, and they differ greatly from one region to another. Consequently, few clearly defined quality standards exist and those participants with limited economic resources resent wealthier proprietors, whom they accuse of running accommodations resembling hotels more than farm stays. Moreover, it does not simplify matters that agritourism is organized in typical Italian fashion, with responsibility divided among three associations, each with its own regulations, politics, and guidelines. Each association produces a directory and may be contacted by writing to:

AGRITURIST, Corso Vittorio Emanuele 101, Rome 00168, Italy
Email: agritur@confagricoltura.it
TERRANOSTRA, Via 14 Maggio 43, Rome 00187, Italy
Email: terranostra@coldiretti.it
TURISMO VERDE, Via E. Franceschini 89, Rome 00155, Italy
Email: info@turismoverde.it

About Bed & Breakfasts

Our goal in this guide is to recommend outstanding places to stay. All of the bed and breakfasts featured have been visited and selected solely on their merits. Our judgments are made on charm, setting, cleanliness, and, above all, warmth of welcome. However (no matter how careful we are), sometimes we misjudge an establishment's merits, or the ownership changes, or unfortunately sometimes standards are not maintained. If you find a recommended place is not as we have indicated, please let us know, and accept our sincere apologies. The rates given are those quoted to us by the bed and breakfast: please use these figures as a guideline only and be certain to ask at the time of booking what the rates are and what they include.

Please visit the Karen Brown website (*www.karenbrown.com*) in conjunction with this book. It provides comments and discoveries from you, our readers, information on our latest finds, post-press updates, the opportunity to purchase goods and services that we recommend (airline tickets, rail tickets, car rental, travel insurance), and one-stop shopping for our guides and associated maps. Most of our favorite places to stay participate in our website where you can find color photos and direct links to their own websites and email.

ACCOMMODATION

The most important thing to remember as you consider an agritourism vacation is that you will be staying in the private homes of families who are obligated to run their bed and breakfasts without hiring additional personnel aside from family and farmhands. Do not forget that, in most cases, the primary responsibility of your hosts is the running of their farm, so, with a few exceptions, do not expect the service of a hotel. **Rooms may not necessarily always be cleaned daily** (sometimes linens are changed every three to seven days). Nevertheless, do anticipate a comfortable and enjoyable stay, because the proprietors will do everything possible to assure it. Cost will vary according to the level of service offered. (For the traveler's convenience, some city hotels have been included that are similar to a bed and breakfast in style, but go by the name *Albergo*, *Pensione*, or Hotel.)

ROOMS: Agritourism accommodations should not be thought of strictly in terms of the British or American definitions of bed and breakfasts, as in Italy they vary greatly according to each proprietor's interpretation of the concept. The bed and breakfasts in this guide have been described in terms of the criteria used in their selection—warmth of hospitality, historic character, charm of the home, scenery, proximity to sites of touristic interest, and quality of cuisine. Obviously, all of these attributes are not always found in each one. Most of them have an average of six rooms situated either within the family's home or in a separate guesthouse. Unless otherwise indicated in the bottom description details, all bedrooms have private bathrooms. Furthermore, we have tried to include only those with en-suite bathrooms, as our readers have requested (although for the budget traveler this may not be a priority). Having another bed or two added to a room at an extra charge for families with small children is usually not a problem. According to laws of the European Community, all new or renovated establishments must now offer facilities for the handicapped. It is best to enquire about the individual bed and breakfast's facilities when making reservations to see if they have accommodation that is suitable for you.

APARTMENTS: Since more and more travelers are learning that it is much more advantageous to stay for longer periods in one place (distances are so short between towns within a specific region), apartment-type accommodations with fully equipped kitchenettes are flourishing. And, in fact, jumping around from one place to another for one or two nights defeats the purpose of a more intimate contact with host families. Apartment accommodation is offered either within the farmhouse along with other units for two to six persons, or as a full house rental for six to ten persons. They are rented by the week from Saturday to Saturday throughout the country, the exception being during the low season. No meals are included unless the bed and breakfast also has a restaurant or makes special arrangements for breakfast. Rates include use of all facilities (unless otherwise indicated), linens, and utilities. There is usually an extra charge for heating and once-a-week cleaning. Average apartments for four persons run $800 weekly, a rate hotels cannot beat.

CREDIT CARDS

Whether or not an establishment accepts credit cards is indicated in the list of icons at the bottom of each description by the symbol ▨. We have also specified in the accommodation description which cards are accepted as follows: AX–American Express, MC–MasterCard, VS–Visa, or simply, all major.

FOOD

A highlight of the agritourism experience is without a doubt the food. Most travelers would agree that a bad meal is hard to find in Italy, a country world-famous for its culinary skills. In the countryside you'll be sampling the traditional regional recipes from which Italian cuisine originates. Since, whenever possible, all of the ingredients come directly from the farms where you'll be staying and are for the most part organically grown, you'll discover the flavorful difference freshness can make. A peek into the farm kitchen is likely to reveal pasta being rolled and cut the old-fashioned way—by hand. Many country cooks prefer to prepare food using traditional methods, and not rely on machines to speed up the process. Guests are usually welcomed into the kitchen for a look around and actual cooking lessons are becoming very popular.

MEALS OFFERED: Bed and breakfasts often serve only a Continental breakfast of coffee, tea, fresh breads, and jams. However, many prepare a buffet breakfast plus other meals and offer (sometimes require) half- or full-board plans. Half board means that breakfast and dinner are both included in the daily per-person room rate. Full board includes the room and all three meals and is less common, since most guests are out and about during the day, or prefer one lighter meal. Dinner is a hearty three-course meal, often shared at a common table with the host family, and normally does not include wine and other beverages. Menus might be set daily, according to the availability of fresh produce, or a limited choice may be given. Some farms have a fully-fledged restaurant serving non-guests as well. Travelers who are not guests at a particular bed and breakfast may take advantage of this opportunity to sample other fare (it is advisable to reserve in advance). When a listing offers dinner by arrangement we indicate this with the icon ▲. If a property has a restaurant, we use the icon ⅋ .

ENGLISH

English and other languages spoken at each bed and breakfast are indicated as follows: fluent, good, some, very little, and none. We would like to note, however, that this is just an indication, as the person who speaks English may or may not be there during your stay. In any case, it is helpful (not to mention rewarding) to have a few basic Italian phrases on hand. A phrase book or dictionary is indispensable. And when all else fails, the art of communicating with gestures is still very much alive in Italy!

FINDING YOUR BED AND BREAKFAST

At the back of the book is a key map of the whole of Italy plus 14 regional maps showing each recommended bed and breakfast's location. The pertinent regional map number is given at the right on the *top line* of each bed and breakfast's description. To make it easier for you, we have divided the location maps with grids of four parts—a, b, c, and d—as indicated on each map's key. Directions to help you find your destination are given after each bed and breakfast description. However, they are only a small clue, as it would be impossible to find the space to give more details, and to know from which direction the traveler is arriving. The beauty of many of these lodgings is that they are off the beaten track, but that characteristic may also make them very tricky to find. If you get lost, a common occurrence, first keep your sense of humor, then call the proprietors and/or ask locals at bars or gas stations for directions. It is important to know that addresses in the countryside often have no specific street name. <u>A common address consists of the farm name, sometimes a *localita* (an unincorporated area, or vicinity, frequently not found on a map and outside the actual town named), and the town name followed by the province abbreviated in parentheses. (The bed and breakfast is not necessarily **in** that town, but it serves as a post office reference</u>.) The *localita* can also be the name of the road where the bed and breakfast is located, to make things more confusing. We state the *localita* in the third line of the bed and breakfast details and many times that name is the map reference name as well. Ask to be faxed a detailed map from the B&B upon confirmation.

Detailed maps for the area in which you will be traveling are essential and we recommend purchasing them in advance of your trip, both to aid in the planning of your journey and to avoid spending vacation time searching for the appropriate maps. We like the *Michelin Tourist and Motoring Atlas of Italy,* a book of maps with a scale of 1:300,000 (1 cm = 3 km). We also find the regional Michelin maps very useful and we state which Michelin 400-series map each listings town is found on in the hotel description. We sell Michelin country maps, city maps, and regional green guides (sightseeing guides) in our website store at *www.karenbrown.com.* Another fine choice is the Touring Club Italiano map set, in an easy-to-read three-volume format divided into North, Central, and South. Even the smallest town or, better, *localita* is listed in the extensive index.

ICONS

We have introduced these icons in the guidebooks and more on our website, *www.karenbrown.com.* ❄ Air conditioning in rooms, ♨ Breakfast included in room rate, ⚷ Children welcome (age given on website), ♨ Cooking classes offered, 💳 Credit cards accepted, ☎ Direct-dial telephone in room, 🔺 Dinner served upon request, 🐕 Dogs by special request, 🛗 Elevator, 'X' Exercise room, 🎁 Gift shop, @ Internet access, ⵏ Mini-refrigerator in room, ⊘ Non-smoking rooms, P Parking available, 🍴 Restaurant, 🛎 Room Service, ♨ Sauna, ❀ Spa, ⚲ Swimming pool, ⟓ Tennis, 📺 TV in bedrooms, 💍 Wedding facilities, ♿ Wheelchair accessible, ⟂ Beach nearby, ⛩ Archealogical site nearby, ⴷ Golf course nearby, ⚇ Hiking trails nearby, 🏇 Horseback riding nearby, 🎿 Skiing nearby, ⚓ Water sports nearby. Icons allow us to provide additional information about our recommended properties. When using our website to supplement the guides, positioning the cursor over an icon will in many cases give you further details. For easy reference an icon key can be found on the last page of the book.

LENGTH OF STAY

Agritourism is most advantageous for those who have more than the standard one week to travel. Bed-and-breakfast accommodations take longer to reach, for one thing, and **often they are neither set up nor staffed for one-night stays**, which increase costs and defeat the purpose of this type of travel. There are numerous exceptions, however, especially in bed and breakfasts near cities, where overnight guests are accepted. It is noted in the description where a minimum stay is required.

RATES

Room rates vary according to size, location, season, and level of service. Rates range from $80 to $200 for two people with breakfast (indicated as B&B in the following descriptions) and from $75 to $150 per person for room with half board (dinner also included). **Approximate prices for two persons in a room for 2003 are indicated in euros and are by no means fixed**. Rates include tax and must be **confirmed at the time of reservation**. If breakfast is included this is indicated with the 🍺 icon. Because of its cost advantages, agritourism is an ideal choice for families. Children under eight are offered a discount and hosts will almost always add an extra bed for a small charge. There are some wonderful benefits to traveling in Italy in the low season (November to March with the exception of holidays). The considerable reduction in bed-and-breakfast rates combined with irresistibly low air fares makes for a super-economical vacation. And then, there's the ultimate advantage of not having to fight for space with crowds of other tourists. Italy is all yours!

Introduction–About Bed & Breakfasts

RESERVATIONS

Whether you plan to stay in several bed and breakfasts or decide to remain for an extended period in just one, **advance reservations are preferred**. Not only do many of the bed and breakfasts have only a few bedrooms available, but also they are often in private homes that are not prepared to take walk-in traffic. It is important to understand that once reservations for accommodation are confirmed, whether verbally by phone or in writing, you are under contract. This means that the proprietor is obligated to provide the accommodation that was promised and that you are obligated to pay for it. If you cannot, you are liable for a portion of the accommodation charges plus your deposit. As a courtesy to your hosts, in the case of cancellation, please advise them as soon as possible. Although some proprietors do not strictly enforce a cancellation policy, many, particularly the smaller properties in our book, simply cannot afford not to do so. Similarly, many airline tickets cannot be changed or refunded without penalty. We recommend insurance to cover these types of additional expenses arising from cancellation due to unforeseen circumstances. A link on our website (*www.karenbrown.com*) will connect you to a variety of insurance policies that can be purchased online.

When making your reservations, be sure to identify yourself as a "Karen Brown traveler." The hosts appreciate your visit, value their inclusion in our guide, and frequently tell us they take special care of our readers. We hear over and over again that the people who use our guides are such wonderful guests!

There are several ways to make a reservation:

Email: This is our preferred way of making a reservation. All hotels/bed and breakfasts featured on the Karen Brown website that also have email addresses have those addresses listed on their web pages (this information is constantly kept updated and correct). You can link directly to a property from its page on our website using its email hyperlink. (Always spell out the month as the Italians reverse the American month/day numbering system.)

Fax: If you have access to a fax machine, this is a very quick way to reach a bed and breakfast. If the place to stay has a fax, we have included the number in the description. Following is a reservation request form in Italian with an English translation. (See comment above about spelling out the month.)

Reservation Service: If you want to pay for the convenience of having the reservations made for you, pre-payments made, vouchers issued, and cars rented, any of the bed and breakfasts in this guide can be booked through **Hidden Treasures of Italy**, a booking service run by the author of this guide, Nicole Franchini. Further information can be found at the back this book.

Telephone: You can call the bed and breakfast directly, which is very efficient since you get an immediate response. (See page 25 for more information on the Italian telephone system.) The level of English spoken is given in each bed and breakfast description. To telephone Italy from the United States, dial 011 (the international code), then 39 (Italy's code), then the city area code (including the "0"), and then the telephone number. Italy is six hours ahead of New York.

BED & BEAKFAST or HOTEL NAME & ADDRESS — clearly printed or typed

Vi richiediamo la seguente prenotazione:
We would like to request the following reservation:

Numero delle camere o appartamenti _____ con bagno o doccia privata a _____ posti letti
Number of rooms or apartments with private bath or shower for how many persons

Numero di adulti _____   Numero di bambini _____Età _____
Number of adults   *Number of children and ages*

Numero delle camere o appartamenti _____ senza bagno o doccia privata _____ posti letti
Number of rooms or apartments without private bath or shower for how many persons

Numero di adulti _____   Numero di bambini _____ Età _____
Number of adults   *Number of children and ages*

Data di arrivo _____   Data di partenza _____
Date of arrival   *Date of departure*

      Tipo di servizio richesto:
      Type of meal plan requested:
      _____ Pernottamento con prima colazione (*B&B*)
      _____ Mezza Pensione (*Half Board—breakfast and dinner included*)
      _____ Pensione Completa (*Full Board—all three meals included*)

Costo giornaliero: B&B (two persons) _____
Daily rate   MP (Half Board—per person) _____
      PC (Full Board—per person) _____

Ci sono ulteriori sconti per bambini e quanto? _____
Is there a discount for children and what is it?

E necessario una caparra e quanto? _____
Is a deposit necessary and for how much?

Ringraziando anticipatamente per la gentile conferma, porgo cordiali saluti,
Thanking you in advance for your confirmation,

YOUR NAME, ADDRESS, TELEPHONE & FAX NUMBER — clearly printed or typed

REGIONAL FARM NAMES

The following names for farms, seen throughout this guide, vary from area to area.

azienda agricola—a general term meaning farm, not necessarily offering hospitality

borgo—a small stone-walled village, usually of medieval origins

casale, casolare—variations of farmhouse, deriving from "casa"

cascina and ca'—farmhouse in Piedmont, Lombardy, and Veneto

fattoria—typically a farm in Tuscany or Umbria

hof and maso—terms meaning house and farm in the northern mountain areas

locanda—historically a restaurant with rooms for travelers passing through on horseback

masseria—fortified farms in Apulia, Sicily

podere—land surrounding a farmhouse

poggio—literally describes the farm's position on a flat hilltop

stazzo—typical stone farmhouse in Sardinia

tenuta—estate

torre—tower

trattoria—a simple, family-run restaurant in cities and the countryside

villa and castello—usually former home of nobility and more elaborate in services

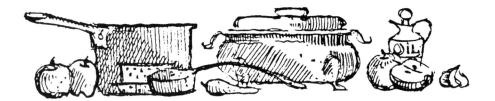

WHEN TO VISIT

Since agritourism accommodation is usually in permanent residences, many remain open all year, but most are open only from Easter through November. If you are traveling outside this time, however, it is worth a phone call to find out if the bed and breakfast will accommodate you anyway (at very affordable rates). The best time for agritourism is without a doubt during the spring and fall months, when nature is in its glory. You can enjoy the flowers blossoming in May, the *vendemia*, or grape harvest, at the end of September, the fall foliage in late October, or olive-oil production and truffle hunts in November and December. Southern Italy can be mild and pleasant in the winter, which might be perfect for travelers who like to feel they are the only tourists around. The vast majority of Italians vacation at the same time, during the month of August, Easter weekend, and Christmas, so these time periods are best avoided, if possible.

WHAT TO SEE AND DO

Bed and breakfast proprietors take pride in their farms and great pleasure in answering questions about their agricultural activity. They will often take time to explain and demonstrate procedures such as wine making, olive pressing, or cheese production. They are the best source for, and are happy to suggest, restaurants and local itineraries including historic sites, picturesque villages, and cultural activities. Your hosts feel responsible for entertaining their guests and many have added swimming pools or tennis courts if they are not already available in the vicinity. Other activities such as archery, fishing, hiking, and biking are sometimes offered. Horseback riding has made an enormous comeback and farms frequently have their own stables and organize lessons and/or excursions into the countryside. In most circumstances, a charge is made for these extra activities.

About Italy

The following pointers are given in alphabetical order, not in order of importance.

AIRFARE

Karen Brown's Guides have long recommended Auto Europe for their excellent car rental services and we are now very pleased to introduce their air travel division, Destination Europe, to our readers. An airline broker working with major American and European carriers, Destination Europe offers deeply discounted coach- and business-class fares to over 200 European gateway cities. It also gives Karen Brown travelers an additional 5% discount off its already highly competitive prices. You can make reservations online via our website, *www.karenbrown.com*, (click "Discount Airfares" on our home page) or by phone at (800) 223-5555. When phoning, be sure to use the Karen Brown ID number 99006187 to secure your discount on the lowest prices they currently offer.

BANKS–CURRENCY

Normal banking hours are Monday through Friday from 8:30 am to 1:30 pm and 3 to 4 pm, with some city banks now opening on Saturday mornings. Cash machines accepting U.S. bank cash cards and credit cards are widely distributed throughout Italy. An increasingly popular and convenient way to obtain foreign currency is simply to use your bankcard at an ATM machine. You pay a fixed fee for this but, depending on the amount you withdraw, it is usually less than the percentage-based fee charged to exchange currency or travelers' checks. *Cambio* signs outside and inside a bank indicate that it will exchange traveler's checks or give you cash from certain credit cards. Also privately run exchange offices are available in cities with more convenient hours and comparable rates. The euro (€) is now the official currency of most European Union countries, including Italy, and has completely replaced European national currencies. Visit our website (*www.karenbrown.com*) for an easy-to-use online currency converter.

CAR RENTAL

An International Driver's Permit is not necessary for renting a car as a tourist: a foreign driver's license is valid for driving throughout Italy. Readers frequently ask our advice on car rental companies. We use Auto Europe, a car rental broker that works with the major car rental companies to find the lowest possible price. They also offer motor homes and chauffeur services. Auto Europe's toll-free phone service from every European country connects you to their U.S.-based, 24-hour reservation center (ask for the card with European phone numbers to be sent to you). Auto Europe offers our readers a 5% discount, and occasionally free upgrades. Be sure to use the Karen Brown ID number 99006187 to receive your discount and any special offers. You can make your own reservations online via our website, *www.karenbrown.com* (select Auto Europe from the home page), or by phone (800-223-5555).

DRIVING

A car is a must for this type of travel—most bed and breakfasts are inaccessible by any other means of transportation. A car gives the traveler a great deal of independence (public transportation is frequently on strike in Italy), while providing the ideal means to explore the countryside thoroughly. It is best to reserve a vehicle and pre-pay by credit card before your departure to ensure the best rates possible.

Italy is not quite the "vehicular-free-for-all" you may have heard about, at least not outside big cities (particularly Rome, Florence, and Milan). When visiting Rome, it's advisable to do so at the beginning or end of your trip, before you pick up or after you drop off your car, and, by all means, avoid driving within the city. Italians have a different relationship with the basic rules of the road: common maneuvers include running stop lights and stop signs, triple-parking, driving at 100 mph on the highways, passing on the right, and backing up at missed highway exits. But once out of the city, you will find it relatively easy to reach your destination. Road directions are quite good in Italy and people are very willing to help.

DISTANCES: Distances are indicated in kilometers (one kilometer equals 0.621 mile), calculated roughly into miles by cutting the kilometer distance in half. Distances between towns are also indicated in orange alongside the roads on the Touring Club Italiano maps. Italy is a compact country and distances are relatively short, yet you will be amazed at how dramatically the scenery can change in an hour's drive.

GASOLINE: Gas prices in Italy are the highest in Europe, and Americans often suspect a mistake when their first fill-up comes to between $45 and $80 (most of it in taxes). Most stations now accept Visa credit cards, and the ERG stations accept American Express. Besides the AGIP stations on the autostrade, which are almost always open, gas stations observe the same hours as merchants, closing in the afternoon from 12:30 to 4 and in the evening at 7:30. Be careful not to get caught running on empty in the afternoon! Many stations have a self-service pump that operates on off-hours (€10 or €20 accepted).

MAPS: An above-average map of Italy is absolutely essential for this type of travel. The Touring Club Italiano maps, in an easy-to-read three-volume format divided into North, Central, and South, are a superior selection. Even the smallest town or, better, *localita* is indicated in the extensive index. Another fine choice is the Michelin series of maps. We use the Michelin 400 series maps (six regional maps) and the *Michelin Tourist and Motoring Atlas of Italy* (a book of maps). We sell these and regional Michelin green guides (sightseeing guides) in our website store at *www.karenbrown.com*.

ROADS: Names of roads in Italy are as follows:
Autostrada: a large, fast (and most direct) two- or three-lane tollway, marked by green signs bearing an "A" followed by the autostrada number. As you enter you receive a ticket from an automatic machine by pushing a red button. Payment is made at your exit point. If you lose your card, you will have to pay the equivalent amount of the distance from the beginning of the autostrada to your exit.
Superstrada: a one- or two-lane freeway between secondary cities marked by blue signs and given a number. Speed limit: 110 kph.

Strada Statale: a small one-lane road marked with S.S. followed by the road number. Speed limit: 90 kph.

Raccordo or *Tangenziale*: a ring road around main cities, connecting to an autostrada and city centers.

ROAD SIGNS: Yellow signs are for tourists and indicate sites of interest, hotels, and restaurants. Black-and-yellow signs indicate private companies and industries.

TOLLS: Tolls on Italian autostrade are quite steep, ranging from $15 to $28 for a three-hour stretch, but offering the fastest and most direct way to travel between cities. Fortunately for the agritourist, tollways are rarely necessary. However, if it suits your needs, a *Viacard*, or magnetic reusable card for tolls, is available in all tollway gas stations for €20–€50, or a MasterCard or Visa card can now be used in specified lanes (the lines for these automatic machines are always the shortest).

HOLIDAYS

It is very important to know Italian holidays because most museums, shops, and offices are closed. National holidays are listed below:

New Year's Day (January 1)

Epiphany (January 6)

Easter (and the following Monday)

Liberation Day (April 25)

Labor Day (May 1)

Assumption Day (August 15)

All Saints' Day (November 1)

Christmas (December 25)

Santo Stefano (December 26)

In addition to the national holidays, each town also has its own special holiday to honor its patron saint. Some of the major ones are listed below:

Bologna—St. Petronio (October 4)

Florence—St. John the Baptist (June 24)

Milan—St. Ambrose (December 7)

Palermo—Santa Rosalia (July 15)

Rome—St. Peter (June 29)

Venice—St. Mark (April 25)

The Vatican Museums have their own schedule and are closed on Sundays (rather than on Mondays as in the case with all other National museums), except the last Sunday of each month when admission is free of charge.

INFORMATION

Italian Government Travel Offices (ENIT) can offer general information on various regions and their cultural attractions. They cannot offer specific information on restaurants and accommodations. If you have access to the Internet, visit the Italian Tourist Board's websites: *www.italiantourism.com* or *www.enit.it*. Offices are located in:

Chicago: Italian Government Travel Office, 500 N. Michigan Ave., Suite 2240, Chicago, IL 60611 USA; tel: (312) 644-0996, fax: (312) 644-3019. (Mail, fax, or phone only.)

Los Angeles: Italian Government Travel Office, 12400 Wilshire Blvd., Suite 550, Los Angeles, CA 90025, USA; tel: (310) 820-1898, fax: (310) 820-6357.

New York: Italian Government Travel Office, 630 5th Ave., Suite 1565, New York, NY 10111, USA; tel: (212) 245-4822, fax: (212) 586-9249.

Montreal: Italian Government Travel Office, 1 Place Ville Marie, Suite 1914, Montreal, Quebec H3B 2C3, Canada; tel: (514) 866-7667, fax: (514) 392-1429.

London: Italian State Tourist Office, 1 Princes Street, London WIR 8AY, England; tel: (020) 7355-1557, fax: (020) 7493-6695.

Sydney: Italian Government Travel Office, Level 26, 44 Market Street, Sydney NSW 2000, Australia; tel: (61292) 621.666, fax: (61292) 625.677.

Rome: ENTE Nazionale Italiano per il Turismo (Italian Government Travel Office), Via Marghera, 2, Rome 00185, Italy, tel: (06) 49711, fax: (06) 4463379.

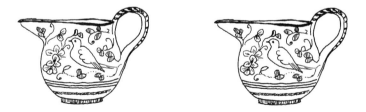

REGIONS

For reference, the 20 regions of Italy from north to south, with their capital cities in parentheses, are as follows:

NORTH—Valle d'Aosta (Aosta), Liguria (Genova), Piedmont (Torino), Friuli Venezia Giulia (Trieste), Trentino-Alto Adige (Trento & Bolzano), Lombardy (Milan), Veneto (Venice), and Emilia-Romagna (Bologna).

CENTRAL—Tuscany (Florence), Umbria (Perugia), Marches (Ancona), Lazio (Rome), Abruzzo (L'Aquila), and Molise (Campobasso).

SOUTH—Campania (Naples), Apulia (Bari), Calabria (Cantazaro), Basilicata (Potenza), Sicily (Palermo), and Sardinia (Cagliari).

SAFETY

If certain precautions are taken, most unfortunate incidents can be avoided. It is extremely helpful to keep copies of passports, tickets, and contents of your wallet in your room in case you need them. Pickpocketing most commonly occurs in cities on buses, train stations, crowded streets, or from passing motorbikes. WARNING: At tollway gas stations and snack bars, **always** lock your car and beware of gypsies and vendors who try to sell you stolen merchandise. This practice is most prevalent south of Rome. In general, **never** leave valuables or even luggage in the car. Also, **never** set down luggage even for a minute in train stations.

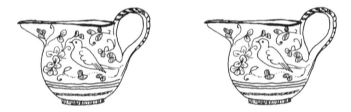

SHOPPING

Italy is a shopper's paradise. Not only are the stores brimming with tempting merchandise, but the displays are works of art, from the tiniest fruit market to the most chic boutique. Each region seems to specialize in something: in Venice hand-blown glass and handmade lace are popular; Milan is famous for its clothing and silk; Florence is a center for leather goods and gold jewelry; Rome is a fashion hub, where you can stroll the pedestrian shopping streets and browse in some of the world's most elegant shops boasting the latest designer creations. Religious items are also plentiful in Rome, particularly near St. Peter's Cathedral. Naples and the surrounding area (Capri, Ravello, and Positano) offer delightful coral jewelry and also a wonderful selection of ceramics. You will be enticed by the variety of products sold at the farms such as wines, virgin olive oil, jams and honeys, cheese, and salami, along with local artisans' handicrafts. NOTE: For reasons of financial control and the tax evasion problems in Italy, the law states that clients **must** leave commercial establishments with an official receipt in hand, in order to avoid fines.

For purchases over €155 an immediate cash refund of the tax amount is offered by the Italian government to non-residents of the EU. Goods must be purchased at an affiliated retail outlet with the "tax-free for tourists" sign. Ask for the store receipt **plus** the tax-free shopping receipt. At the airport go first to the customs office where they will examine the items purchased and stamp both receipts, and then to the "tax-free cash refund" point after passport control.

U.S. customs allows U.S. residents to bring in $400-worth of foreign goods duty-free, after which a straight 10% of the amount above $400 is levied. Two bottles of liquor are allowed. The import of fresh cheese or meat is strictly restricted unless it is vacuum-packed.

TELEPHONES

The Italian phone company (TELECOM) has been an object of ridicule, a source of frustration, and a subject of heated conversation since its inception. More modern systems are gradually being installed, and most areas have touch-tone phones now. Telephone numbers can have from four to eight digits, so don't be afraid of missing numbers. Cellular phones have saved the day (Italians wouldn't be caught dead without one) and are recognized by three-digit area codes beginning with 3. We have added cellphone numbers for the majority of properties in the guide. Cellphones offer the B&B owner great flexibility and give guests the advantage of always finding someone "home."

IMPORTANT NOTE: Since October 1998, all calls to Italy need to include the "0" (previously dropped) in the area code, whether calling from abroad, within Italy, or even within the same city, whereas cellphone numbers have dropped the "0" in all cases.

Dial 113 for emergencies of all kinds—24-hour service nationwide.

Dial 116 for Automobile Club for urgent breakdown assistance on the road.

Dial 118 for Ambulance service.

Remember that no warning is given when the time you've paid for in a public phone is about to expire (the line just goes dead), so put in plenty of change or a phone card. There are several types of phones (in various stages of modernization) in Italy:

Regular rotary phones in bars, restaurants, and many bed and breakfasts, which you can use *a scatti*, meaning you can pay the proprietor after the call is completed.

Bright-orange pay phones, as above with attached apparatus permitting insertion of a *scheda telefonica*, reusable magnetic cards worth €5–€25, or coins.

NOTE: Due to the ongoing modernization process of telephone lines, phone numbers are constantly being changed, making it sometimes very difficult to contact lodgings (many times they are listed under the owner's name instead of the lodging's name). A recording (in Italian) plays for only two months indicating the new number. If you are calling from the United States and your Italian is not up to par, we suggest you ask the overseas operator to contact the Italian operator for translation and assistance.

To call the United States from Italy, matters have been eased by the ongoing installation of the Country Direct System, whereby you can reach an American operator by dialing either 172-1011 for AT&T or 172-1022 for MCI. Be patient and wait the one to two minutes before a recording or U.S. operator comes through. Either a collect call or a credit-card call can then be placed. If you discover this system doesn't work from some smaller towns, dial 170 to place a collect call, or, in some cities, try dialing direct (from a *scatti* phone), using the international code 001 + area code + number.

Introduction–About Italy

TIPPING

Hotels: Service charges are normally included in four- and five-star hotels only. It is customary to leave a token tip for staff.

Restaurants: If a service charge is included, it will be indicated on the bill, otherwise 10–15% is standard tipping procedure.

Taxis: 10%.

TRAIN TRAVEL

Although a car is an absolute necessity to reach most bed and breakfasts, it is often convenient and time-saving to leave the car and take a train for day trips into the city. NOTE: Your ticket must be stamped with the time and date **before** you board the train; otherwise, you will be issued a €20 fine. Tickets are stamped at small and not very obvious yellow machines near the exits to the tracks. Unstamped tickets may be reimbursed with a 30% penalty. In order to avoid long lines at the station it is strongly advised that you purchase your ticket (including seat reservation) in advance through a local travel agency when you arrive in Italy or contact CIT train reservation service to book tickets from the States (tel: 800-248-8687). The IC and EC trains to major cities are the most efficient. If you plan to travel by train throughout Europe, you can research schedules and fares and purchase tickets and passes online. (Note that many special fares and passes are available only if purchased in the United States.) For information and the best possible fares, and to book tickets online, visit our website, *www.karenbrown.com*.

TRANSFERS INTO CITIES

Travelers from abroad normally arrive by plane in Milan, Rome, or Venice (sometimes Florence) and pick up their rental car at the airport. However, if your first destination is the city and you plan on picking up your car after your stay, approximate transfer rates are as follows:

MILAN

From Malpensa to city by taxi (70 min)	€75
From Malpensa to Cadorna station by train (every 30 min)	€8
From Malpensa to central station by bus (every 20 min)	€12
From Linate to city by taxi (20 min)	€31
From Linate to city by bus (every 20 min)	€3

ROME

From Da Vinci to city by train (every 30 min)	€8
From Da Vinci to city by taxi (45 min)	€47–62

VENICE

From airport to city by waterbus (1 hour)	€10
From airport to city by private waterbus	€77
From station to city by waterbus (15 min)	€5
From station to city by private waterbus	€72

FLORENCE

From airport to city by taxi (30 min)	€36

We wish you the best in your travels to Italy and always welcome your comments and suggestions. *Buon Viaggio!*

Places to Stay

A pleasant budget choice for touring the Veneto region is found just outside Padua at Casa Ciriani, a lovely pale-yellow rectangular-shaped home. Silvana and her mother Mariantonia thoroughly enjoy the international cultural exchange that their bed and breakfast business brings. Within the large family home where Silvana grew up are four simply decorated, homey guestrooms which have been left pretty much as they were, with the family's history displayed in photos, drawings, and other personal artifacts. Only one bedroom (with a small terrace) has an en-suite bathroom—a second has its bathroom just outside the door, while a double and single combination with one bathroom serves families well. Downstairs, guests have plenty of common space including a living room, dining room, and outside patio overlooking the garden and grounds where a breakfast of breads, cereals, fruit, cheese, and yogurt is served. Although the house is of newer construction, it has the feeling of an older home that has stood still in time. Your warm and friendly hostesses suggest local itineraries such as historic Padua, Vicenza, and Treviso, or nearby golf courses and thermal spas in Abano. Frequent trains for Venice leave from town (5 km) and take 50 minutes. *Directions:* From the north, exit from A4 at Padova Ovest and follow signs for Abano (10 km); coming from Bologna on A13, exit at Terme Euganee. Silvana gives guests a map.

CASA CIRIANI
Host: Silvana Ciriani
Via Guazzi 1
Abano Terme (PD) 35031, Italy
Tel & fax: (049) 715272, Cellphone: (368) 3779226
4 rooms, Double: €67–€77
Minimum nights required: 2
Open: all year
Other languages: good English
Region: Veneto, Michelin Map: 429
www.karenbrown.com/italy/ciriani.html

In the heart of the wine valley of Piedmont, just above the town of Alba, lies the stately, cream-colored villa belonging to Giuliana Pionzo, her doctor husband Giuseppe, and sons Andrea and Fabrizio—Cascina Reine's warm and gracious hosts. Accommodation is offered within the ivy-covered main house, each room finely decorated with antiques, paintings, and the family's personal objects. A suite consisting of a bedroom, sitting room with two extra beds, bath, kitchenette, and large terrace is ideal for a family of four. Other equally charming rooms and apartments (one with facilities for the handicapped) are on the ground and first floors of the adjoining wing, one with its own private terrace. A full breakfast is served either outside under big umbrellas overlooking the vineyards and woods or inside in the pristine dining room with vaulted ceilings. A swimming pool is set in the best possible position taking in views over the city, soft hillsides, river valley, and distant Alps. Alba boasts some of the finest restaurants in Italy and is also famous for its regional wines and prized truffle festival. The Giacosas have a piece of land dedicated to experimentation (with Torino University) of the cultivation of truffles. *Directions:* From Alba's center follow signs for Barbaresco and Mango. Halfway up the hill on a large curve, watch for a small yellow sign indicating a gravel road on the left and then the wrought-iron gates of the property at the end of the road.

CASCINA REINE (VILLA LA MERIDIANA)
Host: Giacosa family
Localita: Altavilla 9
Alba (CN) 12051, Italy
Tel & fax: (0173) 440112, Cellphone: (338) 4606527
5 rooms, Double: €75
4 apartments: €85 daily
Minimum nights required: 2
Open: all year, Other languages: good English
Region: Piedmont, Michelin Map: 429
www.karenbrown.com/italy/cascinareine.html

I Ginepri opened its doors in 2001 after owners Maria Carla and Roberto decided to make their weekend getaway from Rome into a permanent home and business. The main stone farmhouse offers three guest bedrooms and there are ten additional suites in an extended one-story building adjacent to the home. Along with a large glassed-in multi-use room, the three buildings form a U around an open brick square where guests are received. Rooms upstairs within the home are appointed with more traditional country antiques, while the panoramic suites are more contemporary in design. Each bi-level suite (with independent entrance from the outside) has a loft bedroom and tiled sitting room with single sofa bed and kitchenette below, and each looks out over the 100-acre wooded property with swimming pool. A long list of amenities includes satellite TV, Internet outlet, mini bar, room service, and air conditioning. For extra-special pampering, indulge in the super suite with its own sauna and sunken hydrojet bath for four persons. A local chef prepares excellent meals either on the terrace looking up to the hilltop village of Allerona, or in the intimate dining room. Breakfast is served in the side bar area. Nearby are the thermal waters of San Casciano. *Directions:* Leave the AI autostrada at Orvieto and follow signs from Orvieto center until the turnoff for Allerona. After Allerona Scalo, pass the town of Allerona and follow signs for I Ginepri (5 km).

❄ ☕ ☕ CREDIT ☎ 🏠 ⓨ P ⑪ ≈ 🖼 🐾 ♿

I GINEPRI   New
Hosts: Maria Carla Maggiore & Roberto Marcotulli
Localita: Spiagge
Allerona (TR) 05020, Italy
Tel: (0763) 628020, Fax: (0763) 629548
13 rooms, Double: €73–€130
Open: all year, Credit cards: all major
Other languages: fluent English
Region: Umbria, Michelin Map: 430
www.karenbrown.com/italy/iginepri.html

Seven kilometers from historic Bergamo and within easy reach of beautiful Lakes Como, Iseo, and Garda is the home of the region's agritourist president, Gianantonio Ardizzone. On the property, next to the recently constructed residence where he and his family live, is a sprawling 15th-century farmhouse and barn quad complex of the type known in Lombardy as a cascina. Installed within the cascina are five guest apartments, each including one or two bedrooms, bathroom, and kitchen (though breakfast is served). The apartments are furnished modestly but comfortably, with a decidedly rustic ambiance. The cascina is nestled in pretty surroundings, looking onto the small town of Nese and backing onto the green hills where well-tended riding horses are kept. Gianantonio delights in showing guests his hobbies—a collection of antique farm tools, fruit orchard, and ostrich breeding—and wife Lalla takes care of guests' daily requests including dinner with prior confirmation. The Grumello offers self-catering, conveniently located accommodation and outstanding value. Your hosts are exceptionally helpful and sincerely warm. *Directions:* Exit from the A4 autostrada at Bergamo and follow signs for Alzano Lombardo, Valle Seriana. Exit at Alzano after 6 km and follow hospital signs; go straight on for Nese and turn left on Via Grumello after 300 meters.

CASCINA GRUMELLO
Host: Gianantonio Ardizzone family
Localita: Fraz. Nese
Alzano Lombardo (BG) 24022, Italy
Tel: (035) 510060, Cellphone: (338) 8608708
Fax: (035) 738703
5 apartments: €52 double B&B
Open: all year, Credit cards: VS
Other languages: some English
Region: Lombardy, Michelin Map: 428
www.karenbrown.com/italy/grumello.html

The southernmost tip of Umbria bordering Lazio offers a myriad of interesting sights and villages and La Palombara makes a splendid base for exploring them. Signor Baldoni, a yacht broker from Rome, bought the 400-year-old country home made of stone with its six bedrooms mainly for entertaining. He enjoys the place so much that he had the one-story barn converted into a guesthouse with two apartments each containing three bedrooms, three bathrooms, and living room with kitchenette. They can be rented out either as separate rooms or as an entire apartment. The decor, as in his own home, is one of refined elegance, full of precious antiques and leather sofas. Coordinated color schemes in rooms follow through in English wallpaper, fabrics, and bathroom tiles. The large windows look out to the surrounding garden, which includes a rose garden with many rare species. Guests relax poolside in the summer and are treated to a very special candlelit dinner prepared by the Count himself in the enormous veranda overlooking the pool. Gourmet cooking lessons mingled with the Count's advice on proper service and etiquette (bon ton) are an exceptional experience. In the colder months, afternoon tea is served before the fire in the Count's lovely home. *Directions:* Before entering Amelia, take a right for Acquasparta and drive for 4.5 km, staying left for Castel dell'Aquila. 2.5 km after Sambucetole turn left for Collicello. La Palombara is the first house on the left.

LA PALOMBARA
Owner: Count Giancarlo Baldoni
Strada di Collicello 34
Amelia (TR) 05022, Italy
Tel: (0744) 988373, Fax: (0744) 988414
6 rooms, Double: €110, 2 apartments: €1,450 weekly
Minimum nights required: 3
Open: May 23 to Jan 10
Other languages: good English
Michelin Map: 430
www.karenbrown.com/italy/palombara.html

One of the most attractive features of Florence is that its surrounding countryside hugs the city limits, giving the possibility of staying in the tranquil foothills of Chianti. In the nearby village of Antella warm hosts Azelio and Luisa have completely restored their part of an enormous estate divided into three 14th-century villas. Besides the hosts' private quarters, the downstairs area includes a large living/dining room, main kitchen, and kitchenette for guests' use during the day. The vaulted antique cantina below displays an enviable collection of reserve wines. Up a steep flight of stairs are the four well-appointed guestrooms, all with superb views over countryside all the way to Brunelleschi's cupola. Three regular doubles are individually decorated with country antiques and one has a hydrojet bathtub. The real treat is the large junior suite with its high wood-beamed mansard ceilings, sitting area, and canopy bed. Originally the outdoor loggia, it retains its columns and seven windows looking out to both sides of the property. A country breakfast is served either in the dining room or in the garden. Do not miss a chance to sample one of Luisa's delectable Tuscan meals or, better yet, cooking lessons. *Directions:* Exit from the A1 at Firenze Sud and turn immediately right for Grassina. Go back under the autostrada and at the roundabout turn for Antella. After town continue straight on Via Montisoni for 1 km. 12 km from the center of Florence.

VILLA IL COLLE   *New*
Hosts: Azelio & Luisa Pierattoni
Via Montisoni 45
Antella–Florence (FI) 50011, Italy
Tel & fax: (055) 621822, Cellphone: (347) 8778178
4 rooms, Double: €120–€150
Minimum nights required: 2
Open: all year, Credit cards: MC, VS
Other languages: good English
Region: Tuscany, Michelin Map: 430
www.karenbrown.com/italy/colle.html

Borgo Argenina has all the elements of a "bestseller" bed and breakfast: the perfect location in the heart of Chianti surrounded by vineyards, very comfortable accommodation in an ancient stone farmhouse, glorious countryside views, and, above all, Elena, the Borgo Argenina's gregarious hostess. She left behind a successful fashion business in Milan and bought an entire abandoned village, restoring two of the stone houses for herself and the bed and breakfast. She chose the best artisans in the area and literally worked with them to create the house of her dreams. Everything from painting stenciled borders in rooms through restoring furniture to sewing quilted bedspreads is executed exclusively by Elena herself. The downstairs living rooms and breakfast room are beautifully done in rich cream and soft yellows that complement perfectly the brick-vaulted ceilings and terra-cotta floors. Elena is up at dawn baking cakes for breakfast accompanied by classical music. Every little detail has been attended to in the pink-and-blue bedrooms adorned with white eyelet curtains, patchwork quilts, and dried flower arrangements. Three bedrooms have kitchen facilities and across the way is a very comfortable three-bedroom, independent house. *Directions:* Follow S.S.408 from Siena for Montevarchi and after 15 km turn off to the right at Monti. Just before Monti and S. Marcellina there is a sign on the right for Argenina.

BORGO ARGENINA
Host: Elena Nappa
Localita: Argenina-Monti, Gaiole in Chianti (SI) 53013, Italy
Tel: (0577) 747117, Fax: (0577) 747228
7 rooms, Double: €150–€200
1 house: €450 daily B&B (4 people)
Minimum nights required: 2
Open: all year, Credit cards: all major
Other languages: good English
Region: Tuscany, Michelin Map: 430
www.karenbrown.com/italy/argenina.html

Fabrizio and Bianca, the Milanese hosts originally from this part of Umbria, restored their inherited La Fornace farmhouse, situated in the very desirable touring location of Assisi, with their guests' comfort foremost in mind. With careful attention to detail, six comfortable apartments and two guestrooms were fashioned within the three stone houses. Each apartment has one or two bedrooms, bathroom, fully equipped kitchenette, and eating area. Interesting decorating touches such as parts of antique iron gates hung over beds, terra-cotta and white ceramic tiles in the immaculate bathrooms, and antique armoires give the accommodations a polished country flavor. Le Pannocchie includes a corner fireplace, while Papaveri looks out over the flat cornfields up to magnificent Assisi and the Subasio Mountains beyond. Ambra Cascioli and a young couple look after guests when the owners are away. A small dining room has been created on the ground floor, next to the 18th-century wood oven, for breakfast and healthy light meals upon request. At guests' request guided tours are arranged to Umbria's top sights. Besides a lovely swimming pool for guests, bikes, ping-pong, and games for children are on hand. *Directions:* From Perugia-Spoleto highway 75, exit at Ospedalicchio on route 147, turn left for Tordibetto after the bridge, then right for Assisi and follow signs for La Fornace.

PODERE LA FORNACE
Hosts: Bianca & Fabrizio Feliciani
Via Ombrosa 3, Assisi, Tordibetto di (PG) 06081, Italy
Tel: (075) 8019537 or (338) 9902903, Fax: (075) 8019630
2 rooms, Double: €67–€80
6 apartments: €535–€1,030 weekly, €85– €160 daily
Minimum nights required: 3
Closed: Jan & Feb, Credit cards: all major
Other languages: good English
Region: Umbria, Michelin Map: 430
www.karenbrown.com/italy/lafornace.html

The delightful Malvarina farm with its charming, country-style accommodations, excellent local cuisine, warm and congenial host family, and ideal location has been a long-time favorite of our readers. Just outside town, yet immersed in lush green vegetation at the foot of the Subasio Mountains, the property is comprised of the 15th-century stone farmhouse where the family lives and four independent cottages (converted barn and stalls) divided into bedrooms and suites with en-suite bathrooms, plus three apartments with kitchenettes for two to four persons. Casa Angelo has several bedrooms plus a sweet breakfast room with a corner fireplace and cupboards filled with colorful Deruta ceramics. Great care has obviously been taken in the decor of rooms, using Mamma's family's heirloom furniture. The old wine cellar has been cleverly converted into a cool and spacious taverna dining room with long wooden tables for dining en famille if not out on the veranda terrace. Cooking classes are very popular here. A collection of antique farm tools and brass pots cover walls near the enormous fireplace. Horses are available for three- to seven-day trekking trips into the scenic national park just beyond the house, led by gregarious host, Claudio. A welcome feature is a swimming pool. *Directions:* Exit at Capodacqua from the Perugia-Spello route 75. Turn right then left on Via Massera (Radio Subasio sign) and follow the road up to Malvarina.

MALVARINA
Host: Claudio Fabrizi family
Localita: Malvarina 32, Assisi-Capodacqua (PG) 06080, Italy
Tel & fax: (075) 8064280
10 rooms, Double: €93
3 apartments: €98 daily (2 persons)
Minimum nights required: 3
Open: all year, Credit cards: MC, VS
Other languages: some English
Region: Umbria, Michelin Map: 430
www.karenbrown.com/italy/malvarina.html

After many years of traveling to Italy at any opportunity, Jennie and Alan left England to move to Tuscany and fell in love immediately with Villa Mimosa, a rustic, 18th-century home with a shady front courtyard facing the village street and the church. They have created three sweet bedrooms and one attic mansard suite for four persons, each with a different theme and with lovely mountain views. A cozy sitting room and a library with grand piano are reserved upstairs for guests and decorated with the Pratts' own antiques imported from England. Jennie and Alan delight in sharing their passion for this part of the country known as Lunigiana (very near the Cinque Terre coastal area and one hour from both Parma and Lucca) and give their guests lots of personal attention, while making them feel right at home. Guests are treated to breakfast on the terrace overlooking the pretty garden and swimming pool with the Apennine Mountains as a backdrop and delight in Jennie's creative cuisine based on fresh garden vegetables and local recipes. Tea and homemade cakes are served in the shady garden. *Directions:* Leave the A15 autostrada (Parma-La Spezia) at Pontremoli from the north or Aulla from the south and head north alongside the autostrada to Villafranca, then Bagnone. Enter town through the gateway and turn left at Via N. Quartieri. Go uphill to Corlaga (3 km) and the villa is on the right, before the church.

VILLA MIMOSA
Hosts: Jennie & Alan Pratt
Localita: Corlaga
Bagnone (MS) 54021, Italy
Tel & fax: (0187) 427022, Cellphone: (335) 6264657
4 rooms, Double: €83–€100
Open: all year
Other languages: fluent English
Region: Tuscany, Michelin Map: 430
www.karenbrown.com/italy/mimosa.html

In the heart of the Veneto region, south of Vicenza, you find the Castello winery and estate, a handsome 15th-century villa watching proudly over the sweet town of Barbarano Vicentino and the home of the Marinoni family for the past century. Signora Elda, along with her two young children, Lorenzo and Maddalena, carries on the tradition. The large walled courtyard with manicured Renaissance garden is bordered by the family's home, the guesthouse (originally the farmer's quarters), and converted barn, where concerts and banquets are organized. A lovely courtyard overlooks the family's expansive vineyards from which top-quality (D.O.C.G.) red wines are produced. The independent two-story guesthouse overlooking the garden can be rented out as one house or divided into three apartments. It has recently been renovated, with each apartment having one or two bedrooms, bathroom, and kitchenette with sitting area, and decorated simply but pleasantly with the family's furnishings. This is an excellent, economical base from which to visit the Veneto region. It's an easy drive to Padua and Venice where you may opt to leave your car and take the train. *Directions:* Exit from the A4 at Vicenza Est towards Noventa Vicentino, then Barbarano Vicentino. Follow signs to Castello (20 km).

IL CASTELLO
Host: Elda Marinoni family
Via Castello 6
Barbarano Vicentino (VI) 36021, Italy
Tel: (0444) 886055, Fax: (0444) 777140
3 apartments: €23–€26 daily (per person)
Minimum nights required: 7
Open: all year
Other languages: good English
Region: Veneto, Michelin Map: 429
www.karenbrown.com/italy/ilcastello.html

The area around the city of Alba is true wine country, where vineyards cover every possible inch of land, making Chianti look almost barren! Giovanna, an independent producer of wine, admirably manages her grandparents' farm and bed and breakfast single-handedly. This year she has taken on the ultimate challenge of producing Barbaresco, Barbera, and Docetto wines right on the premises. Giovanna loves welcoming travelers who are looking for a home away from home, wholesome foods, and the simple pleasures of country life. The mustard-colored house backed by striped hillsides has a separate guest entrance. A large informal living room filled with books and local wine itineraries includes a corner kitchen where guests sit at a table for a self-service breakfast. Upstairs are the three country-style bedrooms. The pink room has twin beds and a vineyard view while the green and blue rooms have queen beds. They each have new, immaculate bathrooms, and are decorated with grandmother's lace curtains, old photographs, brass beds, and patchwork quilts. Four similarly appointed apartments are situated on two floors in a wing off the main house. *Directions:* From Alba (6 km) follow signs for Barbaresco. Before town at the sign for Tre Stelle, look for Cascina delle Rose on the left. From Asti follow signs for Alba-Barbaresco-Treiso. After Barbaresco, on the road towards Alba, watch for Tre Stelle and the B&B on the right.

CASCINA DELLE ROSE
Host: Giovanna Rizzolio
Localita: Tre Stelle, Barbaresco (CN) 12050, Italy
Tel: (0173) 638292, Fax: (0173) 638322
3 rooms, Double: €85
4 apartments: €520–€990 weekly, €85–€160 daily
Minimum nights required: 4
Open: all year, Credit cards: all major
Other languages: good English, French, German
Region: Piedmont, Michelin Map: 428
www.karenbrown.com/italy/dellerose.html

La Casa Sola is just that—an ancient villa standing alone atop a hill on a gorgeous 400-acre vineyard estate in the heart of Chianti. The gracious proprietors and hosts, assisted by the local Regoli family, produce prestigious Chianti Classico Riserva, Supertuscan-Montarsiccio, and extra-virgin olive oil of the highest quality. There are six large guest apartments on two floors of a rose-covered stone farmhouse down the road from the main villa. All the apartments consist of a living room, kitchen, bedrooms, and baths, with private entrances and garden (with flowers to match the color scheme of each apartment!). The apartments (numbers 3 and 5 being the loveliest) are furnished stylishly with selected country antiques, and details such as botanical prints hung with bows, eyelet curtains, fresh flowers, and a bottle of wine are welcome touches. Number 5, for up to eight people, is the most spacious, with four bedrooms, a fireplace, and magnificent views over the Barberino Valley and cypress woods. Il Capanno in the converted barn is a delightful "nest" for honeymooners. An inviting swimming pool overlooks the valley surrounding the main villa. Wine-cellar visits with wine tasting are organized once a week and marked hiking trails lead guests through picture-perfect landscapes. *Directions:* Leave the Florence-Siena superstrada at San Donato in Poggio. 1.5 km after San Donato at the church, turn right for Cortine/Casa Sola, and drive for 2.5 km.

FATTORIA CASA SOLA
Host: Count Gambaro family
Localita: Cortine, Barberino Val d'Elsa (FI) 50021, Italy
Tel: (055) 8075028, Fax: (055) 8059194
6 apartments: €800–€1,799 weekly (Jul & Aug)
€70–€84 daily (2 people)
Heating and cleaning extra, Minimum nights required: 2
Open: all year, Credit cards: MC, VS
Other languages: good English
Region: Tuscany, Michelin Map: 430
www.karenbrown.com/italy/fattoriacasasola.html

Strategically positioned midway between Siena and Florence sits the square stone farmhouse with cupola (actually one of the bedrooms!) dating to 1700 owned by Gianni and Cristina, a couple who have dedicated their lives to the equestrian arts. The Paretaio appeals particularly to visitors with a passion for horseback riding, for the de Marchis offer everything from basic riding lessons to dressage training, and day outings through the gorgeous surrounding countryside. In fact, the Paretaio is recognized as one of the top riding "ranches" in Tuscany, with more than 30 horses. On the ground floor is a rustic living room with country antiques, comfy sofas, and piano enhanced by a vaulted brick ceiling and worn terra-cotta floors, off which are two bedrooms. Upstairs, the main gathering area is the dining room, which features a massive fireplace and a seemingly endless wooden table. This room gives access to more bedrooms, each decorated with touches such as dried flowers, white lace curtains, and, of course, equestrian prints. A vast collection of over 300 pieces with an equestrian theme is displayed about the home. Il Paretaio also organizes courses in Italian and is an excellent base for touring the heart of Tuscany. The swimming pool gives splendid views over olive groves and vineyards. *Directions:* Head south from Barberino on route 2 and after 2 km take the second right-hand turnoff for San Filippo. Continue on 1.5 km of dirt road to the house.

IL PARETAIO
Hosts: Cristina & Giovanni de Marchi
Localita: San Filippo, Barberino Val d'Elsa (FI) 50021, Italy
Tel: (055) 8059218
Cellphone: (338) 7379626 or (339) 2314419
Fax: (055) 8059231
8 rooms, Double: €47–€98, 2 apartments: €360–€1,200 weekly
Per person half board: €62–€70
Open: all year, Other languages: good English, French
Region: Tuscany, Michelin Map: 430
www.karenbrown.com/italy/ilparetaio.html

The Mulino dell'Argenna, a 16th-century grain mill miraculously transformed into an elegant bed and breakfast, sits among woods along a small river. Cordial hosts Liliana and Pierpaolo took on the challenging project of restoring the stone mill. Pierpaolo provided the know-how, having worked on the restoration of homes for many years, while Liliana added style in her careful selection of antiques, rich fabrics, and soft color schemes in rooms. Five romantic bedrooms accessed from the exterior of the mill have smart travertine bathrooms and many hotel amenities, with special touches such as embroidered linen sheets. The charm of the home comes not only from its decor, but also from its being built on different levels with terraces, balconies, and archways leading to private corners. Behind the house is an enchanting apartment, Il Mulinetto, a miniature version of the mill, with a one-bedroom loft, kitchenette, and terrace. Breakfast is served in bedrooms, out on private patios, or in the intimate dining room. Divine four-course gourmet dinners are accompanied by a very selective list of wines. Close to the house is a large swimming pool with Jacuzzi. This property lends itself well for a full-house rental by the week for family reunions. *Directions:* Exit at S. Donato from the Florence-Siena highway and after S. Donato town follow signs for Castellina. Turn left at the second road after the La Ripa sign at km 9.5. (Located near the main road.)

RELAIS MULINO DELL'ARGENNA
Hosts: Liliana Cajelli & Pierpaolo Porcù
Localita: S. Silvestro 17, Barberino Val d'Elsa (FI) 50021, Italy
Tel: (055) 8072354, Cellphone: (339) 3906277
Fax: (055) 8072310
5 rooms, Double: €114–€145
1 apartment: €1,291–€1,808 weekly
Minimum nights required: 3, Closed: Nov to Mar
Other languages: very little English
Region: Tuscany, Michelin Map: 430
www.karenbrown.com/italy/dellargenna.html

When the Caccettas and three other families purchased the 250-acre property more than 20 years ago, they were true pioneers in agritourism. After many years of restoring both the land and historic 16th-century hunting lodge, today they have a self-sufficient organic farm producing top-quality Chianti, white and rosé wines, grappa, and virgin olive oil, and the first in Europe to be awarded certification (Uni En Iso) as an "organic agricultural park" for quality level and comprehensive agritouristic activity. Spacious guestrooms are divided between the main house, with two suites and three bedrooms, and an adjacent house. All are decorated with care and attention to detail using lovely family antiques, which blend in perfectly with the overall refined ambiance. The very cozy common rooms include a living room with fireplace and stone walls, card room, small bar area, and dining rooms where breakfast and dinner are served. During the warmer months a buffet breakfast and dinner are served outside under the pergola overlooking deep woods. A set four-course dinner consists of traditional Tuscan recipes using primarily fresh vegetables and aromatic herbs. A swimming pool, grass tennis courts, many hiking trails, and horseback riding at a nearby stables are all available. *Directions:* From the Siena-Florence highway, exit at San Donato, drive to Tavarnelle then Barberino, and turn right at the La Spinosa sign. Take the dirt road to the very end.

LA SPINOSA
Hosts: Caccetta, Presezzi, Ossola & Videsott families
Via Le Masse 8, Barberino Val d'Elsa (FI) 50021, Italy
Tel: (055) 8075413, Fax: (055) 8066214
9 rooms, Double: €150–€180
Per person half board: €105–€120
Minimum nights required: 2
Open: Mar to Nov, Credit cards: MC, VS
Other languages: good English
Region: Tuscany, Michelin Map: 430
www.karenbrown.com/italy/laspinosa.html

The Bad Dreikirchen is situated up in the Dolomite foothills with an enchanting view over a lush green valley and distant snowcapped mountain peaks. The young and energetic Wodenegg family works diligently at making guests feel at home in their lovely residence and at running the busy restaurant, which serves typical local meals to non-guest patrons as well as guests since it shares the site of a unique historical monument—Le Tre Chiese, three curious, attached, miniature medieval churches. This unique inn is accessible only by taxi or Jeep, or on foot. An exhilarating half-hour hike takes you up to the typical mountain-style chalet with long wood balconies in front. The most charming rooms are those in the older section, entirely wood-paneled, with fluffy comforters and old-fashioned washbasins. The rambling house has several common areas for guests as well as a swimming pool. This is truly an incredible spot, near the Siusi Alps and Val Gardena where some of the best climbing in Europe can be found. *Directions:* Exit from the Bolzano-Brennero autostrada A22 at Chiusa, cross the river, and take S.S.12 south to Ponte Gardena. Take the road on the right up to Barbian and call the hotel from the village for a pickup by Jeep (€12).

BAD DREIKIRCHEN
Hosts: Annette & Matthias Wodenegg family
San Giacomo 6
Barbian (BZ) 39040, Italy
Tel: (0471) 650055, Fax: (0471) 650044
30 rooms, Double: €84–€106
Open: May 20 to Oct 26, Credit cards: MC, VS
Other languages: good English
Region: Trentino-Alto Adige, Michelin Map: 429
www.karenbrown.com/italy/baddreikirchen.html

Just 2 kilometers outside Barolo in the area where the famous wine is produced sits the long, rectangular, antique-pink-colored farmhouse of Raffaella Pittatore, passed down to her from her grandparents. After years of working for a major tour-operator company and living in many parts of the world, she came back home with her young son to impart her hospitality experience to her own guests. She is a natural hostess, friendly and accommodating, with a joie de vivre that is truly refreshing. One year after opening, four bedrooms in the attached former barn were added to those already existing on the first floor. These are simply furnished with the family's country furniture and each has its own bathroom. One also has a kitchenette. Downstairs you find an informal living room and breakfast room with original brick ceilings and floors. Guests can use the kitchen or barbecue, if desired, and breakfast is served out on the front patio in fine weather. Although there are no particular views, the crossroads location is convenient for touring this beautiful Piedmont wine country, the price economical, and the hospitality exceptional. Raffaella has put together many interesting local itineraries including quaint villages, castles, wine museums, and vineyards. *Directions:* From Alba (10 km) follow signs for Barolo and at the turnoff stay to the left. The entrance to the bed and breakfast is on the right-hand side of the road just at this fork.

IL GIOCO DELL'OCA
Host: Raffaella Pittatore
Via Crosia 46
Barolo (CN) 12060, Italy
Tel & fax: (0173) 56206, Cellphone: (338) 5999426
6 rooms, Double: €60–€70
1 apartment
Open: Mar to Dec, Credit cards: MC, VS
Other languages: very little English
Region: Piedmont, Michelin Map: 428
www.karenbrown.com/italy/ilgioco.html

The expansive Pomurlo farm, home to the congenial Minghelli family, covers 370 acres of hills, woods, and open fields and is an excellent base for touring Umbria. A winding dirt road leads to the typical stone house, which contains a restaurant featuring organically grown, farm-fresh specialties. An antique cupboard and old farm implements on the walls enhance the rustic setting. A nearby converted stall houses two adorable independent rooms looking out over the lake. Other guestrooms and apartments are found in two large hilltop homes commanding a breathtaking view of the entire valley with its grazing herds of longhorn cattle. The main house, a 12th-century tower fortress where the inn's personable hostess Daniela resides, accommodates guests in three additional suites of rooms. Breakfast fixings are provided in rooms. The acquisition of the neighboring property has resulted in a center (Le Casette) offering more service—two stone farmhouses containing several other rooms and a restaurant around a large swimming pool. Comfortable and cheerful, all rooms are decorated with wrought-iron beds, colorful bedspreads, and typical regional country antiques. Activities such as tennis, soccer, and mountain biking are available. *Directions:* The farm is conveniently located near the Rome-Florence autostrada. Take the Orvieto exit from the A1 and follow signs for Todi, not for Baschi. On route S.S.448 turn right at the sign for Pomurlo.

POMURLO VECCHIO
Hosts: Lazzaro Minghelli & family
Localita: Lago di Corbara
Baschi (TR) 05023, Italy
Tel: (0744) 950190 or 957645, Fax: (0744) 950500
25 rooms, Double: €100–€120*
*Includes breakfast & dinner
Open: all year, Credit cards: MC, VS
Other languages: some English, French
Region: Umbria, Michelin Map: 430
www.karenbrown.com/italy/pomurlovecchio.html

Only 30 kilometers from Milan, the Cascina Caremma is the pure definition of agritourism: a 100-acre working farm using strictly organic methods; offering accommodation and meals using more than 80% of the farm's own produce; and organizing lessons in organic production and the agri-ecosystem. It is also part of the Ticino River Park reserve, which can be explored by bike, horse, or foot only. This typical northern Italian cascina is a quad formation with large inner courtyard lined with multi-coloured houses, stalls, and barns. Over the years the very involved hosts have vastly improved the comfort level and charming decor of the accommodations, which are situated in two colorful side-by-side houses. Cheerful, air-conditioned rooms have country furnishings and beamed ceilings and are accented with matching floral curtains and bedspreads. The delightful downstairs dining rooms maintain their true country flavor with antiques, fireplace, and ancient wood-burning oven. On weekends people from the city come to enjoy the excellent, wholesome meals. Scheduled to open in April 2003 is a "well-being" center with indoor pool, steam bath, sauna, and yoga classes. Within reach are Malpensa airport and the lake region. *Directions:* Exit the A7 (Genova-Milano) at Binasco and head towards Casorate Primo, Besate. In the small town of Besate look for a sign for the cascina and follow this country road for 2 km to the farm.

CASCINA CAREMMA
Host: Gabriele Corti family
Strada per il Ticino
Besate (MI) 20080, Italy
Tel & fax: (02) 9050020, Cellphone: (348) 3049848
14 rooms, Double: €52–€82
Per person half board: €47, Dinner Thur to Sun only
Closed: Aug, Credit cards: all major
Other languages: good English
Region: Lombardy, Michelin Map: 428
www.karenbrown.com/italy/cascinacaremma.html

The Locanda, a pale-yellow and brick house dating from 1830, sits on the border between Tuscany and Umbria and is an excellent base from which to explore this rich countryside. The villa's dining room features a vaulted ceiling in toast-colored brick, an enormous fireplace, French windows opening out to the flower garden, and antiques including a cupboard adorned with the family's blue-and-white china. The upstairs quarters are reserved primarily for guests, and contain five comfortable rooms all off one hallway and an inviting sitting room and library. The cozy bedrooms have mansard ceilings, armoires, lovely linens, and washbasins. Additional guestrooms are located on the ground floor of the converted barn between the house and a small garden, where a swimming pool has been added. These are more spacious, private, and modern in decor. Cordial hostess Palmira assists with local itineraries. Excellent regional fare including divine vegetarian dishes with local produce is prepared by local cooks. Siena is only 45 kilometers away, and the quaint medieval and Renaissance villages of Pienza, Montepulciano, and Montalcino are close by. *Directions:* Exit from the Rome-Florence autostrada at Val di Chiana. Head toward Bettolle, then bear right toward Siena. Follow signs for La Bandita.

LOCANDA LA BANDITA
Host: Palmira Fiorini
Via Bandita 72
Bettolle–Sinalunga (SI) 53040, Italy
Tel & fax: (0577) 624649, Cellphone: (335) 6945920
8 rooms, Double: €95–€105
No dinner Tue
Open: Mar to Dec, Credit cards: all major
Other languages: good English
Region: Tuscany, Michelin Map: 430
www.karenbrown.com/italy/locandalabandita.html

The vast Torre Burchio property is immersed in 1,500 acres of wooded wildlife preserve where wild boar, deer, hare, and pheasant abound. Seemingly far away from "civilization," this Italian version of a ranch offers a relaxing holiday in close touch with nature, while still being in reach of Umbria's top sights. The reception, restaurant, and six guest bedrooms are within the main 18th-century farmhouse, which maintains the ambiance of the original hunting lodge with hunting trophies on the walls, large open fireplace, cozy living room, and library. The upstairs breakfast room, from which the bedrooms lead, is lined with colourful Deruta ceramics. An additional ten bedrooms are found in a single-story house just across from the lodge, while the very comfortable apartments with kitchenettes are in a beautifully restored 230-year-old stone house with inner courtyard 4 kilometers down the road. The rooms and apartments are very nicely appointed with antiques, pretty fabrics, paintings, and large bathrooms, and have telephones and televisions. Guests gather in the busy restaurant in the evening for a hearty meal based on organic products from the farm. Many activities such as cooking classes, horseback-riding weeks, and sports are available. *Directions:* 20 km from either Perugia or Assisi. From the center of Bettona, follow signs for 5 Cerri-Torre Burchio and follow the dirt road through the woods for 5 km to the main house/reception.

TORRE BURCHIO
Host: Alvaro Sfascia
Bettona (PG) 06084, Italy
Tel: (075) 9885017, Cellphone: (336) 544647
Fax: (075) 987150
16 rooms, Double: €101, 13 apartments: €672–€878 weekly
Minimum nights required: 3
Closed: Jan, Credit cards: all major
Other languages: good English
Region: Umbria, Michelin Map: 430
www.karenbrown.com/italy/burchio.html

Luisa and Sergio left their fashion business in Parma and settled in this peaceful and varied landscape 3 kilometers from the coast after the stone farmhouse was extensively restored. The stylish, impeccable home clearly reflects the personalities of the warm and reserved hosts who themselves tastefully designed both the exterior and interiors. Each of the four corner bedrooms upstairs has its own large private terrace and beautiful floral-tiled bathroom and all offer beds made with linen sheets and splendid views over fruit orchards and olive groves to the sea. While the hosts occupy the cupola, guests have a separate entrance to the upstairs rooms, giving utmost privacy to all. Common areas include the living room and open kitchen with large arched window and doors looking out to the surrounding garden. An ample fresh country breakfast with cakes all prepared by Luisa is served here. A separate cottage next to the main house offers a double room and beamed living room with stone fireplace and kitchen, and a second apartment is available within another cottage. Day trips include Elba Island, Volterra and San Gimignano, Lucca, Siena, private beaches, Etruscan itineraries, visits to the wine estates of Bolgheri, and biking in the nearby nature park. *Directions:* Exit from Aurelia on route 1 at Bibbona and turn left. Pass through La California and turn left for Bibbona. Podere Le Mezzelune is before town, well marked to the left. Pisa airport is 40 km away.

PODERE LE MEZZELUNE
Hosts: Luisa & Sergio Chiesa
Via Mezzelune 126, Bibbona (LI) 57020, Italy
Tel: (0586) 670266, Cellphone: (329) 3712287
Fax: (0586) 671814
4 rooms, Double: €145–€176
2 apartments: €155– €176 daily
Open: all year, Credit cards: MC, VS
Other languages: none
Region: Tuscany, Michelin Map: 430
www.karenbrown.com/italy/mezzelune.html

This guide includes some small urban hotels for the convenience of travelers who would like to do some metropolitan sightseeing. For some reason, the city of Bologna is often bypassed by visitors, despite its rich past, beautiful historic center, arcaded streets, and elegant shops. Cristina, Serena, and Mauro Orsi, the owners of the splendid, four-star Hotel Corona d'Oro, mentioned in another of our guides, Italy: Charming Inns & Itineraries, own two other centrally located, smaller hotels: the Orologio and the Commercianti. Just steps away from Bologna's main piazza and Basilica you find the nicely renovated Orologio, so-called because it looks onto city hall with its clock tower. The reception desk on the ground floor leads upstairs to a large sitting and dining room where a buffet breakfast is served. From this level there is an elevator up to the guestrooms with their lovely antiques, fabric walls, and white and gray marble bathrooms. The elegantly decorated rooms have all amenities and most have views of the square. Bicycles are available free of charge to our readers to visit the city's historical center and main monuments. The owners also organize personalized cooking classes, tickets for special events, and private tours of Bologna and surrounding cities. *Directions:* Located in the heart of the old city. Private garage facilities are available upon reservation (restricted traffic in historical center).

❄ ☕ ⬇ 💳 ☎ 🐴 🏃 Y P 🚭 🖼

HOTEL OROLOGIO
Host: Cristina Orsi family
Via IV Novembre 10
Bologna 40123, Italy
Tel: (051) 231253, Fax: (051) 260552
41 rooms, Double: €191–€298
Open: all year, Credit cards: all major
Other languages: good English
Region: Emilia-Romagna, Michelin Map: 429
www.karenbrown.com/italy/hotelorologio.html

Bolsena is a quaint, ancient village 18 kilometers from Orvieto right on picturesque Lake Bolsena with its small ports and two islands. Marco Zammarano, with his long hotelier experience in Rome, took over the family's 60-acre hillside farm property just above town and opened lovely bed and breakfast accommodation offering utter tranquillity. The main stone farmhouse holds eleven beamed bedrooms each with en-suite bathroom, satellite TV, and fridge, simply but comfortably appointed with a mix of wicker furniture and country antiques. All but two have gorgeous views over the manicured garden and swimming pool out to the lake. Four bedrooms are found farther up the wooded road in another house with its own swimming pool and there is a third residence with an additional twelve rooms. Two apartments are available within yet another separate building. A restaurant for guests only has an ample outside terrace enjoying sunsets over the lake and takes advantage of ingredients fresh from the farm. Here you have the convenience of being near town and many interesting Etruscan sights, while the lake itself offers many activities including a fascinating boat ride to the small, historic island of Bisentina. *Directions:* Exit the A1 autostrada at Orvieto and follow signs for Bolsena. Just before town at the Trattoria Castagneta, turn right up to La Riserva. Shuttle service is available from the Rome airport or Orvieto train station.

LA RISERVA MONTEBELLO
Host: Marco Zammarano
Strada Orvietana km 3
Bolsena (VT) 01023, Italy
Tel & fax: (0761) 798965, Cellphone: (335) 5310801
27 rooms, Double: €87–€108, 2 apartments
Per person half board: €65–€81
Closed: Jan, Credit cards: all major
Other languages: good English
Region: Lazio, Michelin Map: 430
www.karenbrown.com/italy/lariservamontebello.html

A pocket of absolutely stunning yet unexplored countryside is the Oltrepo Pavese hills, 60 kilometers south of Milan. It is predominantly wine country producing top-quality Cortese, Pinot, Barbera, and Riesling. Less than an hour's drive away is the Alba/Asti wine region of Piedmont and the Italian Riviera. Also not to be missed are historic Pavia and its celebrated Certosa monastery. What better place to set up a home base than the Castello di Stefanago where a variety of accommodation is available. The two Baruffaldi brothers work diligently at producing wines and maintaining their 600-acre property. The 12th-century castle perched atop a hill and taking in spectacular views houses the host families and five lovely suites for two to five persons. Each has a bathroom, living area, and kitchenette and has been decorated appropriately with the family's period furniture. Below the castle on the road is a restored farmhouse, La Boatta, where a restaurant and six sweet double bedrooms are available. Each room has coordinated Provençal-patterned spreads and curtains with spotless bathrooms. Typical meals are served using fresh produce directly from the farm. (Fixed menu €24, not including beverages.) *Directions:* Exit at Bereguardo/Pavia on the A7 autostrada from Milan. Follow it to Pavia (skirting the city) and then Casteggio. Drive on to Montebello-Borgo Priolo-Fortunago-Stefanago and up the long drive to the castle.

CASTELLO DI STEFANAGO
Hosts: Patrizia & Giacomo Baruffaldi
Borgo Priolo (PV) 27040, Italy
Tel: (0383) 875227 or 875413, Fax: (0383) 875644
11 rooms, Double: €58–€135
Open: Feb to Nov, Credit cards: all major
Other languages: some English
Region: Lombardy, Michelin Map: 428
www.karenbrown.com/italy/stefanago.html

The prestigious Monsignor della Casa property extending over 600 acres is a true country resort with all the trimmings in the beautiful area north of Florence called Mugello. This is the land from which such masters as Giotto, Cimabue, and Fra Angelico came and was the actual home of 15th-century writer and Vatican secretary, della Casa, whose portrait hangs in Washington's National Gallery. The Marzi family meticulously restored a cluster of six stone farmhouses on the vast estate next to their own stately villa. The refined bi-level apartments exude pure Tuscan charm and can accommodate from two to six guests. Two individual villas, each with private swimming pool, can take a group of eight to sixteen. The finest linens and fabrics were chosen to accent exposed stone walls, brick floors, and wood-beamed ceilings. After a day of touring you return to a variety of activities for every age and interest—biking, hiking, or horseback riding in the nearby woods, golf, swimming in one of two pools, tennis, volleyball, and children's playground. An elegantly rustic restaurant and wine bar serves guests in the evening with cordial host Alessio making sure nothing is overlooked. The "wellness center" offers sauna, steam bath, Jacuzzi, and other services. Indulge! *Directions:* From Borgo San Lorenzo follow signs for Faenza. Just after the turnoff for Scarperia (golf course) turn right for Mucciano, coming first to the resort (3 km total). 27 km from Florence.

MONSIGNOR DELLA CASA   New
Host: Alessio Marzi family
Via di Mucciano 16
Borgo San Lorenzo (FI) 50032, Italy
Tel: (055) 840821, Fax: (055) 8408240
21 apartments: €140–€540 daily, 2 villas: €4,460 weekly
Minimum nights required: 2, 7 in high season
Open: all year, Credit cards: MC, VS
Other languages: good English
Region: Tuscany, Michelin Map: 430
www.karenbrown.com/italy/monsignor.html

Just off the busy road that connects the major towns of Umbria—Perugia, Assisi, Spoleto, and Todi—is the elegant country house Giulia, which has been in the Petrucci family since its 14th-century origins. Later additions were built on to the main stone villa, one of which Signora Caterina has opened up to guests. Time seems to have stood still in the six bedrooms, all but one with en-suite bathroom, and filled with grandmother Giulia's lovely antique wrought-iron beds, armoires, and period paintings. They are divided among three floors, accessed by a steep stone staircase, the largest having a ceiling fresco depicting the local landscape. Another room with handicapped facilities has been added on the ground floor. Breakfast is served either in the chandeliered dining room upstairs, with Oriental carpets, lace curtains, and a large fireplace, or under the oak trees in the front garden during the warmer months. The family's frescoed quarters can be rented out for weddings. Part of the barn has been converted into two independent units for up to four persons, including a fully equipped kitchenette. Although the large swimming pool overlooks a rather barren field and the distant main road, it is a welcome respite after a full day of touring, which guests do a lot of from this convenient location. *Directions:* Just off the Perugia-Spoleto route 75 between Trevi and Campello.

CASA GIULIA
Host: Caterina Alessandrini Petrucci
Via S.S. Flaminia km 140.1
Bovara di Trevi (PG) 06039, Italy
Tel: (0742) 78257, Cellphone: (335) 8037147
Fax: (0742) 381632
7 rooms, Double: €91–€98, 2 apartments: €455–€707 weekly
Open: all year, Credit cards: all major
Other languages: some English
Region: Umbria, Michelin Map: 430
www.karenbrown.com/italy/casagiulia.html

The town of Brisighella is a gem and comes to life during the first half of July with its annual Medieval Festival when games of the period are re-enacted, and medieval music, literature, and dance are produced. Locals attire themselves in appropriate costume and torches illuminate the village's narrow streets nightly for the occasion. Just out of town sits the sweet farmhouse of Ettore (a former architect) and Adriana, with its 25 acres of organically cultivated vineyards and orchards. Guests can learn about the production of the hosts' excellent Sangiovese and Chardonnay wines. The renovated barn next to their small brick house holds two guestrooms and a rustic dining area with exposed beams and a large fireplace where guests gather for typical Romagna-style meals. A third bedroom is within their own home and the ex-barn provides two cozy apartments for two to five people. Breakfast is served out on the covered terrace overlooking a quiet valley lined with vineyards. Rooms are decorated with simple country furnishings. The atmosphere is casual and the value excellent. "Must sees" are the mosaics in Ravenna, Bologna's historical center, and the international ceramic museum in Faenza. La Torre golf club is 8 kilometers away. *Directions:* Take the Faenza exit from the A14 between Bologna and Rimini, following signs for Brisighella or Florence. At town turn left for Terme/Modigliana. Il Palazzo is the fourth house on the left after the Hotel Terme.

IL PALAZZO
Host: Ettore Matarese family
Via Baccagnano 11, Brisighella (RA) 48013, Italy
Tel & fax: (0546) 80338
3 rooms, Double: €62–€68
2 apartments: €100–€130 daily
Minimum nights required: 3
Open: Mar to Oct, Credit cards: all major
Other languages: good English
Region: Emilia-Romagna, Michelin Map: 429
www.karenbrown.com/italy/ilpalazzo.html

Tall cypress trees protect the cluster of ancient stone farmhouses making up the idyllic Iesolana property, situated atop 300 acres of cascading vineyards, olive groves, and sunflowers, with 360 degrees of breathtaking Tuscan views. After years of meticulous restoration of the three ochre-stained houses, eight high-level apartments are offered, most with private terraces. Apartments have from one to four bedrooms and are elegantly appointed with rustic furnishings, country fabrics, and modern kitchens and baths that harmonize beautifully with the cool stone floors and original wood-beamed ceilings. Among the many services available are individual telephones, satellite TV, barbecue facilities, swimming pool, and mountain bikes for leisurely rides. The impeccable landscape is studded with terra-cotta pots overflowing with brightly colored geraniums. A recent addition is the fabulously restored barn, which now hosts a stylish wine bar for tastings of Iesolana's own wines, oils, and honey. Breakfast and dinners of regional cuisine are also served in the comfortable restaurant with outdoor seating as an option. A state-of-the-art meeting room is available for groups. Centrally located for day trips to Siena, Florence, and Rome, this is the perfect spot for relaxing and exploring. *Directions:* Leave the A1 at Valdarno for Montevarchi, Bucine (8 km). From town follow signs up to Iesolana, passing over a stone bridge (2 km) to the end of the road.

BORGO IESOLANA
Host: Giovanni Toscano
Localita: Iesolana
Bucine (AR) 52021, Italy
Tel: (055) 992988, Fax: (055) 992879
8 apartments: €120–€180 daily, €900–€2,700 weekly
Minimum nights required: 2
Open: all year, Credit cards: all major
Other languages: good English
Region: Tuscany, Michelin Map: 430
www.karenbrown.com/italy/iesolana.html

The Ripolina farm property is a vast 500-acre farm comprised of several different brick farmhouses. Self-catering apartments (two for up to ten people) and individual guest bedrooms are divided among five farmhouses dotting the soft hills of the property. Two very charmingly authentic apartments are found within the Pieve di Piana, a cluster of houses grouped around an ancient church with bell tower dating to 900. The richly historic Pieve sits on a hill and enjoys panoramic views of vineyards and fields of grain and sunflowers extending for as far as the eye can see. Hostess and owner Laura Cresti resides in the house called S. Ferdinando where one of the double rooms is offered with a separate entrance. The other five rooms are next door in the Ripoli house, each being individually appointed with appropriate country local antiques from the late 1800s. Walls are painted in warm earth colors and the upstairs loggia, a typical open porch with four large arched windows, has been enclosed and transformed into the breakfast room. A full country breakfast buffet includes fresh coffee cakes, fruit, cereals, yogurt, and even cheeses and breads. This is strikingly beautiful countryside and the territory is chock-full of hilltowns to explore. Bicycles are available for guests. *Directions:* From Siena (25 km) take the S.S.2 to Buonconvento and turn right in town following signs for Bibbiano. After crossing the river, turn right at La Ripolina and drive up to the main house.

LA RIPOLINA
Host: Laura Cresti
Pieve di Piana
Buonconvento (SI) 53022, Italy
Tel & fax: (0577) 282280, Cellphone: (335) 5739284
7 rooms, Double: €70–€80
7 apartments: €30–€40 daily (per person)
Open: all year, Credit cards: MC
Other languages: good English
Region: Tuscany, Michelin Map: 430
www.karenbrown.com/italy/laripolina.html

After living in South Africa for 20 years, the Tosi family returned to their homeland in search of a piece of land that in some way resembled their beloved Africa. The gorgeous Montebelli property, situated in Maremma, the wild west of Italy, fit the bill with its 300-plus acres of mountain, hills, and plain, all close to the sea—the one essential element, according to Lorenzo, which brings people "allegria". Lorenzo, his simpatica wife, Carla, and son, Alessandro, now divide their time and energy between their guests and production of wines and olive oil. At the foot of the hills is the main guesthouse where most of the rooms are situated. Others, each with separate entrance, are in two one-story wings connecting to an outdoor dining area. The best rooms are in the main house, decorated tastefully with antiques and including all the amenities of a regular hotel. The half-board requirement allows guests to sample the marvelous cuisine of the area within the characteristic dining room featuring the stone wheel from the original press. This is unexplored territory, full of historical treasures and Etruscan remains. Scenic walks on marked trails (a must for the views!), a swimming pool, tennis courts, horse riding, and summer concerts are available right on the property. *Directions:* From the north, exit at Gavorrano Scalo from Aurelia S.S.1, following signs for Caldana. Just before Caldana, turn at the Montebelli sign and take the dirt road to the end.

MONTEBELLI
Hosts: Carla & Lorenzo Tosi
Localita: Molinetto, Caldana (GR) 58020, Italy
Tel: (0566) 887100, Fax: (0566) 81439
21 rooms, Double: €150–€210*
*Includes breakfast & dinner
Minimum nights required: 2, 7 in high season
Closed: Jan 11 to Feb 13, Credit cards: MC, VS
Other languages: good English
Region: Tuscany, Michelin Map: 430
www.karenbrown.com/italy/montebelli.html

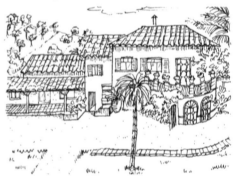

The quaint medieval village of Calvi is just on the border between Lazio and Umbria and conveniently located at 15 kilometers from the autostrada and 70 kilometers from Rome. Louise, from Sweden, divides her time between Rome and the countryside where the farm's activities include production of wine and olive oil, and horse breeding on the 150-acre property. The fascinating family residence in town is a historic 15th-century palazzo filled with period furniture, paintings, and frescoed ceilings. Hospitality is offered in the bright-yellow farmhouse within four comfortable apartments, each with private garden area. Accommodations on the first and second floors are a combination of one or two bedrooms, living room with fireplace, fully equipped kitchen, bathroom, and outdoor barbecue. The house has been restored with new bathrooms and tiled floors while maintaining original beamed ceilings and a country flavor in antique furnishings. Fresh fixings for breakfast are left in the apartments and special arrangements have been made with local restaurants for guests. Besides wandering around the many villages of the Sabina area, you can visit Orvieto, Todi, and Spoleto, or relax by the swimming pool. A children's playground and an exercise course are available. *Directions:* Leave the Rome-Florence autostrada A1 at Magliano Sabina. After Magliano, follow signs for Calvi. Just before Calvi you see signs for San Martino on the right.

CASALE SAN MARTINO
Host: Louise Calza Bini
Colle San Martino
Calvi dell'Umbria (TR) 05032, Italy
Cellphone: (328) 1659514, Fax: (0744) 710644
4 apartments: €57–€140 daily
Minimum nights required: 2, 7 in Jul & Aug
Open: all year
Other languages: good English
Region: Umbria, Michelin Map: 430
www.karenbrown.com/italy/casalesanmartino.html

The Villa Bellaria, situated right in the picturesque village of Campagnatico with its stone streets and houses and magnificent views over the Ombrone Valley and up to Mount Amiata, retains the authentic flavor of a noble country home from centuries past. Credit goes to gracious hostess Luisa who oversees the 900-plus-acre property, once belonging to such powerful families as the Aldobrandeschi and Medici. It was partially destroyed during World War II and completely restored by the Querci della Rovere family. Talented Luisa runs not only the hospitality activity but the entire farm as well, while her husband produces Morellino wine from another property. With its large surrounding balustraded park with cypress-lined trails and swimming pool, one forgets that it is all part of the actual town (with its many conveniences). The spacious bedrooms with family antiques and two of the apartments are situated within the main villa while the other newer but characteristic ones are spread out on three floors in the transformed olive-press building. They have either one or two bedrooms, bathroom, and sitting room with kitchenette and are appointed with the family's country furniture. This is a lovely base for exploring a vast number of prepared and varied itineraries. *Directions:* From Siena (55 km) or Grosseto (20 km) exit from highway 223 at Campagnatico and continue for 4 km to the town. The villa is the second right in town—drive up to a green gate.

VILLA BELLARIA
Host: Luisa Querci della Rovere
Campagnatico (GR) 58042, Italy
Tel: 0564) 996626, Cellphone: (335) 6097438
Fax: (0564) 996626 or (0577) 281716
4 rooms, Double: €60–€80, 10 apartments: €490–€980 weekly
Minimum nights required: 2
Open: all year, Credit cards: all major
Other languages: good English
Region: Tuscany, Michelin Map: 430
www.karenbrown.com/italy/bellaria.html

For those who have a passion for horseback riding, or with an urge to learn, Tenuta La Mandria provides the opportunity to do either while on holiday. Host and horseman Davide Felice Aondio's horse farm has been in existence for over 35 years and has been a model for riding resorts. Situated near the foothills of the Alps and between the cities of Turin and Milan, the vast, flat property borders a 15,000-acre national park, offering spectacular scenery and endless possibilities for horseback excursions. The complex is made up of horse stables, indoor/outdoor ring, haylofts, guestrooms, dining room, and the private homes of the proprietor and his son Marco's family. The whole forms a square with riding rings in the center. As a national equestrian training center, it offers lessons of every kind for all ages. Six very basic bedrooms with bath are reserved for guests and good local fare is served in the rustic dining room. Golf, swimming, and tennis facilities are available nearby. Two side trips that must not be missed are first, to lovely Lake Maggiore, and then to the intriguing medieval town of Ricetto where the houses and streets are made of smooth stones. *Directions:* Take the Carisio exit from the Milan-Turin autostrada. Head toward Biella, but at the town of Candelo turn right for Mottalciata. La Mandria is on the right.

TENUTA LA MANDRIA
Host: Marco Aondio family
Candelo (VC) 13062, Italy
Tel: (015) 2536078, Fax: (015) 2530743
6 rooms, Double: €72
Per person half board: €60
Open: all year
Other languages: good English
Region: Piedmont, Michelin Map: 428
www.karenbrown.com/italy/lamandria.html

Poetically named after a classic Italian tale by Cesare Pavese, a native of this area, the Luna e i Falo (meaning "the moon and the fire") farmhouse was lovingly restored by congenial hosts Ester and Franco Carnero. The ritual described in the story is still performed in August every year when local farmers burn old grapevines under the full moon in hopes of a good crop. On that night, the bonfires dotting hills surrounding the farm create quite a spectacle. The Carneros' brick home has arched windows and arcaded front and side terraces, with three double or triple rooms and one apartment for four persons within the villa, which they have made available to visitors. For a country home, the spacious living/dining area is elaborately furnished with Renaissance period pieces. The bedrooms enjoy a combination of old and new decor and sweeping views of the countryside, known for its wineries. The emphasis at the Luna e i Falo is on the cuisine: the proprietors previously owned a top-rated restaurant in Turin and continue to practice their culinary skills, producing delicacies from ancient recipes to guests' delight. Regardless of the language barrier, they have a way of making guests feel right at home. *Directions:* From Asti follow the signs for Canelli and, before town, take a right up the hill to Castello Gancia. The farmhouse is on the right after Aie.

LA LUNA E I FALO
Hosts: Ester & Franco Carnero
Localita: Aie 37
Canelli (AT) 14053, Italy
Tel & fax: (0141) 831643, Cellphone: (328) 7191567
3 rooms, Double: €110, 1 apartment
Minimum nights required: 2
Open: Mar to Nov
Other languages: French
Region: Piedmont, Michelin Map: 428
www.karenbrown.com/italy/laluna.html

The Canonica a Cerreto property is truly a marvel to behold, with an extraordinary combination of features. Perfectly located in lower Chianti and equidistant to most of Tuscany's highlights, it offers not only very comfortable accommodation in a fascinating historic dwelling but also seemingly endless vistas of gorgeous countryside, and welcoming and gracious hosts. Iron gates open up to an entrance lined with gorgeous terra-cotta pots in the form of lions, overflowing with geraniums and oleander plants giving accents of color to the façade of the ancient stone church and attached canonica, the summer residence of the Vescovo of the Duomo of Siena. Within the walls is a complex including the family's residence, three guest apartments in the monks' former rooms, quarters for the farmhands, and a cantina. Signora Lorenzi proudly shows guests her museum-caliber art collection and magnificent home where large period paintings adorn frescoed walls and elegant antique pieces are displayed. The apartments, in an elegant country style, are tastefully appointed with antiques and include a bedroom, bathroom, and living area with kitchenette. The largest apartment has two bedrooms, each with its own bathroom. A lovely, secluded swimming pool has superb countryside views. *Directions:* From Siena follow the S.S.408 towards Gaiole and just after Pianella, take the first left (Canonica a Cerreto is marked on most maps).

CANONICA A CERRETO
Host: Egidio Lorenzi family
Canonica a Cerreto
Castelnuovo Berardenga (SI) 53010, Italy
Tel & fax: (0577) 363261
3 apartments: €730–€1,250 weekly
Minimum nights required: 7
Open: Apr to Oct, Credit cards: all major
Other languages: good English
Region: Tuscany, Michelin Map: 430
www.karenbrown.com/italy/canonica.html

North of Florence between Prato and Pistoia is a pocket of little-known yet entrancing countryside encompassing the Calvana Mountains and Bisenzio Valley. New owners, Marco and Sonia, together with daughter Erica and partner Andrea, love sharing their enthusiasm for the area by offering accommodation to guests on their 35-acre farm, which produces grain crops and livestock. Although access to the rather plain-looking house is by a congested side entrance, the property is beautifully situated overlooking a wooded valley and private lake at the back. What really counts here is the hosts' warmth and their sincere effort to make their guests feel at home. The bedrooms for two to three persons with accompanying immaculate bathrooms are sweet and simple, decorated with comfortable, old-fashioned furniture. Guests convene downstairs for breakfast and dinner in the rustic dining room with exposed beams and fireplace. Off the dining room is the kitchen, where you can watch Sonia making fresh pasta for meals that reflect the influence of the bordering regions of Tuscany and Emilia. A visit to the welcoming Ponte alla Villa offers an opportunity to familiarize yourself with the customs of an area off the beaten track. *Directions:* From Prato, take route 325 north for 25 km to Vernio, then bear left toward Cantagallo. Watch for signs for the bed and breakfast at Luicciana.

PONTE ALLA VILLA
Hosts: Andrea Barni, Erica & Marco Ciolini
Via della Villa 18, Loc. Luicciana
Cantagallo (PO) 59025, Italy
Tel & fax: (0574) 956244, Cellphone: (339) 5792603
7 rooms, Double: €48–€54
Per person half board: €40
Open: all year
Other languages: some English, German
Region: Tuscany, Michelin Map: 429
www.karenbrown.com/italy/allavilla.html

The turreted medieval village of Capalbio, perched on a hilltop, has the double advantage of being close to one of the prettiest seaside spots—Argentario—plus having the beautiful countryside and villages of Maremma to explore. Monica and husband Filippo run an efficient little bed and breakfast operation, having left a long career in the restaurant business. Breakfast, composed of fresh homemade cakes, breads, and jams, is served in the stone-walled dining room or out on the patio. Ten rooms in a row, each with independent entrance from the garden, are situated next door to the main house, while four new bedrooms have been added in the adjacent converted barn. Rooms are nicely decorated in a uniform blue or pink color scheme, and have such amenities as television, telephone, hairdryer, and air conditioning. This comes in handy on hot summer evenings, although there is always a cool breeze passing through (hence the Etruscan name "Iced Woods") and the swimming pool is wonderfully refreshing. The farm property extends over 30 acres of olive groves and fields of grain and oats. Not to be missed is an unforgettable meal at Tullio's famed restaurant in town, run by relatives of the Olivi family. *Directions:* From Rome on the coastal highway 1, exit before Capalbio at Pescia Fiorentina. At Pescia stay left for 3 km. Ghiaccio is just 1 km after the fork for Manciano.

❄ ⚓ ■ ✄ ☎ 🧍 👥 🏇 P ≈ 🖼 ⛵ 🍇

GHIACCIO BOSCO
Hosts: Monica Olivi & Filippo Rinaldi
Strada della Sgrilla 4
Capalbio (GR) 58011, Italy
Tel & fax: (0564) 896539, Cellphone: (339) 5662578
14 rooms, Double: €78–€99
Open: all year
Other languages: some English
Region: Tuscany, Michelin Map: 430
www.karenbrown.com/italy/ghiaccio.html

Up in the northeastern reaches of Tuscany bordering Umbria and near several nature reserves in mountains reaching heights of 1500 meters is the agritourism bed and breakfast, Borgo Tozzetto. Owning a bed and breakfast is nothing new to Luciano Fabrizi, whose family owns the very popular La Malvarina in Assisi. Luciano fell in love with this lesser-known, virgin countryside and has put the business in the capable hands of a young local couple, Daniela and Marco. Tozzetto is located in a group of private homes, encompassing two restored stone houses plus a mini apartment in the transformed stalls (Gnacco). The Contadina is a large apartment on two floors with three bedrooms and kitchen/living room in the same building as the stone-walled taverna dining room where Daniela serves local specialties. Just across from this is a small house with two identical one-bedroom apartments enjoying sweeping views over the bucolic hillsides. All rooms are immaculate and neat, with simple reproduction country furniture and fresh paint in soft hues set off by stencil motifs. There is a lawn area in front with swimming pool and playground for children. The impressive city of Arezzo with its beautiful historical center and antique market is 45 kilometers away. *Directions:* Exit at Arezzo from the A1 and drive towards Sansepolcro, Anghiari, and Caprese Michelangelo (Michelangelo's birthplace and museum). In town there are signs for Tozzetto—2 km.

BORGO TOZZETTO
Host: Luciano Fabrizi
Localita: Tozzetto
Caprese Michelangelo (AR) 52033, Italy
Tel: (0575) 793853, Fax: (0575) 793545
4 apartments: €57–€129 daily
Minimum nights required: 2
Open: all year
Other languages: very little English
Region: Tuscany, Michelin Map: 430
www.karenbrown.com/italy/tozzetto.html

The Villa Krupp, built in 1900, is a delightful, small, family-run hotel, whose claim to local fame can be found in its guest book, boasting such illustrious names as Lenin and Gorky. The warm Coppola family, who turned the property into a hotel in the '60s, offer charming accommodation in 12 bedrooms within a somewhat modern and boxy white building alongside their own residence. The Krupp is dramatically situated in one of the most beautiful corners of Capri's Augusto Park, atop a steep, sheer cliff dropping to the sparkling turquoise sea beneath. The site overlooks the Faraglioni rock formation and Marina Piccola, one of Capri's two ports. A set of stairs leads up to the best vantage point from which to admire this spectacular and privileged panorama away from crowds of tourists. The renovated light-filled guestrooms, featuring individual balconies, are decorated with scattered antiques and pastel-colored ceramic tiles and some have air conditioning. Breakfast is served either out on the front terrace overflowing with potted flowers or in the luminous veranda bar/dining room. Mother-daughter team Valentina and Donatella do an excellent job of caring for their guests, many of whom are regulars. Reserve well in advance. *Directions:* Take the cable car up to Capri center (la piazzetta). Walk to Via Emanuele, past the Quisisana hotel, down to Viale Matteotti. The hotel is to the right up a ramp, as indicated (ten minutes from the main square).

❄ ⊥ ☕ 🛥 ▭ ☎ 🚶 🖼

VILLA KRUPP
Hosts: Valentina & Donatella Coppola
Viale Matteotti 12, Capri (NA) 80073, Italy
Tel: (081) 8370362 or 8377473, Cellphone: (338) 1954155
Fax: (081) 8376489
12 rooms, Double: €115–€150
Minimum nights required: 2, 3 in high season
Open: Mar 20 to Oct 31, Credit cards: MC, VS
Other languages: some English, French, German
Region: Campania, Michelin Map: 431
www.karenbrown.com/italy/krupp.html

La Minerva, a full-fledged hotel with many amenities, is located in a quiet section of Capri, slightly off the beaten track, yet still quite central, permitting easy access to the more bustling areas of town—a walkers' paradise with no motorized transportation allowed. Glass entrance doors look straight through the capacious reception/sitting area across glossy blue-and-white tiled floors out to a view of the sea through another set of glass doors at the opposite end of the room. The captivating sea views through umbrella pine trees will strike you every time you come and go, as well as from most bedrooms. Rooms, all below this level, are reached by elevator, as is a small breakfast area, although most guests prefer breakfast served in rooms on their private balconies. The hotel's royal-blue-and-white tile theme follows through in the luminous guestrooms (standard or larger superior doubles), which are accented by an occasional antique piece. Newly renovated deluxe doubles have larger terraces with sea view, and Jacuzzi bathtubs. A rooftop solarium is an unusual bonus. *Directions:* Stop at the tourist office as you get off the hydrofoil for a detailed map indicating Via Occhio Marino. The cable car or a taxi takes you from the port to the piazza at the center of town. From there it's a ten-minute walk to the hotel. Prearrange to have your luggage picked up at the port, otherwise, pack light!

❄ ⚓ ☕ 💳 ☎ 🏨 👫 🍸 🖼 🚤 🕊

LA MINERVA
Host: Luigi Esposito
Via Occhio Marino 8
Capri (NA) 80073, Italy
Tel: (081) 8377067, Fax: (081) 8375221
18 rooms, Double: €150–€260
Closed: Feb, Credit cards: all major
Other languages: good English
Region: Campania, Michelin Map: 431
www.karenbrown.com/italy/laminerva.html

Capri has long had a reputation as an exclusive island, with prices only the elite were able to afford. However, the cost of tourism across Italy has soared, bringing other destinations more in line with Capri in terms of expense and making it relatively more affordable than it once was. Besides the many hotels, there are just a few true bed and breakfasts and Villa Vuotto is one of the best. Antonino Vuotto and his wife, a local couple both with hotel experience, opened up their centrally located, prim white home in the town of Capri, making four bedrooms down one hall available to guests. The very pleasant and airy rooms are extremely clean and neat, with typical tiled floors, and private baths and balconies in each. All have a full or partial view of the sea. Breakfast is not served because there are no common rooms for guests but the Villa Vuotto's convenient location makes it easy to get to any of Capri's fine restaurants for breakfast, lunch, and dinner. It would be impossible to find another accommodation with such an absolutely incredible price/quality rapport. A marvelous value! *Directions:* Take the cable car up to Capri. Go through the main town square to Via Emanuele, past the Quisisana Hotel, and continue to the end of the street. Turn left onto Via Certosa, then left again on Cerio. The Villa is on the corner of Campo di Teste and is marked with its original name, Villa Margherita.

VILLA VUOTTO
Host: Antonino Vuotto family
Via Campo di Teste 2
Capri (NA) 80073, Italy
Tel & fax: (081) 8370230
4 rooms, Double: €72–€80
Open: all year
Other languages: very little English
Region: Campania, Michelin Map: 431
www.karenbrown.com/italy/vuotto.html

The Ombria farmhouse nestles amidst the foothills just 30 kilometers from both beautifully austere Bergamo and Lecco on Lake Como. Bed-and-breakfast/restaurant activity in this 1613 stone house began after meticulous restoration by owner Luciano Marchesin, who has now retired, leaving the business in the capable hands of the Vergani brothers, part of his staff from the beginning. An arched entryway leads into a stone courtyard with gazebo and open grill, where tables are set for summer meals. The Ombria is well known for its exceptional restaurant where locals enjoy candlelit regional cuisine at long tables in the intimate stone-walled dining room—as long as they make reservations three months in advance! For those retiring to bed early, it would be best to avoid weekends. The spacious double bedrooms, which accommodate up to four persons, are decorated with country antiques and wrought-iron beds. Original fireplaces, exposed beams, warm wood floors, and stone walls make them very appealing and cozy. Special attention has been given to bathrooms, which are beautifully tiled and rather luxurious. Readers give Ombria a high rating. *Directions:* From autostrada A4, exit at Dalmine and follow signs for Lecco on route 36. After Pontida, turn right at the sign for Celana and continue on to Celana, then Ombria (total 15 km).

OMBRIA
Hosts: Alberto & Giuseppe Vergani
Localita: Celana
Caprino Bergamasco (BG) 24030, Italy
Tel & fax: (035) 781668
3 rooms, Double: €67
Dinner Thur to Sun only
Open: all year
Other languages: some English
Region: Lombardy, Michelin Map: 431
www.karenbrown.com/italy/ombria.html

Between the cities of Bergamo and Brescia is a vast commercial area that incorporates the wine region known as Franciacorta—or "land of bubbles." The Ricci Curbastro vineyards, made up of 60 acres, are located in the heart of the area based at the foot of Lake Iseo. The family is one of the most renowned producers of top-quality (D.O.C.G.) Franciacorta Brut champagne, among 12 other varieties of wine. The large and busy family estate just on the main road is made up of a complex of houses, which include the family's villa, wine cellars, a wine-tasting showroom, an antiques store, and an interesting agricultural museum and library filled with ancient farm tools and wine presses. Across the street is the farmhouse, transformed into guest apartments of various sizes (studio, one and two bedrooms), each with living area and kitchenette facilities. Rooms are simply decorated with country antiques and stenciled borders around windows and doorways. Here you have the advantage of being close to town while having views of the flat vineyards from bedroom windows. Sports facilities in the area include golf, horseback riding, and biking. This is a conveniently located accommodation for independent travelers. *Directions:* Exit at Palazzolo from the A4 autostrada and follow signs to Capriolo (2 km). Turn right in town at the sign for Adro. After half a kilometer the farm is on the left-hand side of the road.

❄ ⚓ 🚵 💳 🏠 🎿 🐴 ▼ P 🖼 🏊

AZIENDA AGRICOLA RICCI CURBASTRO
Host: Ricci Curbastro family
Via Adro 37
Capriolo (BS) 25031, Italy
Tel: (030) 736094, Fax: (030) 7460558
7 apartments: €62–€70 daily
Minimum nights required: 2
Open: all year, Credit cards: all major
Other languages: good English
Region: Lombardy, Michelin Map: 428
www.karenbrown.com/italy/curbastro.html

After 20 years of managing guided tours throughout Italy, Welsh-born Maureen, along with husband, Roberto, brought her expertise "home" to La Torretta. Restoration work on the three-story 15th-century building, tucked away in this yet-undiscovered medival hilltop village, took three years to complete. The entrance stairway leads to a large open and elegant living room with a collection of the family's paintings, stone fireplace, and 16th-century frescoes discovered during the restoration process. All seven bedrooms are individually and tastefully decorated in soft beige tones, which harmonize with travertine bathrooms, and have stunning views over the town's rooftops. Meals are served upstairs in a dining area with panoramic terrace overlooking olive groves and the wooded Sabine hills. This virgin territory is filled with hilltop villages to explore, besides being on the border of Umbria, and is just a 45-minute train ride from Rome. Maureen and her daughters customize itineraries for guests and organize cooking courses, while Roberto specializes in ancient Roman architecture and archaeology. A separate self-catering apartment across the street is available. *Directions:* From Rome or Florence exit the A1 at Ponzano-Soratte (a new exit not marked on maps). After the railroad crossing turn right and continue to the T-junction. Turn left and follow signs to Casperia (20 mins). Cars are easily parked on the street below and luggage is delivered by special vehicle.

LA TORRETTA
Hosts: Maureen & Roberto Scheda
Via Mazzini 7
Casperia (RI) 02041, Italy
Tel & fax: (0765) 63202, Cellphone: (333) 4997014
7 rooms, Double: €70–€90
1 apartment: €80–€90 daily
Minimum nights required: 2
Other languages: fluent English
Region: Lazio, Michelin Map: 430
www.karenbrown.com/italy/torretta.html

A stay at the Villa Aureli with Count di Serego Alighieri (descendant of Dante) and daughter Flavia can only be memorable. With its back to the town and looking out over the Italian Renaissance garden and surrounding countryside, the imposing brick villa has been standing for the past 300 years. When it was bought by the di Serego family in the 18th century, it was meticulously restored and embellished with plasterwork, decorative painted ceilings, richly painted fabrics on walls, ornately framed paintings and prints, colorful tiles from Naples, and Umbrian antiques. Left intentionally intact by the Count, who disdains overly restored historical homes, the elegant apartments for guests maintain their original ambiance. They can accommodate from four to six persons and are spacious, having numerous sitting rooms with fireplaces; although do not expect updated bathrooms or kitchens. A small swimming pool set against the villa's stone walls is a refreshing spot for dreaming. The villa serves as an ideal base from which to explore Umbria and parts of Tuscany, as well as special local itineraries prepared for guests by the Count. *Directions:* Exit from the Perugia highway at Madonna Alta and follow route 220 for Citta della Pieve. After 6 km, turn left for Castel del Piano Umbro.

VILLA AURELI
Host: Leonardo di Serego Alighieri family
Via Cirenei 70,
Castel del Piano Umbro (PG) 06071, Italy
Tel: (075) 5140444 or (075) 5159186
Fax: (075) 5149408
2 apartments: €852–€1,136 weekly
Heating extra, Open: all year
Other languages: good English
Region: Umbria, Michelin Map: 430
www.karenbrown.com/italy/villaaureli.html

Castelfiorentino is 40 kilometers from Florence, Siena and Pisa, and although its outskirts are very commercial, it is a strategic touring base and the surrounding countryside is lovely. Continuing a long tradition of making guests feel at home—their hotel in Florence has been in the family for four generations—Massimo and Susanna opened this bed and breakfast five years ago after major restoration of two hilltop farmhouses. The completely refurbished rooms, with many modern amenities (some have a kitchenette), new bathrooms, fresh landscaping, and recently installed swimming pool and tennis court, have a very new feeling. Spacious bedrooms are appointed with authentic and reproduction antiques and have colorful Sicilian ceramic tiles above beds, with matching ones in bathrooms. The former barn was converted into a small restaurant decorated with contemporary art, a kitchen with viewing window, and a common living room/library upstairs. The preparation of delectable Tuscan fare using ancestral recipes is another strong tradition and cooking lessons are happily arranged for those eager to take home family secrets. A buffet breakfast is served. The side terrace, overlooking soft hills, is where guests can both enjoy breakfast and watch the sunset in the evening. *Directions:* From Castelfiorentino turn off at signs for Renai (this can be tricky to locate) and follow signs for Locanda Country Inn Le Boscarecce (5 km).

LE BOSCARECCE
Hosts: Susanna Ballerini & Massimo Ravalli
Via Renai 19
Castelfiorentino (FI) 50051, Italy
Tel: (0571) 61280, Fax: (055) 283391
7 rooms, Double: €110–€145
Minimum nights required: 2
Open: all year, Credit cards: all major
Other languages: good English
Region: Tuscany, Michelin Map: 430
www.karenbrown.com/italy/boscarecce.html

The Villa Gaidello farm has been written up on several occasions (in Bon Appetit, Cuisine, Eating in Italy), mostly for its superb cuisine. There is nothing extravagant about hostess Paola Bini's recipes—rather, the secret to her success seems to lie in the revival of basic traditional dishes using the freshest possible ingredients. Pasta is made daily (a great treat to watch) and features all the local variations on tagliatelle, pappardelle, and stricchettoni. Reservations for dinner must be made several days in advance. Paola is one of the pioneers in agritourism, transforming her grandmother's nearly-200-year-old farmhouse into a guesthouse and restaurant more than 26 years ago. One to five guests are accommodated in each of the eight apartments, which include kitchen and sitting room. The apartments are cozy and rustic with exposed-brick walls, country antiques, and lace curtains. Two double bedrooms are found in a fourth house on the property, San Giacomo, each decorated in the style of Paola's two favorite countries, France and the U.S. The dining room, set with doilies and ceramic, is situated in the converted hayloft and overlooks the vast garden and a small pond. This is a convenient stopover just off the Bologna-Milan autostrada. *Directions:* Exit the A1 autostrada at Modena Nord (or Bologna Nord from the south). Follow Via Emilia/route 9 towards Castelfranco. Turn left (or right) on Via Costa (hospital) and follow signs to Gaidello.

VILLA GAIDELLO
Host: Paola Bini
Via Gaidello 18
Castelfranco Emilia (MO) 41013, Italy
Tel: (059) 926806, Fax: (059) 926620
2 rooms, Double: €88
8 apartments: €120–€217 daily B&B
Closed: Aug, Credit cards: all major
Other languages: very little English
Region: Emilia-Romagna, Michelin Map: 429
www.karenbrown.com/italy/villagaidello.html

There is no doubt that the spectacular Amalfi coast must be seen, but in high season when the traffic is unbearable and Positano's streets are packed, a welcome retreat is the coast farther south at Castellabate. This is a very quiet and modest resort area where the majority of summer tourists are Italians. The winding road climbs up to the medieval village of Castellabate and La Mola, the summer home of the Favilla family, is right on the road entering town. Rather nondescript from the roadside entrance, the four-story former olive-press building, perched on the cliffside, faces out to the bay. Each room takes in some angle of this amazing panorama, two having balconies and the two-bedroom suite having a terrace. With an occasional antique, the bedrooms and living room with spiral staircase are pleasantly uncluttered so as not to detract from the inspiring sea views. On a clear day the Amalfi coastline and even Capri are visible. Hostess Loredana takes care of guests, preparing cakes and bread for breakfast, which is served on a table made from the old stone press on the main terrace. It is difficult to tear oneself away to try one of the interesting itineraries with an emphasis on either nature or ancient history (temples of Paestum, Certosa, or Padula). *Directions:* 60 km from Salerno. Take the road up to the town center and La Mola is marked on the side of the gray building on the right, the first house as you enter town on Via Cilento.

LA MOLA
Host: Francesco Favilla
Via A. Cilento 2
Castellabate (SA) 84048, Italy
Tel: (0974) 967053, Cellphone: (335) 1292800
Fax: (0974) 967714
5 rooms, Double: €104–€120
Open: Apr to Oct, Credit cards: all major
Other languages: some English
Region: Campania, Michelin Map: 431
www.karenbrown.com/italy/lamola.html

While wandering in Umbria through picture-perfect landscapes, we came upon the Giardino degli Ulivi bed and breakfast and were immediately intrigued. The absolutely charming accommodation is actually part of a 12th-century stone village and faces out to the rolling hills splashed with bright patches of yellow sunflowers. The scenery per se is enough to leave one in awe, let alone Maria Pia's marvelous cuisine with its Michelin rating. The carefully restored building, left ingeniously intact, thanks to her architect husband, Sante, includes the stone-walled restaurant with its many intimate nooks, centered around the ancient wine-making press. The five bedrooms upstairs off two sitting rooms with fireplace have wrought-iron beds, antique bedside tables, and beamed ceilings. The favorite corner bedroom (at a higher rate) has a large arched window taking in the breathtaking view. A small apartment for two persons with living area and kitchenette has been incorporated within the large house. While their son, Francesco, tends to the breeding of horses, daughter Raffaele assists guests with the many interesting itineraries in the area (Camerino, San Severino, Matelica, and Fariano—famous for its paper industry). A real sense of discovery is experienced in this region, which keeps its traditions and folklore intact. *Directions:* From Castelraimondo follow route 256 towards Matelica, turning first left for Castel S. Maria then Castel S. Angelo.

IL GIARDINO DEGLI ULIVI
Host: Sante Cioccoloni family
Localita: Castel S. Angelo, Castelraimondo (MC) 62022, Italy
Tel: (0737) 642121, Cellphone: (338) 3056098
Fax: (0737) 640441
5 rooms, Double: €89–€120, 1 apartment: €89 daily
Reduced rates for 3 or more nights
Closed: 2 weeks in Nov & Jan 8 to Mar 7, Credit cards: AX, VS
Other languages: good English
Region: Marches, Michelin Map: 430
www.karenbrown.com/italy/ilgiardino.html

Tucked away off a winding mountain road in the enchanting Siusi Alps is a typical Tyrolean farmhouse where the Jaider family has resided ever since the 15th century, traditionally running a dairy farm. Their inviting home, with its authentic ambiance of the past, is colorfully accented with green shutters and flower-laden windowboxes. Two wooden barns are connected to the residence via a stone terrace. Paula Jaider runs her home with the hotel efficiency expected by visitors to this predominantly German-speaking area. Meals are served either out on the vine-covered terrace or in the original dining room, whose charm is enhanced by the low, wood-paneled ceiling and little carved wooden chairs. Be sure to reserve dinner: the food is excellent and it is just too far to go out for a meal. Cuisine in this region has an Austrian flavor, featuring speck ham, meat and potatoes, and apple strudel, and regulars come from afar to this well-known restaurant. Lovely country antiques are dispersed throughout the house and the eight very nice bedrooms, which are wood-paneled from floor to ceiling and all have balconies with pretty valley views. A real charmer and a bargain. Book well in advance. *Directions:* Exit from the Bolzano-Brennero autostrada at Klausen and drive south to Ponte Gardena where you turn left across the river and first right towards Castelrotto. After 3.5 km make a sharp right for San Osvaldo and follow the narrow road for 2.5 km.

※ 📠 🎿 💳 🐎 🚶 🏇 P ¶ 🎿 🍇

TSCHOTSCHERHOF
Host: Jaider family
San Osvaldo 19
Castelrotto–Osvaldo (BZ) 39040, Italy
Tel: (0471) 706013, Fax: (0471) 704801
8 rooms, Double: €46–€52
Per person half board: €31
Open: Mar to Nov, Credit cards: all major
Other languages: very little English, German
Region: Trentino-Alto Adige, Michelin Map: 429
www.karenbrown.com/italy/tschotscherhof.html

Il Loghetto is located 10 kilometers east of Bologna and is a combination of converted farmhouse and the efficiency and service of a small hotel. Run by Ulicia and her son, Andrea, the yellow house surrounded by a large garden and then flat fields has ten beamed bedrooms upstairs and a restaurant downstairs. There is a reception area at the entrance and also an elevator up to the rooms, which are all new with rather standard wood furniture and amenities such as television and air conditioning. The dining room with fireplace and hanging brass pots, where fresh pasta dishes and other local specialties are served, is filled with a variety of antiques collected by Andrea. Beyond is an enormous living room with arched glass doors overlooking the garden and outdoor tables, a bar, billiard table, piano, and two sitting areas. There may be minimal noise from the nearby road. Transfers are arranged to Bologna or the airport. Besides this being a convenient stopover, marvels such as Ravenna, Ferrara, and Faenza (ceramic museum) can be visited from here. *Directions:* From the ring highway of Bologna, exit at S. Vitale (N11) and continue towards Villanova. After the commercial area of Castenaso, turn left for Budrio. Il Loghetto is indicated on the left.

❄ ☕ 🚲 ♨ 💳 ☎ 🐕 🛗 🕴 🏇 🍸 P 🍴 🎭 🔔 ♿

IL LOGHETTO
Host: Mazza family
Via Zenzalino Sud 3-4
Castenaso (BO) 40050, Italy
Tel: (051) 6052218, Fax: (051) 6052254
10 rooms, Double: €95
Closed: Jan & Aug, Credit cards: MC, VS
Other languages: some English
Region: Emilia-Romagna, Michelin Map: 429
www.karenbrown.com/italy/loghetto.html

This small bed and breakfast has been added to the new group of agritourism accommodation in the Aosta Valley region. It offers a pleasant place to stay right in the center of charming Champoluc and is associated with the agritourism cheese farm, La Tchavana, up on the mountainside overlooking town (they plan to offer rooms by late 2003). In the summer months the two establishments offer a very worthwhile four-day itinerary featuring a country lunch and tour of the Bagnod family's fontina cheese farm, a visit to an ancient mountain village with sabotier artisans, and two other mountain hikes. The scenic ride up through the valley leading to Champoluc takes you by many picturesque villages, ending at the ski/summer resort. Raul and Lorena took over the family's early-19th-century home in the center of town and recently had it refurbished into a small bed and breakfast. The prim white house with wood-trim balconies, conveniently located right next to the cable-car lift entrance, contains six (non-smoking) bedrooms divided among the top two floors, decorated plainly and practically with new tiled flooring and wood-beamed mansard ceilings. The main entrance to the home opens directly into a welcoming living room with dark-wood furniture, burgundy armchairs, and combination wood and slate floors. A loft balcony overlooks the room. Breakfast is served downstairs in the dining room. *Directions:* On the main road in Champoluc.

LO MIETE VIEI   *New*
Hosts: Raul Chasseur & Lorena Blondin
Rue Prabochon 6
Champoluc (AO) 11020, Italy
Tel: (0125) 308713, Fax: (0125) 308449
6 rooms, Double: €80–€110
Open: all year, Credit cards: MC, VS
Other languages: some English, French
Region: Aosta Valley, Michelin Map: 428
www.karenbrown.com/italy/lomiete.html

If you were ever one of Stella Casolaro's fortunate guests in her former B&B accommodation in Chianti, you would understand why travelers still come back and stay with her year after year. Casa Italia, 35 kilometers west of Siena, is in the lesser-known, more rugged part of the Tuscan countryside. In fact, much to the delight of son, Paolo, who has a passion for hunting for porcini mushrooms, dense woods cover the entire area. The white 60-year-old house with encircling garden is right on the edge of the quaint village of Ciciano. Three sweet bedrooms, each with its own bathroom (two just outside the room), and a living room have been reserved for guests on the family's first floor, while they reside on the upper floor. All rooms have a double wrought-iron bed with a variety of country antiques in keeping with the simple, old-fashioned ambiance. A country breakfast is served downstairs in the cantina. Not to be missed are the nearby mystic ruins of San Galgano cathedral. *Directions:* From Siena, take route 73 towards Grosseto. After Frosini, turn off right for Chiusdino, then Ciciano (45 km from the seaside). Casa Italia is right on the main street in town.

CASA ITALIA
Hosts: Stella & Paolo Casolaro
Via Massetana 5
Ciciano, Chiusdino (SI) 53010, Italy
Tel & fax: (0577) 750656
3 rooms, Double: €62
Open: all year
Other languages: some English
Region: Tuscany, Michelin Map: 430
www.karenbrown.com/italy/casaitalia.html

In the hills between Tuscany and Umbria and overlooking the Tiber and Chiana valleys, you find the Nannotti family's typical farm property. Renato and Maria Teresa used to run a restaurant nearby before deciding to open a bed and breakfast and serve delicious Tuscan-Umbrian recipes at home. The two adjacent red-stone houses include five guestrooms, one apartment, and the family's private quarters. Two rooms are on the ground floor, another has an upstairs terrace, and all are decorated in a simple, pleasant country style with a mix of armoires, wrought-iron beds, and some modern pieces. Renato specializes in organic produce and makes his own honey, jams, grappa, wine, and olive oil, which are brought directly to the dining-room table or served out under the porch. Maria Teresa creates an easy, informal ambiance and young daughter Aureliana and son Ernesto both help out. Being close to the charming, historical village and having easy access to the autostrada make this a super touring location. There are also bikes, a swimming pool, hiking trails, a special spa package at nearby thermal waters, a park for children, many farm animals, a fitness track, and horses to ride. *Directions:* Exit at Chiusi from the north or Fabro from the south and follow signs for Citta della Pieve. In town follow signs for Ponticelli—the bed and breakfast is well marked before this town.

MADONNA DELLE GRAZIE
Host: Renato Nannotti family
Via Madonna delle Grazie 6
Citta della Pieve (PG) 06062, Italy
Tel & fax: (0578) 299822, Cellphone: (340) 8210564
5 rooms, Double: €90–€110, 1 apartment: €600–€800 weekly
Per person half board: €55–€70
Open: all year
Other languages: some English, German, French
Region: Umbria, Michelin Map: 430
www.karenbrown.com/italy/madonna.html

British expatriate Dawne Alstrom finally found the farmhouse property of her dreams 17 years ago and immediately set about organizing major restoration work on the crumbling stone house—the ground floor was completed in record time and the final results are indeed splendid. Dawne's organizing skills learned in film production enabled her to coordinate the various artisans quite naturally, and her years of stylist experience were put to use in ingenious decorating, incorporating fireplaces and antique pieces she bought to create an authentic Italian country home. Two lovely, luminous bedrooms with large bathrooms are located on the ground floor off the cozy living room with its music and reading library. The remaining three upstairs are also decorated with fine antiques and are all corner rooms with another sitting room, allowing privacy and total silence. The atmosphere is that of a continual house party and guests convene in the delightful country kitchen around an enormous table for delectable five-course dinners (€40). The vineyards out back creep right up to the swimming pool where a light lunch can be served. From here Tuscany, Umbria, and unusual "backroad" local attractions are all at your fingertips. Truly special. *Directions:* From Rome leave the A1 autostrada at Attigliano and head left towards Bomarzo, turning right towards Castiglione for 12 km. Turn left at the silos (Battisti Cereali) to the first house on the right with a small tower.

L'OMBRICOLO
Host: Dawne Alstrom-Viotti
Via Ombricolo
Civitella d'Agliano (VT) 01020, Italy
Tel & fax: (0761) 914735
5 rooms, Double: €120–€130
Open: all year, Credit cards: all major
Other languages: fluent English
Region: Lazio, Michelin Map: 430
www.karenbrown.com/italy/lombricolo.html

The Villa Alpina is another good choice for an efficient and moderately priced family-run bed and breakfast (or meublè, as they are called) right in Cortina. The inviting white stucco house with front bay windows has a large veranda on one side lined with flowerboxes where a buffet breakfast is set out for guests. Tables and umbrellas are set up outside in the summer months. Elio and his mother reside in a part of the large home, which was recently renovated, with the addition of an elevator up to the bedrooms. Each carpeted room (standard and superior) is decorated individually in characteristic style using mostly wood furniture and paneling. Some have balconies in the back looking over town and up to the mountains, and all have satellite TV and telephones. There is also a comfortable sitting room with Tyrolean printed fabrics on sofas and curtains whose focus is the ceramic-tiled wood-burning stove heater so typical in this mountain area. *Directions:* Just a few minutes' walk to the pedestrian-only main street (Corso Italia) with all its famous shops. Follow signs through town to Via Roma—Villa Alpina is well marked.

VILLA ALPINA
Host: Elio Zardini
Via Roma 72
Cortina d'Ampezzo (BL) 32043, Italy
Tel: (0436) 2418, Cellphone: (335) 1244801
Fax: (0436) 867464
12 rooms, Double: €80–€195
Open: all year, Credit cards: all major
Other languages: good English
Region: Veneto, Michelin Map: 429
www.karenbrown.com/italy/villaalpina.html

Cortina has enjoyed a long-standing reputation as one of the most "in" resorts of the Dolomites, helped also by its center-stage location. Prominent politicians, stars of television and cinema, socialites, and nobility have vacation homes here and congregate three times a year at Christmas, Easter, and during the month of August. In town, there is a large range of accommodation available, but if you want to be part of the scene yet desire a quiet place to sleep, the Menardi family's Baita Fraina is the perfect choice. A baita is a typical chalet farmhouse where home and barn are incorporated into one building. Overlooking mountains to the back and a large park for children to the front, the Fraina is primarily a well-established and esteemed restaurant cited in top restaurant guides and specializing in pastas with fresh mushrooms as well as the exquisite local fartaies dessert with wild-berry sauce. Three paneled and intimate dining rooms have ceramic-tiled stove heaters, lace curtains, antique kitchen tools, and dried flower arrangements. The six simply decorated bedrooms done in pinewood were added later on the top two floors. A sauna, Jacuzzi, and sun terrace are extra features of this characteristic bed and breakfast. *Directions:* Entering Cortina on route 48, turn left before town for Fraina and take the road for 1.2 km.

BAITA FRAINA
Host: Adolfo Menardi family
Localita: Fraina
Cortina d'Ampezzo (BL) 32043, Italy
Tel: (0436) 36 34, Fax: (0436) 87 62 35
6 rooms, Double: €92–€130
Closed: Apr 15 to Jun 25, Sep 25 to Oct 6
Credit cards: MC, VS
Other languages: good English
Region: Veneto, Michelin Map: 429
www.karenbrown.com/italy/fraina.html

Cortina is one of the most frequented spots for travelers passing through the Dolomites on their way up to Austria, or those who just want to get a taste of a mountain resort Italian-style. The multitude of ski lifts and variety of slopes along with the absolutely gorgeous scenery make it an easy winner. For shorter stays, accommodation right in town is convenient to restaurants, ski slopes, and hiking trails. The Meublè Oasi is a pleasant, recently updated bed and breakfast on the outskirts of town (easily reached by foot) at the beginning of a pretty residential street. This former private residence dating to 1925 has ten rooms located on the ground and first floors, while the Luchetta family, the original owners, reside on the top floor. New bedrooms are comfortably appointed with pinewood beds topped with fluffy comforters and soft-pea-green curtains and matching chairs. Amenities include satellite TV and phones in the rooms. A good buffet breakfast is served in the downstairs breakfast room with bay window. A small garden to the side of the house offers a restful spot. This is an efficient little hotel maintaining the warmth of a home and the Seppis are true hosts. *Directions:* The Meublè Oasi is in town on the road leaving Cortina towards Dobbiaco and well marked.

MEUBLÈ OASI
Hosts: Lorenza Seppi & Tranquillo Luchetta
Via Cantore 2
Cortina d'Ampezzo (BL) 32043, Italy
Tel: (0436) 862019, Cellphone: (329) 9888167
Fax: (0436) 879476
10 rooms, Double: €70–€160
Open: all year, Credit cards: MC, VS
Other languages: German, good English
Region: Veneto, Michelin Map: 429
www.karenbrown.com/italy/meubleoasi.html

Borgo Elena, located in the hills outside one of our favorite Tuscan towns, Cortona, belongs to Mario Baracchi, whose brother owns the gorgeous inn, Il Falconiere (listed in our Inns guide). In fact, you can reach Borgo Elena by passing through the Falconiere property (stop in for an exquisite meal) on a narrow, steep gravel road that ends at the cluster of stone houses bordered by dense chestnut woods. Here you are totally immersed in nature and complete silence, with hilltop Cortona to one side and the immense Chiana Valley spread out before you. Seven quaint apartments, each with independent entrance, are dispersed among the various stone houses, which were the quarters for the farmhands of the Falconiere estate a century ago. Their original rustic ambiance remains while convenient modern utilities and amenities have been incorporated. The apartments, all charmingly appointed with Tuscan country pieces, accommodate from two to six persons and are all different in layout, most being on two levels. A lovely swimming pool sits higher up and takes in even more of the expansive view. The Borgo Elena is an ideal base for independent travelers who want to settle in one place for easily touring Tuscany's highlights. *Directions:* Instead of going into the center of Cortona, follow signs for Arezzo and drive past Camucia on the outskirts of town to Tavarnelle. Turn right at San Pietro a Cegliolo and drive 2 km up to Borgo Elena.

BORGO ELENA
Host: Mario Baracchi
Localita: San Pietro a Cegliolo
Cortona (AR) 52042, Italy
Tel & fax: (0575) 604773, Cellphone: (333) 9319320
7 apartments: €500–€827 weekly
Minimum nights required: 3
Open: all year
Other languages: very little English
Region: Tuscany, Michelin Map: 430
www.karenbrown.com/italy/borgoelena.html

For British couple, Scarlett and Colin, the fantasy of restoring a farmhouse in the Tuscan hills and enjoying a slower-paced life became reality when they found their dream property, Stoppiacce. Set amongst the lush green mountains separating Tuscany and Umbria beyond Cortona, the ancient stone farmhouse was meticulously restored and tastefully appointed with country antiques and matching fabrics. Within are the hosts' quarters plus three lovely guestrooms, the "tower" room having its own independent entrance. Scarlett, an excellent cook, prepares light lunches or, by prior arrangement, dinners accompanied by top-choice local wines (€44 per person). Below the main house is a cozy nest for two (Il Castagno) with sitting room and kitchenette, terrace on the first floor, and bedroom with bathroom on the second floor. This is an ideal place for those who like to combine leisurely local touring with pure relaxation, taking advantage of the lovely swimming pool with the most incredible views over the valley. *Directions:* Exit from the A1 autostrada at Val di Chiana and follow the highway towards Perugia. Exit at the second turnoff for Cortona, pass the city, and continue for Citta del Castello on a small winding road. After 5 km turn left at Portole and call Stoppiacce for instructions on how to find the house.

STOPPIACCE
Hosts: Scarlett & Colin Campbell
Localita: San Pietro a Dame
Cortona (AR) 52044, Italy
Tel & fax: (0575) 690058, Cellphone: (349) 8657088
3 rooms, Double: €130
1 house: €400 weekly
Minimum nights required: 2
Open: Apr to Oct, Other languages: fluent English
Region: Tuscany, Michelin Map: 430
www.karenbrown.com/italy/stoppiacce.html

The Antica Fattoria came highly recommended by several readers who stayed there in the first year it opened. It is indeed a delightful combination of pretty countryside, strategic touring position, comfortable rooms, excellent meals, and warm hospitality. Following the increasingly popular lifestyle trend of abandoning the city for a rural pace, Roman couple Alessandro and Anna left their offices to become, essentially, farmers. They bought and restored two connected stone farmhouses and incorporated a combination of seven rooms and two apartments, decorated pleasantly with a characteristic country flavor, for guests. While Alessandro tends to the crops and farm animals, Anna lives out her passion for cooking, much to guests' delight. Meals are served either outside at one long table or in the transformed horse stalls below with cozy sitting area and fireplace. At times the allegria and good food keep guests at the table until the wee hours. A lovely swimming pool looks over the wooded hills to the valley. The busy hosts take time to assist guests with the many local itineraries and organize a wide variety of games. Perfect for families and a great base for exploring Umbria. The town of Deruta is world-famous for its painted ceramic pottery and is lined with workshops and showrooms. *Directions:* From Perugia (18 km), exit from E45 at Casalina. Take the first right and follow signs to the fattoria.

ANTICA FATTORIA DEL COLLE
Hosts: Anna & Alessandro Coluccelli
Strada Colle delle Forche 6
Deruta (PG) 06053, Italy
Tel & fax: (075) 972201, Cellphone: (329) 9897272
7 rooms, Double: €96, 2 apartments: €780–€1,035
Minimum nights required: 7 in Jul & Aug
Open: Easter to Jan 10
Other languages: good English
Region: Umbria, Michelin Map: 430
www.karenbrown.com/italy/anticafattoriadelcolle.html

At the edge of the Mugello area north of Florence is the property of Enrico and Elisa Lippi and their growing family. The primary activity on the farm is the production of the highest-grade quality (D.O.C.G) Chianti Rufina, something that guests can observe up close as the cantinas, guests' farmhouses, and main villa are closely integrated, forming a borgo. Independent houses have from one to three bedrooms, living room, kitchen, and small garden with sitting area. They have been freshly redone, retaining wood-beamed ceilings and some exposed brick features. Country antiques were also restored and fit in well with the general ambiance. Rosmarino and Bosco, within or attached to the ancient medieval tower, are most characteristic of all the apartments. Il Cavaliere is designed for longer stays and is a nice base for exploring this lesser-known part of northern Tuscany and Emilia-Romagna, divided by the Apennines with their villages of medieval and even Etruscan origins. Mountain bikes can be rented, a pool is open to guests from June through September, and courses in Italian wine and olive-oil production are arranged. *Directions:* From Florence head for Pontassieve and continue to Dicomano. At 1 km before town, turn right for Frascole and follow signs to Il Cavaliere.

FRASCOLE-IL CAVALIERE
Hosts: Elisa & Enrico Lippi
Via di Frascole 27
Dicomano (FI) 50062, Italy
Tel & fax: (055) 8386340, Cellphone: (339) 3050554
5 apartments: €80–€220 daily (high season)
Minimum nights required: 3
Open: all year, Credit cards: VS
Other languages: some English, French
Region: Tuscany, Michelin Map: 430
www.karenbrown.com/italy/frascole.html

The prestigious Luigi Einaudi wine estate (he was the first president of the Italian republic), established in 1897, is the oldest in the area and extends over 300 acres of land of which some 60 acres are covered entirely with vineyards. Today, Luigi's granddaughter Paola and husband Giorgio Ruffo continue this strong family tradition as leading producers of top Barolo, Barbera, and Dolcetto wines. They have transformed one of the family residences dating to the 18th century into a refined bed and breakfast that preserves an authentic essence of the past. The very attractive and spacious bedrooms, all on the first floor and appointed with fine antiques and gorgeous fabrics, are joined by an elegant common living room where plenty of material on what the region offers is readily available. There is also a large terrace for guests on this same floor and a full country breakfast is served in the sunny dining room off the kitchen. Corner rooms and the one suite have terraces and all rooms have splendid views of the undulating hillsides with a backdrop of the Alps in the distance. Elvira, who takes care of guests, lives with her family in the apartment downstairs next to the cantina. In the works for spring of 2003 is the addition of six more bedrooms opposite the main house with arched glassed-in living room, swimming pool, and tennis court. *Directions:* The Foresteria dei Poderi is 2 km outside of Dogliani on the road towards Belvedere.

❄ ▬ ☆ 💳 🏠 🐕 🍴 🏇 P ⇌ 🎿 ♿ 🍇

FORESTERIA DEI PODERI   *New*
Host: Elvira Raimondi family
Localita: Borgata Gombe 31
Dogliani (CN) 12063, Italy
Tel: (0173) 70414, Fax: (0173) 742017
10 rooms, Double: €114
Open: all year, Credit cards: MC, VS
Other languages: some English
Region: Piedmont
www.karenbrown.com/italy/enaudi.html

The Villa Goetzen is an excellent choice as a base for visiting the villas of Palladio and the stunning historical centers of Verona and Padua (plus being 20 minutes from Venice). With a long tradition in hospitality, the local Minchio family bought the peach-colored home (dating from 1739) sitting on the Brenta Canal in town and transformed it into an elegant bed-and-breakfast accommodation. Although the house borders the main road, silence reigns within. You enter the iron gates into a courtyard, where on the right is a miniature coachhouse with two of the twelve rooms. These are the favorites and most romantic, with beamed mansard ceilings, parquet floors, and canal view. All rooms are decorated with classic good taste in the selection of antique pieces, wrought-iron beds, and coordination of fabrics and individual color schemes. Immaculate bathrooms have black-and-white checked tiles. Fortunate guests can sample delectable Venetian meals prepared by Paola and her son, Massimiliano, in one of the three intimate dining rooms. Brother Cristian receives guests and attends to their needs with great charm and finesse. It would be virtually impossible to find a hotel with similar standards in Venice at this rate. *Directions:* Exit at Dolo from the A4 autostrada and go straight into town until you arrive at the canal. Turn left and follow signs for Venezia. The villa is on the right.

VILLA GOETZEN
Host: Minchio family
Via Matteotti 6
Dolo (VE) 30031, Italy
Tel: (041) 5102300, Fax: (041) 412600
12 rooms, Double: €131
Restaurant closed Aug
Open: all year, Credit cards: all major
Other languages: good English
Region: Veneto, Michelin Map: 429
www.karenbrown.com/italy/goetzen.html

Picturesque Courmayeur, on the Italian side of the tunnel cutting through Mont Blanc into France, is a popular ski and summer resort. In the summer months comfortable temperatures and spectacular mountain scenery along with activities such as hiking, golf, horseback riding, and kayaking attract many visitors. The warm Berthod family have been offering hospitality to guests for some time, greeting them by name as they return "home" year after year. The old stone chalet and barn, squeezed between other houses in the center of the centuries-old village of Entreves, outside Courmayeur, has been restored using old and new materials. The cozy reception area maintains its original rustic flavor with flagstone floors and beams, hanging brass pots, typical locally made pine furniture, and homey touches like dried-flower arrangements and lace curtains. The 23 simply appointed rooms, divided between two buildings, offer the amenities of a standard hotel. A hearty breakfast is the only meal served; however, half-board arrangements can be made with local restaurants for longer stays. La Grange is an efficiently run bed and breakfast right at the foot of the snow-capped Alps. *Directions:* From Aosta where the A5 autostrada ends, continue on route 26 to Courmayeur. Entreves is 5 km beyond.

LA GRANGE
Host: Berthod family
Entreves-Courmayeur (AO) 11013, Italy
Tel: (0165) 869733, Fax: (0165) 869744
23 rooms, Double: €104–€130
Closed: May, Jun, Oct, Nov
Credit cards: all major
Other languages: good English
Region: Valle d'Aosta
Michelin Map: 428
www.karenbrown.com/italy/lagrange.html

Although the Apulia region is decidedly one of the most intriguing and unusual areas of the less-traveled Italy, it is short of accommodation with that combination of comfort, charm, and history we search high and low for. The 350-year-old Masseria Marzalossa, however, is a true exception, being a romantic inn strategically placed between the highlights of the region with its unique trulli cone-shaped houses. The stunning 100-acre property, which produces top-quality olive oil, has belonged to the Guarini family since its origins and they take pride in sharing their piece of paradise with world travelers. A wall surrounding the ancient masseria conceals several inner courtyards leading to the massive stone main house and connecting houses where the elegant, ground-level bedrooms enjoy their own private courtyard entrances. The tastefully decorated rooms are appointed with period antiques in harmony with the stone floors and vaulted or beamed ceilings. Also available is a magnificent suite with high, vaulted ceilings, frescoes, and a marble bathroom. A passageway from the front garden leads to a divine enclosed swimming pool surrounded by columns, lemon trees, bougainvillea vines, potted geraniums, and utter silence. Full country breakfasts and occasional dinners are served in the intimate dining room. This property is impeccable. *Directions:* Two km from Fasano on the S.S.16 going towards Ostuni, turn right at their sign.

❄ ⚓ ☕ 🍵 CREDIT 🏔 ☎ 🎿 👫 🐎 ♈ P 🚭 ≋ 🚶 🖼 ⛵ 🌿

MASSERIA MARZALOSSA
Hosts: Mario & Maria Teresa Guarini
Contrada da Pezze Vicine 65, Fasano (BR) 72015, Italy
Tel & fax: (080) 4413780 or (080) 4413024
5 rooms, Double: €156–€186
1 apartment: €93–€115 daily B&B
Minimum nights required: 3
Open: all year, Credit cards: VS
Other languages: some English
Region: Apulia, Michelin Map: 431
www.karenbrown.com/italy/marzalossa.html

Casa Palmira, directly north of Florence, was originally a group of rural buildings attached to an 11th-century tower guarding the road to the Mugello area of Tuscany. Stefano and Assunta, the amiable hosts, named their bed and breakfast after the old lady who lived in the house her entire life. She represents perhaps the spirit of the place, reminding everyone of the basic values of simple country living. The seven bedrooms on the top floor are decorated in a fresh, simple, country style, with hardwood floors, dried and fresh flowers, patchwork quilts, botanic prints, and local country antiques. Rooms are accessed by a large open sitting area with skylights and green plants. The hosts' naturally informal style of hospitality has guests feeling so at home that they can't resist assisting as Assunta works wonders in the open kitchen. This is part of a multi-functional space incorporating kitchen, dining room, and cozy living area with wicker chairs and large fireplace. Meals based on fresh vegetables are served either here or out in the garden under the portico. Daily cooking lessons for individuals or weekly cooking courses for small groups are arranged. Transfers from train station or airport are also offered. *Directions:* Halfway between Borgo S. Lorenzo and Florence on route 302 (Via Faentina), 2 km after Olmo coming from Florence (16 km). Casa Palmira is on the right at the sign for Ristorante Feriolo. From the north leave the A1 at Barberino del Mugello.

CASA PALMIRA
Hosts: Assunta & Stefano Mattioli
Via Faentina–Polcanto
Feriolo–Borgo S. Lorenzo (FI) 50030, Italy
Tel & fax: (055) 8409749, Cellphone: (339) 3331190
7 rooms, Double: €65–€85
Minimum nights required: 3
Open: Mar to Dec
Other languages: very little English, French
Region: Tuscany, Michelin Map: 430
www.karenbrown.com/italy/casapalmira.html

The stunning ancient cities of Ferrara, Ravenna, and Mantova have recently become part of the more curious traveler's itinerary and Il Bagattino could not be a more perfect base for exploring this triangle of Emilia-Romagna as well as making day trips to Bologna or Venice. Congenial hostess Alessandra left a ten-year restaurant business and opened her six-room bed and breakfast in the apartment next door to her own. Just off the main square of the historic center with its impressive fortress Castello Estense, Il Bagattino is on the second floor (with elevator) of a completely refurbished brick building dating to the 1400s. You are warmly greeted in the cheery yellow front room where a breakfast of fresh croissants and homemade cakes is served at one table. The six bedrooms are divided on both sides of the main room, with a small sitting room for extra privacy. Each comfortable, identically-sized bedroom, with air conditioning, television, mini bar, and hairdryer, has its own color scheme reflected in matching bedspreads and curtains, and a new checked-tiled bathroom. The entire historic center of this fascinating ancient city is closed off to traffic and is a cyclist's haven (bikes can be rented through Alessandra). Ferrara is a city not to be missed! *Directions:* Although this is a restricted traffic area, you can unload luggage in front of the bed and breakfast. Follow signs for the city center and Duomo—Corso Porta Reno begins from the piazza at the clock tower.

IL BAGATTINO
Host: Alessandra Maurillo
Corso Porta Reno 24
Ferrara 4410, Italy
Tel: (0532) 241887, Cellphone: (349) 8696683
Fax: (0532) 217546
6 rooms, Double: €85–€95
Open: all year, Credit cards: all major
Other languages: good English
Region: Emilia-Romagna, Michelin Map: 429
www.karenbrown.com/italy/bagattino.html

Best friends Luciano and Tommaso, refugees from city life, have over the past dozen or so years transformed the 1,000-acre property, La Casella, made up of woods, rivers, and valleys, into a veritable countryside haven for vacationers. Foremost attention has been given to the 28 rooms, which are divided between three separate stone houses. The Noci house contains seven doubles upstairs appointed with country antiques, and a large vaulted room downstairs used for small meetings or dining. La Terrazza, originally a hunting lodge, has nine rooms, one with namesake terrace looking over the poplar woods. On the highest point sits San Gregorio, with small chapel, where guests revel in the utter silence and a spectacular 360-degree view over the entire property. The lively dining room offers delectable cuisine, with ingredients direct from the farm. The many sports facilities include a beautiful big swimming pool, tennis, archery, and an equestrian center where numerous special outings and events are organized. There is also a spa program with natural treatments. Well-marked trails lead the rider, biker, or hiker to such marvels as Todi, Orvieto, or even Perugia. *Directions:* Exit at Fabro from the Rome-Florence A1 autostrada. Follow signs for Parrano (7 km), turning right at the Casella sign, and continue for another 7 km on a rough gravel road.

LA CASELLA
Hosts: Luciano Nenna & Tommaso Campolmi
Localita: La Casella, Ficulle (TR) 05016, Italy
Tel: (0763) 86588, Fax: (0763) 86684
28 rooms, Double: €160–€182*
*Includes breakfast & dinner
Minimum nights required: 7 in Jul & Aug
Open: all year, Credit cards: all major
Other languages: fluent English
Region: Umbria, Michelin Map: 430
www.karenbrown.com/italy/lacasella.html

Hotel Albergotto, situated on a corner of the elegant Via de Tornabuoni with its austere Renaissance palazzos and designer boutiques, could not be more central. It existed for the past century as a small hotel once hosting illustrious musical and literary artists like Verdi, Elliot, and Donizetti, but had been virtually forgotten in recent decades. A complete renovation has brought it back to life and it is an excellent choice in the middle price range. From the street entrance you take a red-carpeted flight of stairs to reach the elevator up to the rooms on the top three floors. Beyond the reception desk are two breakfast rooms and a comfortable living room decorated in royal-blue tones with large windows looking out to Tornabuoni. Light-wood floors throughout the hotel give the place a fresh and newer look. Very pleasant, cheerful bedrooms in mustard hues with matching floral bedspreads have amenities such as air conditioning, satellite TV, and mini bar. The double-paned windows keep out any traffic noise from the main street. Most delightful is the large mansard suite with wood-beamed ceilings and views over the city's rooftops and bell towers. *Directions:* Via de Tornabuoni is three blocks north of the River Arno and two blocks west of Piazza della Repubblica.

❄ ☕ ✄ 💳 ☎ 🛗 🚶 👫 🐎 🍸 P 🏨 🐾 🍇

HOTEL ALBERGOTTO
Host: Carlo Martelli
Via de Tornabuoni 13
Florence 50123, Italy
Tel: (055) 2396464, Fax: (055) 2398108
26 rooms, Double: €155–€290
Open: all year, Credit cards: all major
Other languages: good English
Region: Tuscany, Michelin Map: 430
www.karenbrown.com/italy/albergotto.html

The Hotel Aprile, owned by the Cantini Zucconi family for almost four decades, is located in a 15th-century Medici palace behind the Piazza Santa Maria Novella, near the train station and many fine restaurants and shops. The historical building was restored under the strict ordinance of Florence's Commission of Fine Arts. The small and charming hotel is full of delightful surprises: from 16th-century paintings and a bust of the Duke of Tuscany to the frescoed breakfast room and quiet courtyard garden. The old-fashioned reception and sitting areas are invitingly furnished with Florentine Renaissance antiques, comfy, overstuffed red armchairs, and Oriental carpets worn with time. There are 28 double bedrooms, all with private bathrooms. The wallpapered rooms include telephones and mini bars, and feature parquet floors and high vaulted ceilings, but vary widely in their size and decor—some are too basic and modern. Request one of the quieter rooms at the back of the hotel, overlooking the garden. At the desk you find Roberto Gazzini and Sandra Costantini looking after guests' needs. *Directions:* Use a city map to locate the hotel, three blocks north of the Duomo. There is a parking garage.

HOTEL APRILE
Host: Valeria Cantini Zucconi family
Via della Scala 6
Florence 50123, Italy
Tel: (055) 216237, Fax: (055) 280947
28 rooms, Double: €175
Open: all year, Credit cards: all major
Other languages: good English
Region: Tuscany, Michelin Map: 430
www.karenbrown.com/italy/aprile.html

The relaxed and friendly Hotel Ariele has been in the Bertelloni family for more than 40 years. Located in a quiet residential section across from the Opera House, it is within a short walking distance of the center of town. The entrance and reception area are made up of several old-fashioned-style sitting rooms, giving an immediate sense of the private home it used to be (dating back to 14th century). These spaces include a breakfast room and wallpapered sitting room with antique reproductions, gold velvet armchairs, fireplace, and Oriental carpets on tiled floors. A pleasant side garden with white wrought-iron tables and chairs offers a shady spot for breakfast. Hidden off in a corner is an unusual independent double room in its own separate house. There is also space here for parking at a minimal charge. The spacious, high-ceilinged bedrooms on the upper floor (accessed by elevator) are individually decorated using a mix of old and new furnishings and have either wood parquet or marble floors. Extra amenities include air conditioning, telephone, and satellite TV. Unfortunately, the fluorescent lighting does not help brighten up the sometimes drab color scheme. Guests can depend on the kind assistance of the staff for restaurant and itinerary suggestions. *Directions:* Between Piazza Vittorio Veneto and the River Arno. Use a detailed city map to locate the hotel.

HOTEL ARIELE
Host: Bertelloni family
Via Magenta 11
Florence 50123, Italy
Tel: (055) 211509, Cellphone: (337) 696604
Fax: (055) 268521
40 rooms, Double: €100–€150
Open: all year, Credit cards: all major
Other languages: good English
Region: Tuscany, Michelin Map: 430
www.karenbrown.com/italy/hotelariele.html

Another nice discovery in the category of small, renovated hotels in Florence is the Botticelli, hidden away on a narrow back street behind the Central Market. Many original features of this 16th-century building, once a private home, have been preserved including evidence of a tiny alley that divided the two now-united buildings. Guests enter into a painted, vaulted reception area appointed with large blue and gold armchairs and side sitting room. Other architectural features so typical of the Renaissance period in Florence are the austere gray stone doorways, beamed ceilings in bedrooms, and the delightful open loggia terrace on the second floor lined with terra-cotta vases of cascading red geraniums. The bedrooms are situated on the three upper floors, with two being up in the mansard and enjoying the best views, and are comfortably and practically decorated with clean wooden furniture and an occasional antique piece blending well with the pea-green fabrics. A full buffet breakfast is offered in the breakfast room with bar just behind the reception area. All the necessary modern amenities such as air conditioning, elevator, modern telephone system, and satellite TV were incorporated during the recent renovation. Fabrizio and his American wife, Janet, run two other hotels in Florence, one being the Villa Carlotta near Piazzale Michelangelo. *Directions:* The hotel is one block north of Piazza San Lorenzo and the Medici Chapels.

HOTEL BOTTICELLI
Hosts: Fabrizio & Janet Gheri
Via Taddea 8
Florence 50123, Italy
Tel: (055) 290905, Fax: (055) 294322
34 rooms, Double: €170–€204
Open: all year, Credit cards: all major
Other languages: good English
Region: Tuscany, Michelin Map: 430
www.karenbrown.com/italy/botticelli.html

In the center of the city and around the corner from the Accademia Gallery where Michelangelo's David has stood for the past 400 years or so, you find the pleasant and intimate Hotel delle Arti. In 2002 this small hotel, which opened just two years before, was passed on to the Logorio family, owners of the nearby Hotel Loggiato dei Serviti. Comfort, quiet, and a feeling of being pampered guests in a friend's home were the foremost objectives in the renovation process and the decorating was handled with the same care and attention one would give to a private home. Three tasteful bedrooms are located on each of the three upper floors reached by an elevator or green-carpeted staircase. New white-tiled bathrooms were added to the rooms, which are appointed with coordinated floral drapes and bedspreads, parquet floors, an occasional antique piece, and amenities such as air conditioning and satellite TV. On the top floor you find a cozy living room and a breakfast room with small balcony looking out over rooftops where a full buffet breakfast is offered. Warm and gracious hostess Cinzia is personally on call for guests and is a marvelous source of information on special less-touristy places to visit and what is happening in the city. *Directions:* Four blocks north of the Duomo cathedral.

HOTEL DELLE ARTI
Host: Lagorio family
Via dei Servi 38/a
Florence 50122, Italy
Tel: (055) 2645307, Fax: (055) 290140
9 rooms, Double: €144–€180
Open: all year, Credit cards: all major
Other languages: good English
Region: Tuscany, Michelin Map: 430
www.karenbrown.com/italy/arti.html

The Hotel Hermitage is a dream of a small, well-manicured hotel housed in a 13th-century palazzo with efficient service and breathtaking views over the city's most famous monuments. The location could not be more central—on a small street between the Uffizzi Gallery and the River Arno. The fifth-floor reception area looking out to the Ponte Vecchio bridge has a cozy living-room feeling with selected antique pieces, Oriental rugs, and corner fireplace. Across the hall is the veranda-like breakfast room dotted with crisp yellow tablecloths and topped with fresh flowers where privileged guests view the tower of Palazzo Signoria. Color-coordinated, air-conditioned rooms, some with hydrojet baths, have scattered antiques, framed etchings of the city, and more views. However, the highlight of a stay at the Hermitage is spending time dreaming on the rooftop terrace. The view embraces not only the previously mentioned marvels of Florence, but also the famous dome of the Duomo cathedral and Giotto's tower. Guests are served a Continental breakfast under the ivy-covered pergola and among the many flower-laden vases lining its borders. Reserve well in advance. *Directions:* Consult a detailed city map. There is a parking garage in the vicinity. Call for instructions as car traffic in this part of the city is strictly limited.

HOTEL HERMITAGE
Host: Vincenzo Scarcelli
Piazza del Pesce
Florence 50122, Italy
Tel: (055) 287216, Fax: (055) 212208
23 rooms, Double: €233–€244
Open: all year, Credit cards: MC, VS
Other languages: good English
Region: Tuscany, Michelin Map: 430
www.karenbrown.com/italy/hermitage.html

Good location.

The bed and breakfast In Piazza della Signoria is just that—in the piazza, hidden away on the corner of Florence's most famous square hosting the imposing city hall, Palazzo della Signoria. Splendid hosts Sonia and Alessandro initially bought the four-story ancient building as an investment but were touched by the magic spell of this very special historic spot just up the street from the house of Dante and decided to restore it and share it with friends. The fascinating restoration project became something of an archaeological adventure, with documents discovered dating back to 1427 along with a pair of woman's shoes from that same period, and 18th-century frescoes. Up one flight from street level, Sonia, Alessandro, and their three young sons greet guests in a small living room with tables where breakfast is served. The eight bedrooms, named after Renaissance masters, are spread about the two floors, with the top floor being crowned with three apartments for those able to enjoy this marvelous city for a full week. To-die-for views from this level include the piazza, Giotto's tower, and Brunelleschi's cupola. Impeccably styled rooms with unique personalities display the architectural discoveries, lovely antique furnishings, parquet floors, and rich colors of teal, peach, and rust. None of the innovative bathrooms are identical. A real treat. *Directions:* On the northeast corner of the square at the beginning of Via dei Magazzini.

❄ ☕ ✂ ☕ CREDIT ☎ ⛪ 🍴 🏃 🏇 P ⊘ ≋ 🎿 🖼 ⛵ 🎭

IN PIAZZA DELLA SIGNORIA   New
Hosts: Sonia & Alessandro Pini
Via dei Magazzini 2
Florence 50122, Italy
Tel: (055) 2399546, Fax: (055) 2676616
8 rooms, Double: €190–€240
3 apartments
Open: all year, Credit cards: all major
Other languages: good English
Region: Tuscany, Michelin Map: 430
www.karenbrown.com/italy/piazza.html

Orto de'Medici was named for the Medici family's extensive gardens and orchards that once existed on the site of this hotel. Capable father-and-son team Giulio and Giacomo Bufalini (ex-Splendor hotel, a reader favorite) recently took over the reins and took on the challenge of completely refurbishing the family's prim, centuries-old palazzo. Public areas maintain the ambiance of an elegant private home—the frescoed foyer and sitting rooms are graced with portraits, chandeliers, overstuffed armchairs, and Oriental carpets—while services and facilities in bedrooms conform to European Community standards. The spacious upper-floor guestrooms are reached by an elevator and are decorated with classic style. They have matching armoires and beds and all but ten have smart new gray-and-white-marble bathrooms. Several rooms on the top floor have a terrace or balcony with dreamy views over red Florentine rooftops. Perhaps the architectural highlight is the gracious breakfast room (breakfast is a buffet), with high ceilings, original parquet floors, and frescoed panels depicting garden scenes all around. French doors lead from this area to an outdoor terraced flower garden with white iron chairs and tables and a lovely view of San Marco church. Wine and cheese tastings are held here in the late afternoon. Dynamic young host Giacomo and his efficient and friendly staff ensure a perfect city sojourn. *Directions:* Four blocks north of the Duomo.

❄ ▣ ⚷ ☕ 💳 ☎ ⛩ 🏃 👫 🏇 ⅄ P 🚭 🏞 👕 ♿ 🍇

HOTEL ORTO DE'MEDICI
Host: Giacomo Bufalini family
Via San Gallo 30
Florence 50129, Italy
Tel: (055) 483427, Fax: (055) 461276
31 rooms, Double: €140–€250
Open: all year, Credit cards: all major
Other languages: good English
Region: Tuscany, Michelin Map: 430
www.karenbrown.com/italy/demedici.html

Need car, out of town, Not too great on hospitality & amenities. Expensive

| Florence | Villa Poggio San Felice | Maps: 7c, 8a |

The country residences of wealthy Florentine families dating back to Renaissance times were all concentrated on the hills above the city. Villa Poggio San Felice is one of these, reached by way of a labyrinth of narrow (unbelievably two-way) winding roads past stone-walled gardens concealing magnificent villas. Livia inherited not only the actual property of her great-grandfather but also a long-standing tradition in the hospitality field—he was the founder of two of Florence's most prominent hotels, today called the Grand and the Excelsior. This bed and breakfast is special indeed as guests are given full run of the main part of the two-story villa with its library, gracious, portrait-lined sitting rooms, and high-ceilinged dining room where a full buffet breakfast is served overlooking the formal gardens through French doors. Enthusiastic Livia and her husband Lorenzo's desire was that their guests experience the true flavor of a noble villa and consequently minimum possible modifications were made. This authentic ambiance prevails throughout the bedrooms, which are spread out on the upper floor and contain the family's original furniture. The romantic I Sposi honeymoon bedroom has fireplace, parquet floors, and hunter-green color scheme, while the spacious room Nonni features a large terrace looking out over hills to the famous dome of Florence's cathedral. *Directions:* Ten minutes from the center of Florence. A detailed map is provided.

VILLA POGGIO SAN FELICE
Hosts: Livia Puccinelli & Lorenzo Magnelli
Via San Matteo in Arcetri 24
Florence 50125, Italy
Tel: (055) 220016, Cellphone: (335) 6818844
Fax: (055) 2335388
5 rooms, Double: €200–€250
Open: Mar to Dec, Credit cards: all major
Other languages: good English
Region: Tuscany, Michelin Map: 430
www.karenbrown.com/italy/borgosanfelice.html

It is not hard to find accommodations in a 15th-century palace in downtown Florence — the historical center of the city has little else. La Residenza is no exception, but it offers the added attraction of being situated on Florence's most elegant street, with its famous boutiques, the Tornabuoni. For the last two generations the gracious Giacalone family has owned the palazzo's top three floors and operated them as a three-star hotel. An antique mahogany elevator takes you up to the reception area, which opens onto a pretty dining room with pink tablecloths and shelves lined with a collection of bottles, vases, and ceramics. Twenty-four rooms with an eclectic mix of old and new furnishings and amenities including air conditioning are divided between three floors, capped with a rooftop terrace burgeoning with flowerpots and surrounded by city views. A second, slightly worn sitting room with high, beamed ceilings and a satellite television for guests is located on the upper floor. Rooms and bathrooms are in a continual phase of renovation, so ask for one of the newer ones. This is one of the last of the old-fashioned pension-style hotels in the city. *Directions:* Use a detailed city map to locate the hotel in the heart of Florence between Palazzo Strozzi and Piazza Repubblica.

LA RESIDENZA
Hosts: Gianna Vasile & Paolo Giacalone
Via Tornabuoni 8
Florence 50123, Italy
Tel: (055) 218684, Fax: (055) 284197
24 rooms, Double: €190–€210
Without private bath: €129
Open: all year, Credit cards: all major
Other languages: good English
Region: Tuscany, Michelin Map: 430
www.karenbrown.com/italy/laresidenza.html

In the past two years, a new breed of bed and breakfasts has developed in Italy's favourite cities, especially in Florence and Rome. In order to keep costs down and be a competitive alternative to hotels, fewer amenities are offered and breakfast is self-service style in rooms (coffee, tea, breads, jam, cakes) and therefore is more adapted to an independent type of traveler. In fact, it is like having your own home in Florence with keys to the front door. Hostess Lea Gulmanelli had such success with her first B&B that she opened three additional places at a superior level, all in the same neighbourhood. At the Johlea three floors of two neighboring 19th-century buildings were restored, producing twelve bedrooms of varying sizes for guests (Johlea I and II). Lea has a real flair for decorating and, as in someone's home, each well-proportioned bedroom retains its own character. All are very cozily appointed in muted soft colors, with an occasional antique, Oriental carpets, paintings by the owner, and original tiled or parquet floors. There is someone on duty all day to assist guests with their needs. Both I and II have a common living room for guests, with II having a delightful flower-potted terrace with dreamy views over Florence's rooftops to the cupola of the Duomo. Tasteful and very economical. *Directions:* The B&B is located between San Marco Square and Piazza della Libertà, directly north of the Duomo, reached in 12 minutes on foot.

❄ ☎ 🛆 🏛 🚶 🏃 P 🖼

LE RESIDENZE JOHLEA   *New*
Host: Lea Gulmanelli
Via San Gallo 76 & 80
Florence 50129, Italy
Tel: (055) 4633292, Fax: (055) 4634552
12 rooms, Double: €90–€125
Open: all year
Other languages: good English
Region: Tuscany, Michelin Map: 430
www.karenbrown.com/italy/johlea.html

The refurbished Hotel Silla is located on the left bank of the River Arno opposite Santa Croce, the famous 13th-century square and church where Michelangelo and Galileo are buried. This position offers views from some of the rooms of several of Florence's most notable architectural attractions—the Duomo, the Ponte Vecchio, and the tower of the Palazzo Vecchio. Housed on the second and third floors of a lovely 15th-century palazzo with courtyard entrance, 36 new and spotless double rooms (non-smoking upon request) with private baths are pleasantly decorated with simple dark-wood furniture and matching bedspreads and curtains. Air conditioning and an elevator were recently added necessities. The fancy, cream-colored reception area is appointed in 17th-century Venetian style, with period furniture, a chandelier, and large paintings. Breakfast is served on the splendid and spacious second-floor outdoor terrace or in the dining room overlooking the Arno. The Silla is a friendly, convenient, and quiet hotel, near the Pitti Palace, leather artisan shops, and many restaurants. It offers tourists a good value in pricey Florence. A parking garage is available. *Directions:* Refer to a detailed city map to locate the hotel.

❄ ▆ ☇ CREDIT ☎ ⌂ ♿ ♟ ⚐ 🐎 ⛯ P 🚭 🏞 ♿ ⚘

HOTEL SILLA
Owner: Gabriele Belotti
Via dei Renai 5
Florence 50125, Italy
Tel: (055) 2342888, Fax: (055) 2341437
36 rooms, Double: €170
Open: all year, Credit cards: all major
Other languages: good English
Region: Tuscany, Michelin Map: 430
www.karenbrown.com/italy/hotelsilla.html

La Torricella, just on the outskirts of Florence, offers travelers the advantage of staying in a Tuscan home in a quiet residential area, yet with the city easily accessible by public transportation. Marialisa completely restored her great-grandfather's home and converted it into a comfortable and efficient lodging. She decided to offer all the trimmings of a hotel, with amenities such as satellite TVs, mini bars, and telephones in rooms, plus daily cleaning service. The terraced front of the pale-yellow villa is lined with terra-cotta vases of flowers and intoxicating wisteria vines. Upon entering the home, you pass through a small reception area with brick arches and equestrian prints into the luminous breakfast room where a buffet is served in the morning. Accommodations are scattered about the large, pristine home on various levels and are each similarly appointed in soft-green and mustard hues with sparkling new white bathrooms. Reproduction armoires and desks and wrought-iron beds harmonize well with the brick floors and high, beamed ceilings. Marialisa offers cooking classes, teaching secrets of genuine Tuscan dishes, and is a rich source of information on the area. There is a small pool at the back of the house. *Directions:* From the Certosa exit of the A1, head for the center of the city, turning right at the stoplight in Galluzzo at Piazza Acciaiuoli. Take Via Silvani for several blocks, turning right on Via Vecchia di Pozzolatico just before the fork in the road.

LA TORRICELLA
Host: Marialisa Manetti family
Via Vecchia di Pozzolatico 25, Florence 50125, Italy
Tel: (055) 2321808, Cellphone: (340) 2798856
Fax: (055) 2047402
7 rooms, Double: €114–€140, 1 apartment: €930–€1,292 weekly
Minimum nights required: 2
Open: Mar 1 to Nov 20, Credit cards: VS
Other languages: good English
Region: Tuscany, Michelin Map: 430
www.karenbrown.com/italy/torricella.html

On a hilltop overlooking the valley surrounding Foligno and covering over 1,000 acres is the enchanting Rocca Deli bed and breakfast. A winding gravel road takes you up to the crest of the mountain covered with olive groves and Scotch broom where views are truly remarkable and utter silence reigns. The rich history of the ancient tower here dates back to the year 1100 when it served as a watchtower, then through the centuries it was a stopping point on the pilgrims' path from the Adriatic Sea to Rome. Fabio, whose family bought the property in 1820, had the dream to see this mystic, meditative spot brought back to life by offering hospitality to travelers. Inside the wrought-iron gates, the first house attached to the original stone walls holds four bedrooms on two floors, reached by a spiral staircase and appointed with appropriate antiques. Within these medieval walls, immaculate bathrooms with characteristic Deruta tiles were added for each room. The fifth bedroom is in an adjacent house next to the remains of the original tower, with typical Umbrian wrought-iron bed and fireplace. Meals are served in the charmingly authentic taverna with long wooden tables or out in the panoramic garden. The family also owns the Le Due Torri on the other side of Spello, which offers very comfortable apartments for weekly stays. *Directions:* From Spoleto to Foligno, exit for Foligno Centro/Macereta and head for Carpello and La Rocca—follow the road to the end.

ROCCA DELI
Host: Fabio Ciri family
Localita: Scandolaro di Foligno
Foligno (PG) 06034, Italy
Tel: (0742) 651249, Cellphone: (335) 7783400
Fax: (0743) 270273
5 rooms, Double: €62–€72
Open: Easter to Oct, Credit cards: all major
Other languages: some English, French
Region: Umbria, Michelin Map: 430
www.karenbrown.com/italy/roccadeli.html

The bed and breakfast boom of the last decade in Italy has brought about a vast variety of accommodation from classic, in-home hospitality to places with many amenities that more resemble small hotels. Il Torrino brings us back to the more traditional example, with four bedrooms offered within the hostess's home. The large, old-fashioned family home of Signora Cesarina's grandparents is located in the Montechiari hills between Florence and Pisa east-west and between Volterra and Lucca north-south—a prime touring location. Here you will not find standardized rooms all decorated alike, but rather individual rooms filled with the family's personal belongings, heirloom furniture, and the authentic feeling of a Tuscan home. With her children grown and residing in various parts of the world, the very sweet hostess, Cesarina Campinotti, opened her home to travelers and welcomes guests into the downstairs living room and upstairs breakfast room where an abundant meal is served. A separate garden apartment for two persons has glass doors overlooking the small pool and countryside beyond. The four bedrooms with living room and kitchen can also be rented separately. Here you are in the center of Tuscany and there is a golf course 12 kilometers away. *Directions:* From Forcoli follow signs for Montechiari and Montacchita, continuing past Montacchita up to the group of houses called Montechiari (2 km). Il Torrino has the black iron gate and no sign.

IL TORRINO
Host: Cesarina Campinotti
Montechiari
Forcoli (PI) 56030, Italy
Tel & fax: (0587) 629181, Cellphone: (347) 3643411
4 rooms, Double: €93–€104
1 apartment: €440– €490 weekly
Minimum nights required: 3, Open: all year
Other languages: French, Spanish, very little English
Region: Tuscany, Michelin Map: 430
www.karenbrown.com/italy/iltorrino.html

The Locanda San Rocco is located in the heart of the Marches region, in spectacularly unspoilt countryside virtually unknown to international tourists. Here you have a chance to experience at first hand the beauty and simplicity of Italian country life. Nearby you can explore the historic hilltop towns of Camerino, Jesi, Osimo, Macerata, Loreto, and Recanati. The Pirri family from Rome return to their native Marches in the summer months and gracious hostess Signora Gisla opened her summer bed and breakfast business in order to share her love for this beautiful piece of the country. She offers very charming accommodation within an 18th-century stone farmhouse, part of a small village near their 132-acre property. Guests have full run of the house, which includes a large living area in a cozy exposed-stone and wood-beamed room, billiard room, and dining room looking out to a patio and garden at the back. The home is very tastefully appointed with fine country antiques, crisp striped fabrics on overstuffed armchairs, and sofas in sea-green and burgundy tones. The six bedrooms, divided between two floors and reached by an elevator, have wrought-iron beds, fine linens, and original brick floors. *Directions:* From Castelraimondo head towards San Severino and after 2 km turn left for Gagliole. The Locanda San Rocco is located in a small group of houses in Collaiello, before Gagliole.

LOCANDA SAN ROCCO   *New*
Host: Gisla Pirri Conforti
Frazione Collaiello 2
Gagliole (MC) 62020, Italy
Tel: (0737) 641900, Fax: (0737) 642324
6 rooms, Double: €85
Minimum nights required: 2
Closed: Oct to May, Credit cards: MC, VS
Other languages: some English
Region: Marches, Michelin Map: 430
www.karenbrown.com/italy/rocco.html

In the heart of the beautiful Chianti wine region, a cypress-lined lane leads up to the handsome, 13th-century Castello di Meleto, set upon a gentle hill just outside Gaiole. The fairytale-perfect castle with its imposing round watchtowers and arched stone doorway embraced by fragrant roses makes an enchanting stop while exploring the back roads of Tuscany. There is a double treat in store because you can not only sample delicious wines in the attractive tasting room, but also visit the interior of this splendid castle with its walls and ceilings lavishly enhanced by superb frescoes, lovely antique furnishings, and even an adorable baroque theater dating back to the mid-1700s (call ahead for tour times). The castle also offers nine attractively decorated guestrooms with antique furnishings, five within the castle and four in the chapel. Breakfast is served each morning in the cozy kitchen with huge open fireplace. The castle gardens stretch out to a line of lacy trees that frame a superb vista of the idyllic Tuscan countryside. There is also a stunning view from the swimming pool, which is bordered on three sides by a flagstone terrace and on the fourth flows seamlessly into the horizon. If you are traveling with friends or family and want a place to call home for a longer stay, the castle offers nine beautifully furnished stone cottages with well-equipped kitchens and from one to three bedrooms. *Directions:* From Gaiole in Chianti, follow signs to the castle.

CASTELLO DI MELETO *New*
Hosts: Lucia Pasqualini & Roberto Garcea
Gaiole in Chianti (SI) 53013, Italy
Tel: (0577) 749217, Fax: (0577) 749762
9 rooms, Double: €134
9 cottages: €700–€1,700 weekly
Open: all year, Credit cards: all major
Other languages: fluent English
Region: Tuscsany, Michelin Map: 430
www.karenbrown.com/italy/castellomeleto.html

The Castello di Tornano, a strategically situated hilltop tower dating back almost 1,000 years, has a 360-degree vista of the surrounding valley and has been of great historical significance in the seemingly endless territorial battles between Siena and Florence. The current owners are the Selvolini family, whose lovely daughter, Patrizia, welcomes guests to the wine estate. Eight simply appointed apartments for independent stays, with a mix of old and new, are situated in a stone farmhouse in front of the tower. Each has a living area, kitchen, one or two bedrooms, and small outdoor area. The pièce de résistance, however, is the three-floor apartment within the monumental tower, sparsely furnished with the family's antiques and featuring two bedrooms, three living rooms with fireplace, dining room, kitchen, and tower-top terrace with a view not easily forgotten. Six double bedrooms are now available within the central part of the castle. Meals can be taken at the restaurant on the property. Tennis courts and horseback riding facilities are available as well as the exquisite pool cut into the rock and spanned by a stone bridge. Patrizia also organizes cooking classes upon request for small groups. Patrizia may not always be present as she commutes from Florence, but a hostess is always on hand for guests. *Directions:* From the A1 exit at Valdarno and follow the sign to Cavriglia. Take the S.S.408 towards Siena. Passing Gaiole on the left, you will see the sign for Tornano.

CASTELLO DI TORNANO
Hosts: Patrizia Selvolini & Francesca Gioffredda
Gaiole in Chianti (SI) 53013, Italy
Tel: (0577) 746067, Cellphone: (335) 7606699
Fax: (0577) 746094
6 rooms, Double: €160–€300, 9 apartments: €900–€2,300 weekly
Trattoria on premises
Open: Mar to Dec, Credit cards: VS
Other languages: good English
Region: Tuscany, Michelin Map: 430
www.karenbrown.com/italy/castelloditornano.html

The heel of Italy offers a wealth of natural beauty but, because of its remoteness, few really charming places to stay. The Masseria Lo Prieno is run by the delightful Castriota family, whose crops are representative of the staples of the Apulia region, and include olives, almonds, fruits, and grains. Spartan accommodations are offered in bungalows scattered among the pine woods and palms on the family property. Each mini guesthouse includes one bedroom, kitchenette, bathroom, and an eating area containing basic necessities. Nine simply decorated rooms with bathrooms are now available within a newly constructed house on the property. Former animal stalls have been converted into a large dining space rustically decorated with antique farm tools and brass pots. Along with warm hospitality, the family makes meals a top priority and it is the food that makes the stay here special. For an exquisite and authentic traditional meal, the restaurant here is incomparable. Both Maria Grazia, the energetic daughter who runs the show, and her charming mother take pride in demonstrating how local specialties are prepared. This is a budget choice for touring this area. *Directions:* From Taranto take N174 to Galatone, then follow signs for Secli. From Bari take the Gallipoli-Galatone road. After the first traffic light, continue to the sign on the right for Masseria and follow signs to the farm.

MASSERIA LO PRIENO
Host: Francesco Castriota family
Localita: Contrada Orelle, Galatone (LE) 73044, Italy
Tel: (0833) 865898, Cellphone: (335) 8432610
Fax: (0833) 861879
9 rooms, Double: €72, 5 bungalows: €78–€104 daily
Per person half board: €51, Minimum nights required: 2
Open: Apr to Sep, Credit cards: all major
Other languages: some English
Region: Apulia, Michelin Map: 431
www.karenbrown.com/italy/masserialoprieno.html

On the extreme outskirts of Florence, the Fattoressa offers a location for dual exploration of both the city and the Tuscan countryside. One of the many marvelous attractions of Florence is how the countryside comes right up to the doors of the city and just behind the magnificent Certosa monastery you find the 15th-century stone farmhouse of the delightfully congenial Fusi-Borgioli family. They have transformed the farmer's quarters into guest accommodations: four sweetly simple bedrooms plus two triples, each with its own spotless bathroom. Angiolina and Amelio, who have tended to this piece of land for many years, treat their guests like family and, as a result, enjoy receiving some of them year after year. Daughters-in-law Laura and Katia, who speak English, have been a great help in assisting guests with local itineraries. Visitors take meals en famille at long tables in the cozy, rustic dining room with a large stone fireplace (€31 for dinner). Here Angiolina proudly serves authentic Florentine specialties using ingredients from her own fruit orchard and vegetable garden. *Directions:* Entering Florence from the Certosa exit off the Siena superstrada, turn left one street after the Certosa monastery stoplight onto Volterrana. After the bridge, turn right behind the building. The house is just on the left.

LA FATTORESSA
Hosts: Angiolina Fusi & Amelio Borgioli
Via Volterrana 58
Galluzzo-Florence (FI) 50124, Italy
Tel & fax: (055) 2048418
6 rooms, Double: €95–€100
Minimum nights required: 2
Open: all year
Other languages: some English, French, German
Region: Tuscany, Michelin Map: 430
www.karenbrown.com/italy/lafattoressa.html

Casa Mezzuola is part of a small group of farmhouses atop a hill 3 kilometers outside Greve where the land was divided into separate smaller properties. Friendly hosts, Riccardo, an antiques and jewelry dealer, Nicoletta, and their two girls live in the main house while hospitality is offered within three apartments for two to four persons in the adjacent stables and fienile where the hay was once stored. The stone walls, beams, and original brick openings to allow air into the barn were all preserved in the tower-like construction housing two of the apartments. A two-story apartment has a tiled kitchen/living area on one floor and bedroom and bathroom upstairs, while the snug studio apartment crowns the top of the tower. They are all nicely furnished with colorful rugs, local country furniture, satellite TV, and fully equipped kitchens. Breakfast is served within the apartments or outside under one of the pergola terraces. Just below the apartments is a swimming pool, which enjoys the expansive vistas, and there are bikes for guests' use. This is a convenient base for travelers in the heart of Chianti. Greve has a full program of festivals, concerts, and events, especially during the summer. *Directions:* Entering Greve from the north (Florence), turn right at the first stoplight. Follow signs for Mezzuola, Cologne, not Montefioralle. After 3 km of unpaved, bumpy road, you will come across the marked property.

CASA MEZZUOLA
Host: Riccardo Franconeri family
Via S. Cresci 30
Greve in Chianti (FI) 50022, Italy
Tel & fax: (055) 8544885, Cellphone: (347) 6135920
3 apartments: €550–€850 weekly, €90–€130 daily
Minimum nights required: 3, 7 Jun to Sep
Open: all year, Credit cards: MC, VS
Other languages: good English
Region: Tuscany, Michelin Map: 430
www.karenbrown.com/italy/mezzuola.html

In the northern reaches of Lazio, bordering Umbria and Tuscany, is the stately, 17th-century castle of the noble Mancini Caterini family. Sociable hosts Antonello and Cristina decided to transfer their young family from Rome and reside permanently on the vast wooded property, overseeing the agricultural activity as Antonello's ancestors once did. They have done an admirable job of restoring the large, ivy-covered farmhouse just below the family's residence and creating four charming apartments plus twelve bedrooms for guests. The bi-level apartments maintain their original rustic flavor and are cheerfully decorated with antique armoires and dressers, country fabrics for curtains and bedspreads, and wrought-iron beds. Accommodation in low season and for shorter stays is offered in the Granaio 1 and 2, with four bedrooms on each floor and individual living rooms, which can also be used as separate apartments. On the ground floor you find outdoor and indoor eating areas, billiard room, and game room overlooking a lovely swimming pool. Activities include tennis, horseback riding, wine itineraries, and boat rides and sailing on nearby Lake Bolsena, besides exploration of the many ancient Etruscan towns in this very beautiful countryside. *Directions:* From the A1 autostrada exit at Orvieto and follow signs first for Bolsena then Castel S. Giorgio-S. Lorenzo Nuovo-Grotte di Castro. Just past town turn right at the Castello sign.

CASTELLO DI S. CRISTINA
Hosts: Cristina & Antonello Mancini Caterini
Grotte di Castro (VT) 01025, Italy
Tel & fax: (0763) 78011, Cellphone: (339) 8605166
12 rooms, Double: €90–€100
6 apartments: €500–€1,500 weekly
Minimum nights required: 2, 7 in high season
Open: all year
Region: Lazio, Michelin Map: 430
www.karenbrown.com/italy/cristina.html

The Aosta mountain area is known primarily as a ski resort, sharing the majestic Alps with France and Switzerland. Tourism during the rest of the year is in the developing stages and offers a myriad of attractions in a beautifully unspoilt environment, including mountain hikes on well-marked trails (the famous Walser trail stretches straight across the region starting on the Swiss border and ending on the French border), medieval castles, quaint villages, Roman archaeological sites, local artisans, artisan cheese production, and wine tours. Lo Triolet offers a strategic point from which to visit these treasures within two comfortable apartments in the restored 16th-century house with cantina next door. The group of stone houses near the road includes the family's own house, the guesthouse, and surrounding neighbors all backed by the hillside and woods. Everything in the one- and two-bedroom apartments—tiles on floors, kitchenettes, bathrooms, and furniture—is brand new. The immediate area lends itself well to the production of various grapes and Marco took advantage of this climate for the production of various Pinot Gris, which he enthusiastically explains to guests. His wife's family owns another winery in the next valley. *Directions:* Exit from A5 at Aosta Ovest, driving towards Courmayeur. After 5 km, just after the village of Velleneuve, follow signs for Introd. After another 2 km, Lo Triolet is marked on the left.

LO TRIOLET   *New*
Hosts: Marco Martin & Paola Bionaz
Fraz. Junod 7
Introd (AO) 11010, Italy
Tel: (0165) 95067, Cellphone: (339) 1387092
Fax: (0165) 95437
2 apartments: €48–€57 daily (2 people)
Open: all year
Other languages: French
Region: Aosta Valley, Michelin Map: 428
www.karenbrown.com/italy/triolet.html

Lorenza and her family enjoy hosting guests right in their own home within two studio apartments on the ground floor of a typical chalet-style house. The property sits on a hillside with nice views over the valley and mountain ranges near other homes on the outskirts of Introd. Each apartment has a double bed, bathroom, kitchenette with eating area, and garden space and is simply but comfortably appointed with typical furniture made of pinewood from the area. Although no meals are served, there are many restaurants in the vicinity where you can sample typical local products, especially the rich variety of cheeses, hams, and salamis. As far as "in-home" activities are concerned, Lorenza can arrange lessons in the study of local flowers, herbs, and plants for the specific use of natural medicine, or the art of basket weaving. Guests also take full advantage of the fact that Lorenza's husband is an official guide and ranger at the Gran Paradiso National Park and conducts full-day excursions up the mountain for some spectacular views of Mont Blanc. The central location offers easy access to Courmayeur, Cogne, Champoluc, and other valleys of the Aosta region. *Directions:* Exit from A5 at Aosta Ovest, driving towards Courmayeur. After 5 km, just after the village of Velleneuve, follow signs for Introd (Villes Dessous).

PLANTEY   New
Host: Lorenza Silvestri Brunet family
Fraz. Villes Dessous 65
Introd (AO) 11010, Italy
Tel: (0165) 95531, Fax: (0165) 920991
2 apartments: €46 daily (2 people)
Open: all year
Other languages: French
Region: Aosta Valley, Michelin Map: 428
www.karenbrown.com/italy/plantey.html

La Morra is a quaint village dominating the Langhe wine valley with spectacular views over undulating layers of striped hillsides. The village, dating back to the 12th century, has six historic churches and a bell tower from the 1600s. There is a comprehensive enoteca in town where most regional wines are presented and sold, plus five other wine bars and six restaurants. The Vibertis have returned to their farm property after living in Alba for some years and now the retired couple enjoys hosting guests from around the world in their pristine white brick farmhouse dating to 1885. Signora Teresa has done a wonderful job of maintaining an authentic ambiance of the farmer's home. Rooms with worn brick floors retain all the original country antiques, are decorated with embroidered curtains and bedspreads, and have immaculate new bathrooms. All four bedrooms face the road and are off a hallway up on the first floor of one half of the house, while the hosts' quarters remain separate on the opposite side. A country breakfast with fresh-baked cakes is served downstairs in the guests' common room. Son Franco speaks English well and is present mostly in the afternoons and weekends, while brother Bruno has just opened his own 14-room hotel in La Morra. Genuine hospitality and ambiance. *Directions:* Leaving Alba, follow signs for Barolo. At the town of Gallo d'Alba, turn right for La Morra-Santa Maria. Casa Bambin is right on the road 2 km before La Morra.

CASA BAMBIN   New
Host: Teresa Viberti family
Frazione Santa Maria 68
La Morra (CN) 12064, Italy
Tel & fax: (0173) 50785
4 rooms, Double: €50
Minimum nights required: 2
Closed: Dec to Mar
Other languages: good English
Region: Piedmont, Michelin Map: 428
www.karenbrown.com/italy/bambin.html

Among the many identical, perfectly practical chalet-style accommodations available throughout the Dolomites, we gratefully came upon a unique treasure. Easily spotted on the hillside above the main road from La Villa to Corvara, the 16th-century castle with its surrounding stone wall, rock foundation, and two corner lookout towers is the most important and best-preserved monument of its kind remaining in the Badia Valley. Ciastel Colz is something very magical and intimate and has been restored and tastefully decorated with the utmost attention to detail and to the preservation of the castle's rich history. The upstairs floor is dedicated entirely to the restaurant where traditional local dishes are served. Set up like a private home, you find a very cozy rust-and-gray-colored breakfast room with a wood-burning oven where fresh bread is made, a comfortable sitting room, and two simply elegant dining rooms. These luminous paneled rooms, decorated in pastel colors accented with green and rust, have a light and airy ambiance, which contrasts with the building's massive volume. One large bedroom is found on the next floor while the other three are located in the external towers and offer extra privacy. The castle offers guests an authentic ambiance in a most romantic setting. *Directions:* Leave the A22 at Val Gardena and drive through Ortisei, Selva, and Corvara to La Villa. Follow signs to the Ciastel Colz before reaching La Villa center. (A total of 45 km.)

CIASTEL COLZ
Hosts: Wilma & Stefan Weiser
Strada Marin 80, La Villa (BZ) 39030, Italy
Tel: (0471) 847511, Cellphone: (348) 8219284
Fax: (0471) 844120
4 rooms, Double: €176–€268
Restaurant closed Tue
Closed: May & Nov, Credit cards: all major
Other languages: good English
Region: Trentino-Alto Adige, Michelin Map: 429
www.karenbrown.com/italy/colz.html

An outstanding alternative to the city hotels of Venice is the perfectly charming Gargan bed and breakfast situated in the countryside just 30 kilometers away. The Calzavara family renovated the family's expansive 17th-century country house and opened the restaurant and guestrooms, offering four sweetly decorated bedrooms each with its own bathroom on the top floor plus two suites consisting of bedroom, sitting room, and bathroom. Signora Antonia, son Alessandro who looks after the farm, and his wife Nicoletta enjoy making their guests feel as "at home" as possible by having fresh flowers in the cozy, antique-filled bedrooms. The downstairs sitting and dining rooms display the family's country antiques as well as a large fireplace and nice touches such as lace curtains and paintings. Guests are treated to a full breakfast of home-baked cakes and exceptional four-course dinners prepared especially for guests by Signora Antonia herself, using all ingredients from the farm. The Gargan is an ideal choice in this area, being a short drive from such marvels as Padua, Venice, Treviso, Vicenza, Verona, and Palladian villas plus many smaller medieval villages. *Directions:* From Venice take route 245 to Scorze, turning right for Montebelluna at the stoplight 1 km after town. After the town of S. Ambrogio turn left at the stoplight. Turn right at the church in Levada up to the house.

GARGAN
Host: Calzavara family
Via Marco Polo 2
Levada di Piombino Dese (PD) 35017, Italy
Tel: (049) 9350308, Fax: (049) 9350016
6 rooms, Double: €62–€83
Per person half board: €51–€62
Closed: Jan & Aug
Other languages: some English
Region: Veneto, Michelin Map: 429
www.karenbrown.com/italy/gargan.html

When Lois Martin, a retired teacher, spotted the lovely restored farmhouse at San Martino, she knew it literally had her name on it and immediately purchased it. She has been running a bed and breakfast for the past seven years and offers travelers all possible amenities of home. The house is completely open to guests, from the upstairs cozy living room with large stone fireplace, which divides the four bedrooms, to the downstairs country kitchen and eating area. A full breakfast is served either outside on the patio or in the kitchen with its impressive display of Deruta ceramics. One bedroom with king bed is joined by a bathroom to a small room with twin beds, ideal for a family. Each of the other two doubles has a bathroom, with one being en suite. Besides a swimming pool overlooking the wooded hills and valley, other extras are satellite TV, a travel library, American washer and dryer, bikes, guest bathrobes, and dinner upon request, served out on the back porch where tobacco was once hung to dry. Being right on the border of Umbria and Tuscany, Lake Trasimeno and towns such as Gubbio, Perugia, Cortona, Assisi, and Deruta are all easily accessible. The entire house can also be rented weekly for a group of up to eight persons. *Directions:* From Lisciano square, pass the bar and turn left for San Martino. Continue for 2 km and take a right up the hill at the sign for San Martino for just over 1.5 km to the house.

CASA SAN MARTINO
Host: Lois Martin
Localita: San Martino 19
Lisciano Niccone (PG) 06060, Italy
Tel: (075) 844288, Fax: (075) 844422
4 rooms, Double: €145
1 house: €2,000–€5,000 weekly
Minimum nights required: 3
Open: all year, Other languages: fluent English
Region: Umbria, Michelin Map: 430
www.karenbrown.com/italy/casasanmartino.html

Mario and Gabriella Tortella left an intense corporate life and returned to their peaceful Abruzzo region with the intention of concentrating on organic farming and hospitality. They have succeeded and today the 90-acre property overlooking the Apennines is made up of olive groves, woods, a kiwi plantation, orchards, pastures for farm animals, and fields of grain and cereals. Guests are welcomed like old friends and are accommodated within the six country-style bedrooms upstairs in the main 300-year-old house or in one of the more independent apartments next door. Very much in keeping with the simple rustic features of the farmhouse, they have wrought-iron beds, antique armoires, new tiled bathrooms, and a common living room. The largest has a fireplace and kitchenette. Guests convene in the evening for conversation and an excellent regional meal prepared with ingredients straight from the farm by Gabriella's mother, Olga, either out on the covered porch or in one of the vaulted brick dining rooms. This is a very pleasant base for exploring Loreto, Penne, Pescara, Atri, and three national parks, among other attractions. Alternatively, you can relax poolside and just enjoy the views, the tranquillity, and superb meals. *Directions:* Exit the A25 at Pescara-Villanova and drive towards Penne on S.S.81. Six km before Penne, just before S. Pellegrino, turn right after a bar (or call from there) onto a gravel road up to Le Magnolie. (18 km total from exit.)

LE MAGNOLIE
Hosts: Mario & Gabriella Tortella
Contrada Fiorano 83, Loreto Aprutino (PE) 65014, Italy
Tel & fax: (085) 8289534, Cellphone: (335) 384180
6 rooms, Double: €60–€80
2 apartments: €450–€750 weekly
Minimum nights required: 4
Closed: Jan & Feb, Credit cards: MC, VS
Other languages: good English
Region: Abruzzo, Michelin Map: 430
www.karenbrown.com/italy/magnolie.html

Still another undiscovered area is the peaceful countryside northeast of Todi, where you find the Castello di Loreto. After having meticulously restored part of this medieval fortress castle as a country home, Nino Segurini now coordinates restoration work on ancient buildings, besides continuing his own business as a consultant to antiques dealers. Nino is very knowledgeable on a variety of subjects from history and art to music, and delights in introducing guests to the undiscovered treasures he has found in the immediate area. (Upon request he can organize and lead small groups to various cities.) Nino and Francesca's home is a veritable museum, with collections of ancient artifacts naturally inhabiting the historical building. Within the base of the thick-walled fortress you find the main living room, two small bedrooms (one twin, one double) connected by a sitting area, and three bathrooms. The kitchen leads outside to the spacious patio with grape pergola overlooking the landscaped garden and swimming pool. The preferred and largest bedroom, arranged as a suite with its own sitting room, is reached by two flights of stairs past another living room with fireplace, appointed with antique armour and weaponry and an enclosed loggia. *Directions:* Leave highway E45 at Todi/Orvieto, heading for Pian di Porto, then San Terenziano. After 2 km, fork right towards Loreto for another 4 km. The entrance gate is across the street from the church.

CASTELLO DI LORETO
Hosts: Nino & Francesca Segurini
Loreto-Todi (PG) 06059, Italy
Tel & fax: (075) 8852501, Cellphone: (335) 6249734
3 rooms, Double: €105–€130
Minimum nights required: 3
Open: all year, Credit cards: MC, VS
Other languages: good English, Spanish
Region: Umbria, Michelin Map: 430
www.karenbrown.com/italy/loreto.html

Lucca is decidedly one of the loveliest cities of Italy with its historical churches and circular piazzas interspersed among beautiful shops featuring original storefronts and signage. Besides the well-known summer Puccini Festival (this is his birthplace), there are antiques markets, artisan fairs, and some of the most beautiful formal gardens and villas in Italy surrounding the city. In March the villas and gardens open for a special tour when the area's famed flower, the camellia (tree size), is in bloom. Over the years we have patiently awaited the arrival of a charming place to stay within the city walls and we were eventually rewarded with the Alla Corte degli Angeli. The Bonino family, already very familiar with the hospitality business, took over a private residence in the very heart of Lucca and created six spacious bedrooms with guests' comfort in mind. The ground-floor reception area includes a cozy dining room with fireplace where an abundant buffet breakfast is served, if not in your own room. Bedrooms on the upper two floors are reached by an elevator, and all follow a specific flower theme, with pastel-colored walls giving an overall fresh feeling. Complementing the well-put-together decor are antique dressers, parquet floors, and amenities such as air conditioning, Jacuzzi tubs, mini bars, TVs, and Internet access. *Directions:* In the pedestrian-only center of Lucca near the famous Piazza Anfiteatro. Private garage parking can be arranged.

ALLA CORTE DEGLI ANGELI
Host: Pietro Bonino
Via degli Angeli 23
Lucca 55100, Italy
Tel: (0583) 469204, Fax: (0583) 991989
6 rooms, Double: €155
Open: all year, Credit cards: all major
Other languages: some English
Region: Tuscany, Michelin Map: 430
www.karenbrown.com/italy/allacorte.html

For those seeking a base for exploring the hilltowns of Tuscany while sojourning in very characteristic accommodation with a rich historical past, the Lucignanello is a sublime choice. Imagine residing in one of the cluster of stone houses that make up the quaint village immersed in the type of picture-perfect, timeless Tuscan landscape seen in Renaissance paintings. The illustrious Piccolomini family still owns the 15th-century property where lovers of Italy can live out a dream. Five two-bedroom houses have been masterfully restored, preserving the original architectural features while ensuring modern facilities. The irregularly shaped interiors are filled with lovely antiques, Oriental carpets, beautifully tiled bathrooms, and kitchens with travertine counters, and all but one have large fireplaces. High above the village is a pool set among olive trees with inspiring views. Although breakfast ingredients are supplied, guests are self-sufficient (they find the hamlet's grocery shop and osteria most convenient) but a permanent staff is at their disposal for any suggestions or assistance. A separate five-bedroom farmhouse with private swimming pool is rented out by the week. Country charm exudes from every corner and the ambiance is so authentic you will feel almost Tuscan before you leave! *Directions:* From San Quirico go towards Siena, taking the first right to San Giovanni d'Asso. Two km before town, turn right for the 2-km drive to Lucignano d'Asso.

LUCIGNANELLO BANDINI
Host: Giacomo Stuart
Lucignano d'Asso-S. Giovanni d'Asso (SI) 53045, Italy
Tel: (0577) 803068, Fax: (0577) 803082
5 apartments: €1,550 weekly, 1 villa: €4,000 weekly
Minimum nights required: 3
Open: all year, Credit cards: MC, VS
Other languages: good English
Region: Tuscany, Michelin Map: 430
www.karenbrown.com/italy/lucignanello.html

A few years ago the Luz family of Luino refurbished another home, creating a second, more economical accommodation just 2 kilometers up the road from their hotel on Lake Maggiore. The Colmegna is run by their young and energetic daughter Lara and caters well to families—in fact, there is no charge for children under four. The two pale-yellow buildings run right along the waterfront bordered by an old stone port. There are several terraces for dining outdoors and another with a lawn for sunning or relaxing and enjoying the view. Beyond this is a gorgeous shaded park with romantic trails, tall trees, and wildflowers at one of the prettiest points of the lake. Simply appointed bedrooms are all situated lakeside on the two floors and accommodate from two to four persons. Swimming, sailing, and windsurfing sports can be arranged. Luino is famous for its open market on Wednesdays, a long-standing tradition since 1541. Within touring distance are the lakes of Lugano and Como, the ferry from Laveno across Lake Maggiore, and the Swiss border. *Directions:* Luino is halfway up the lake on the eastern side near the Swiss border. Heading north, Colmegna is on the left-hand side of the main road just past the town of Luino.

CAMIN HOTEL COLMEGNA
Host: Lara Luz
Localita: Colmegna
Luino (VA) 21016, Italy
Tel: (0332) 510855, Fax: (0332) 501687
25 rooms, Double: €95–€125
Open: Mar to Dec, Credit cards: all major
Other languages: good English
Region: Lombardy, Michelin Map: 428
www.karenbrown.com/italy/caminhotelcolmegna.html

The noble Albertario family have four large countryside properties in Umbria and Tuscany that they have opened up to accommodate travelers. Macciangrosso, bordered by ancient cypress trees, is the most beautiful, with its hilltop position overlooking the sweeping valley. The large stone villa, which has been added on to at various times throughout its long history (15th-century origins), belonged to the noble Piccolomini ancestors. You enter through the side gate, walk over a large patio looking onto the delightful rose garden, and climb an external stairway up to the six bedrooms. These are all accessed by a main living room, more like a museum with its rare antique pieces and gilded frame paintings. Bedrooms, each with a small bathroom, are simpler, appointed with wrought-iron beds and coordinated bedspreads and curtains. Other common living areas are the transformed cantina and dining and game rooms. The swimming pool is bordered by a stone wall from the Etruscan period and a tennis court is nearby. Ten apartments of various sizes are found in the rest of the home and in a nearby house next to the chapel. Close to the thermal spas, Macciangrosso is on the edge of Umbria and Tuscany, offering easy access to the highlights of both regions. *Directions:* From Chiusi drive 3 km towards Chianciano. Turn right at the grocery store and go 1.5 km to the house.

MACCIANGROSSO
Hosts: Sonia & Luigi Albertario
Localita: Macciano, Chiusi (SI) 53044, Italy
Tel: (0578) 274198, Cellphone: (347) 3204472
Fax: (0578) 21459, 6 rooms, Double: €135
10 apartments: €700–€950 weekly, Heating extra
Minimum nights required: 3, 7 in apartments
Closed: Nov, Credit cards: MC, VS
Other languages: French, good English
Region: Tuscany, Michelin Map: 430
www.karenbrown.com/italy/macciangrosso.html

Ca'delle Rondini opened its doors first as a restaurant and then six years ago as a bed and breakfast. The typical rectangular-shaped, pale-yellow farmhouse with incorporated barn, built in 1800, faces out to the main road in town and at the back to acres of flat fields, fruit orchards, and horse stables. In a section of the long house live gregarious host Ilo and his brother Alessandro, who helps Mamma in the kitchen with the creation of delectable local fare whose ingredients come directly from the farm. Entering the lofty restaurant with fireplace, gray-stone floors, beamed ceilings, and large arched windows, one has the sense of being part of a truly authentic local gathering place—especially for Sunday lunch. Guests sit down in one of the two dining rooms and are offered a variety of inventive antipasti served on cutting boards. The comfortable bedrooms upstairs and one below (with access for the handicapped) all have telephones and air conditioning, and are very pleasantly appointed in typical country style with mansard beamed ceilings, pine-wood floors, and country antiques. Outings by bike or horseback are arranged in the nearby nature park reserve. Ilo can suggest many original itineraries, including a tour of Venice's abandoned islands on a friend's boat. Ca'delle Rondini is a great base for visiting Venice, Padua, Treviso, Verona, and Vicenza. *Directions:* Ca'delle Rondini is in the town of Maerne, northwest of Mestre, just 10 km from Venice.

CA'DELLE RONDINI
Host: Silvestri family
Via Ca' Rossa 26
Maerne (VE) 30030, Italy
Tel & fax: (041) 641114
6 rooms, Double: €85
Restaurant open Thu to Sun
Open: all year, Credit cards: MC, VS
Other languages: none
Region: Veneto, Michelin Map: 429
www.karenbrown.com/italy/rondini.html

It would be difficult for anyone with a passion for the outdoors to resist the challenge offered Federico when he inherited this 1,000-plus-acre estate in the wilderness of Maremma. He and his energetic wife, Elisabetta, plunged in and in two years made this dream come true. The results are notable and very ambitious, with the complete restoration of four stone farmhouses scattered about the vast property comprised of wooded hills, olive groves, and cultivated fields of grain and sunflowers. Guests first arrive at the imposing 1850s main villa, which houses the reception office and private family quarters. Comfortable apartments and rooms divided among the various farmhouses are nicely furnished with country pieces old and new and can accommodate from two to ten persons. Guests have the use of four swimming pools, mountain bikes, sauna, exercise and game rooms, Jacuzzi, and massage therapy. They convene at Podernovo where Tuscan meals are served in the exposed-stone dining room with fireplace, or on the patio looking out over the valley and up to Massa Marittima. The Etruscan towns of Massa Marittima, Volterra, Vetulonia, and Populonia are waiting to be explored and you are also close to the seaside. The summer months offer a rich musical program of operas and classical concerts in the main piazza and villas. *Directions:* Drive for 2 km on the gravel road from Massa Marittima where signs indicate Il Cicalino.

TENUTA IL CICALINO
Hosts: Elisabetta & Federico Vecchioni
Localita: Cicalino, Massa Marittima (GR) 58024, Italy
Tel: (0566) 902031, Cellphone: (347) 6444130
Fax: (0566) 904896
8 rooms, Double: €75–€85, 23 apartments: €82–€323 daily
Minimum nights required: 2
Open: Mar to Nov, Credit cards: MC, VS
Other languages: some English
Region: Tuscany, Michelin Map: 430
www.karenbrown.com/italy/cicalino.html

La Biancarda is the beautiful country home of the Florio family of Ancona, overlooking the colorful hilly countryside. Just south of Ancona begins one of the prettiest coastlines of the eastern Adriatic shores, with a combination of seaside villages, hilly countryside, and dramatic mountains cascading into the sea, making up the Conero National Park. Signora Giovanna had the salmon-colored farmhouse dating to 1760 restored to provide her family with a relaxing country retreat, and adorned it with many of the family's precious antiques. The impressive, stone-walled living room upstairs with enormous fireplace, plus cozy library and billiard room are all open to guests. Six guest bedrooms are divided between the two floors of the home. A real treat is waking up to breakfast in the delightful country kitchen with fireplace, long family table, beamed ceilings, and collection of hanging brass pots. Exquisite dinners based on fresh fish and local produce can also be arranged. Outdoor activities in the area include golf, tennis, horseback riding, and swimming (beaches are ten minutes away). The historical towns of Macereto, Loreto, and Urbino are nearby. *Directions:* From the A14, exit at Ancona Sud, following signs for Numana. Keep on this road for several kilometers to Coppo, turning left onto a dirt road just after the bar—follow it to the end.

LA BIANCARDA
Hosts: Giovanna Florio & family
Via Biancarda 129, Coppo di Sirolo
Massignano (AN) 60125, Italy
Tel & fax: (071) 2800503, Tel & fax (winter): (071) 34331
6 rooms, Double: €90–€103
Minimum nights required: 2
Open: May to Sep
Other languages: good English
Region: Marches, Michelin Map: 430
www.karenbrown.com/italy/biancarda.html

The simple and economical Oasi Verde ("green oasis") is just that: a convenient roadside stop for those traveling between Umbria and the Marches region. Carla and Andrea Rossi inherited the sprawling 200-year-old stone farmhouse and surrounding land, ideally located midway between Perugia and Gubbio (a not-to-be-missed medieval stone village set high up in the hillside), and decided to convert it to a bed and breakfast and restaurant. The eight rooms in the main house, each with its own bathroom, have been decorated like model room number 3, with its original beamed ceiling and country-antique bed and armoire. White-tiled floors may be out of character, but give a sense of cleanliness nonetheless. Another wing of the complex houses three simply furnished suites (two bedrooms and a bathroom) for longer stays, perfect for a family of four. Additional rooms, each with separate ground-floor entrance, are found in a wing renovated within the last few years. The windows at the back of the house open out to green hills with alternating patches of woods and sunflower fields. Facilities tempting you to linger for a while include a swimming pool, bikes available for rent, and a horseback riding school. *Directions:* Traveling from Perugia on route 298, after 25 km you find the bed and breakfast on the left-hand side, at Mengara, 10 km before Gubbio.

OASI VERDE MENGARA
Hosts: Andrea & Carla Rossi
Localita: Mengara 1, Scritto (PG) 06020, Italy
Tel: (075) 9227004 or (336) 633534, Cellphone: (335) 1225738
Fax: (075) 920049
19 rooms, Double: €50–€66
Minimum nights required: 4 in high season
Open: Mar to Dec, Credit cards: MC, VS
Other languages: very little English
Region: Umbria, Michelin Map: 430
www.karenbrown.com/italy/oasiverde.html

Florentine sisters Francesca and Beatrice Baccetti eagerly accepted the challenge of converting the family's country home and vineyards into an efficient bed and breakfast. Restoration work began immediately on the two adjacent stone buildings dating back to 1400. All original architectural features were preserved, leaving the five guestrooms and eleven apartments (for two to four people) with terra-cotta brick floors, wood-beamed ceilings, and mansard roofs, and many with generous views over the tranquil Tuscan countryside. The very comfortable and tidy rooms are furnished with good reproductions in country style and feel almost hotel-like with their telephones and modern bathrooms. A beautiful swimming pool with hydro-massage, tennis court, billiards room, and nearby horse stables are at guests' disposal, although finding enough to do is hardly a problem with Florence only 18 kilometers away and practically all of Tuscany at one's fingertips. Breakfast is served at wooden tables in the stone-walled dining room or out on the terrace. Readers give Salvadonica a high rating for service and warm hospitality. *Directions:* From Florence take the superstrada toward Siena for 6 km, exiting at San Casciano Nord. Follow signs for town, turning left at the sign for Mercatale. Salvadonica is on this road and well marked.

SALVADONICA
Hosts: Francesca & Beatrice Baccetti
Via Grevigiana 82, Mercatale Val di Pesa (FI) 50024, Italy
Tel: (055) 8218039, Fax: (055) 8218043
5 rooms, Double: €99–€115
11 apartments: €220–€245 daily B&B
Minimum nights required: 3
Open: Mar to Nov, Credit cards: all major
Other languages: good English
Region: Tuscany, Michelin Map: 430
www.karenbrown.com/italy/salvadonica.html

In an industrial city where the word “charm” is practically nonexistent, the Hotel Regina, although not inexpensive, came as a pleasant surprise among the rather nondescript modern hotels in Milan. For those flying in and out of Milan, with a desire to catch a glimpse of the city center (and newly restored Last Supper of Da Vinci—by advance reservation only), this is an ideal selection. The attractive, typically 18th-century façade and entrance invite guests into a luminous reception area converted from the original courtyard with stone columns, arches, marble floors, large plants, and a small corner bar with sitting area and tables. Completely refurbished rooms (non-smoking upon request) include all modern amenities and are very quiet, being set off the street. Decorated comfortably and uniformly with identical furniture, rooms are warmed with soft-pastel-colored walls, parquet floors, and scattered Oriental rugs. A full buffet breakfast is served below and is included in the room rate. Manager Michela is helpful in satisfying guests’ requests and bicycles are available for visting the city’s historical center. Linate airport is easily reached by cab in 20 minutes, while the Malpensa airport can be reached by bus from the train station. *Directions:* Via Correnti is just off the Via Torino, which leads to Milan’s famous cathedral and shopping area, and is between the basilicas of San Lorenzo and San Ambrogio.

HOTEL REGINA
Host: Michela Barberi
Via Cesare Correnti 13
Milan 20123, Italy
Tel: (02) 58106913, Fax: (02) 58107033
43 rooms, Double: €165–€250
Open: all year, Credit cards: all major
Other languages: good English
Region: Lombardy, Michelin Map: 428
www.karenbrown.com/italy/hotelregina.html

Just 20 kilometers from Siena, at the foot of Chianti is the Godiolo stone farmhouse with its double loggia and cupola dating back to 1350. Red geraniums cascade from every one of the balconies and terra-cotta urns. While Signor Giuliano tends to the acres of vineyards and wine production, gracious Signora Bianca dedicates her time to making their guests feel very much at home. What used to be the children's rooms are now four charming guestrooms with nice, homey touches such as embroidered linen sheets, dried flower arrangements, and heirloom furnishings. Breakfast in the typical tiled kitchen consists of homemade baked goods to which guests help themselves. Signora, with her Roman-Tuscan origins, is an excellent cook and guests can treat themselves to a delightful dinner with the family upon request. Downstairs is a large informal living and game room for guests. Nearby are the thermal baths of Rapolano where massages, mud baths, and other spa services are available—true relaxation—and the stark and fascinating crater-like landscapes (Le Crete Senesi) south between Rapolano and Montalcino. *Directions:* Exit from the A1 autostrada at Val di Chiana and head towards Siena on route 326 towards Serre di Rapolano, but turn right up to Godiolo rather than left into town.

GODIOLO
Hosts: Giuliano & Bianca Perinelli
Modanella–Serre di Rapolano (SI) 53040, Italy
Tel & fax: (0577) 704304
4 rooms, Double: €130
Open: all year
Other languages: some English
Region: Tuscany, Michelin Map: 430
www.karenbrown.com/italy/godiolo.html

On the same road as the Godiolo bed and breakfast, a more independent self-catering type of accommodation is offered at the 13th-century Castello di Modanella. This is a sprawling stone complex complete with towers and turrets, many separate houses where the farmers of the vast wine estate once lived, a church, and even a school. The castle is in a constant state of restoration and along the way 33 rental apartments for two to nine persons have been incorporated in various sections. Some apartments can be found in the old schoolhouse just outside the castle walls on two floors with one, two, or three bedrooms, bathrooms, kitchen, and living room. They maintain a true rustic flavor with original beams, mansard ceilings, worn brick floors, stone walls, and a mix of old and new wood furniture. All have lovely views over the countryside. Other comfortable apartments are located in four separate houses on the vast property and one house is available for rent. Although currently there are no accommodations in the castle itself, it is worth a visit with its arched entrance, iron gates, stone courtyard, and clock tower. The estate is under the direction of Gabriella Cerretti who assists guests with their every need. Guests also enjoy sports facilities such as tennis courts, two swimming pools, and two lakes for fishing. *Directions:* Travel for 30 km from Siena on route 326 towards the autostrada, then turn left at the sign for the Castello, opposite Serre di Rapolano.

CASTELLO DI MODANELLA
Host: Gabriella Cerretti
Modanella–Serre di Rapolano (SI) 53040, Italy
Tel: (0577) 704604, Fax: (0577) 704740
33 apartments: €106–€273 daily
1 house: €5,162–€6,195 weekly
Minimum nights required: 2
Open: all year, Credit cards: all major
Other languages: some English
Region: Tuscany, Michelin Map: 430
www.karenbrown.com/italy/moda.html

While many agritourism farms are run by transplanted urbanites, many are still owned and operated by farmers whose families have worked the land for generations. Such is the case with Onofrio Contento and his family, proprietors of Masseria Curatori, not far from the city of Monopoli and the Adriatic Sea, where, for five generations, the family has produced olives, almonds, and cattle. Inside the main coral-color house are very modest and immaculate quarters for guests, consisting presently of a large three-bedroom apartment with kitchen and living room, plus two doubles with private bathrooms. Old and new family furniture has been combined to decorate the rooms. The view is pleasingly pastoral, overlooking olive-tree-studded hills. Two apartments for two to four persons are found in a nearby one-story building overlooking a lovely stone-walled garden and fruit orchard. Breakfast and extra meals are taken together with the hospitable family in their dining room where Lucrezia delights guests with local dishes. Horseback riding can be arranged for guests. Curatori is an excellent base from which to visit the highlights of this unique region of Italy. *Directions:* 40 km from Bari. Take coastal route S.S.16 south, leaving at the sixth exit for Monopoli called Monopoli-San Francesco da Paola. Turn right for 300 meters and then left on S.C. Conchia Road, to a pink house on your right.

MASSERIA CURATORI
Hosts: Onofrio & Lucrezia Contento family
Contrada Cristo delle Zolle 227 (S.C. Conchia)
Monopoli (BA) 70043, Italy
Tel & fax: (080) 777472, Cellphone: (338) 6242833
2 rooms, Double: €56, 3 apartments
Per person half board: €45
Open: all year
Other languages: very little English
Region: Apulia, Michelin Map: 431
www.karenbrown.com/italy/masseriacuratori.html

A well-kept secret among off-the-main-road travelers is the countryside north of Rome known as "Sabina" after the mountain range. It is unusual that agritourism has not developed close to Rome compared to what has occurred around Florence, but locals are beginning to wake up. Ancestors of the Gabbuti family came from this area and the principal palazzos in both medieval towns of Casperia and Montasola, plus a large farm with olive groves, have been in the family for generations. One of the daughters, Letizia, decided to leave a law career in Rome to work on restoration of these properties and offer hospitality in the form of apartments and one bedroom within her home. Spacious apartments include one to three bedrooms, living room, kitchen, and bathrooms, all warmly decorated with the family's own antiques. Characteristic architectural features have been preserved, and two apartments have terraces with a breathtaking panoramic view (our favorite is the mansard Le Stelle). There is something very special indeed about being a "resident" of an intact medieval village with its narrow stone alleyways. Guests can lounge under the shady trees of a stone-walled garden close by and dine at the characteristic osteria in the village. Other charming villages dot the area, Umbria is nearby, and Rome is just a 45-minute train ride away. Suitable for independent explorers. *Directions:* Arrangements to be made at the time of reservation.

MONTEPIANO
Host: Maria Letizia Gabbuti
Via dei Casalini 8
Montasola (RI) 02045, Italy
Tel & fax: (0765) 63252, Cellphone (328) 3813145
1 room, Double: €90
4 apartments: €476–€855 weekly, €96–€174 daily
Minimum nights required: 2, Open: all year
Other languages: some English
Region: Lazio, Michelin Map: 430
www.karenbrown.com/italy/montepiano.html

As you travel southwest toward Florence through the foothills of the Appenines, the scenery transforms itself dramatically from the flatlands of the padana into soft green hills textured with alternating fields of wheat and grapevines. From Bologna, the Tenuta Bonzara farm and vineyard is a half-hour drive up a road that winds through scented pine forest, arriving at a group of houses owned by several farming families. The wine estate is owned by Dottor Lambertini of Bologna, and is run by warm-hearted Mario and his family, whose main responsibility is overseeing the wine production. Guest accommodation on the estate consists of two small houses containing two apartments, each with one or two bedrooms, bathroom, kitchenette, and sitting room—the nicest are the one-bedroom apartments in the older house with small corner fireplaces, red-brick floors, and beamed ceilings, rustically furnished with simple pinewood pieces. A trattoria on the premises serves meals and a museum has been set up in the old barn displaying antique farm tools, carts, and agricultural machines. A tennis court is available and participation in the grape harvesting is encouraged. *Directions:* Take the Bologna/Casalecchio exit from the A1 autostrada and continue to Gesso, Rivabella, Calderino, Monte San Giovanni, and left up the hill to San Chierlo.

TENUTA BONZARA
Host: Dottor Francesco Lambertini
Via San Chierlo 37
Monte San Pietro (BO) 40050, Italy
Tel: (051) 6768324, Cellphone: (335) 8110018
Fax: (051) 225772
4 apartments: €377–€455 weekly
Minimum nights required: 2 in low season
Open: May to Oct, Other languages: some English
Region: Emilia-Romagna, Michelin Map: 429
www.karenbrown.com/italy/bonzara.html

Lucca, one of our favorite Italian cities, is well situated near Pisa, with the beautiful Valdera countryside to the south, the Apuane mountain range to the north, the seaside 20 kilometers away, and many splendid villas and famous gardens scattered in the vicinity. The city, however, is directly surrounded by a heavily commercial area until you get to the wine country around the charming hilltop town of Montecarlo, 15 kilometers east of town. This medieval stone village with fortress walls has several restaurants and cafés, its own theatre where Puccini was known to put on operas, and many olive-oil-producing farms and wineries close by. Silvia Moncini left her hometown of Montecatini where her parents have a prominent hotel to reopen the Antica Casa bed and breakfast with her husband Francesco and small child. The family resides across the street and in the early morning the perfume of fresh bread comes wafting up to the eight small rooms on the two upper floors. All but two have en-suite bathrooms and are simply appointed with wrought-iron beds, floral bedspreads, and painted stencil borders, which go well with the beamed ceilings. Breakfast is served either out on the patio where you can observe the daily life of the locals, or in the miniature breakfast room to the left of the reception and living room area. *Directions:* From the A11 autostrada, take the Altopascio exit. Head towards Pescia (3 km) and turn left for Montecarlo for another 2 km.

ANTICA CASA DEI RASSICURATI
Hosts: Silvia & Francesco Romani
Via della Collegiata 2
Montecarlo–Lucca (LU) 55015, Italy
Tel: (0583) 228901, Cellphone: (347) 5365343
Fax: (0583) 22498
8 rooms, Double: €68
Open: all year, Credit cards: MC, VS
Other languages: some English
Region: Tuscany, Michelin Map: 430
www.karenbrown.com/italy/rassicurati.html

Within the same quaint village as the previous listing is an alternative kind of accommodation that allows the traveler to stay in one of Montecarlo's private, historical homes. The large building on the main street of town with Pompeiian-red worn façade (a color that is predominant in the interior) dates back to the 1500s and its foundation was part of the original walls of the castle. Gracious hostess Bianca's desire was to bring back life to the ancient, antique-filled home by offering unique accommodation to travelers. Even though space would allow it, she has made no alterations or added extra rooms, preferring to keep the original architectural features of her ancestral home intact. Limited accommodation, therefore, is offered either within an enormous double bedroom with en-suite bathroom overlooking the street, or in a family suite incorporating three sleeping areas (separate double bedroom plus two sleeping alcoves for an additional three people), bathroom, and grand hall with French windows looking out over the lovely terraced garden. Breakfast is served in the formal dining room with antique tapestries or in the absolutely charming country kitchen with open fireplace and French plates adorning the walls. Take a step back in time in this castlelike home filled with precious antiques and paintings. *Directions:* From the A11 autostrada, take the Altopascio exit. Head towards Pescia (3 km) and turn left for Montecarlo for another 2 km.

CASA SATTI
Host: Bianca Satti Tori
Via Roma 31
Montecarlo–Lucca (LU) 55015, Italy
Tel: (0583) 22347, Fax: (0583) 22007
2 rooms, Double: €120–€230
Minimum nights required: 2
Open: Apr to Nov 15
Region: Tuscany, Michelin Map: 430
www.karenbrown.com/italy/casasatti.html

The scenic approach to the Fattoria di Vibio passes through lush green hills, by picturesque farms, and is highlighted by a romantic view of the quaint town of Todi, 20 kilometers away. Two handsome brothers from Rome run this top-drawer bed and breakfast consisting of several recently restored stone houses. The houses sit side by side and share between them 14 double rooms with private baths. Common areas for guests include a cozy, country-style living room with fireplace, games room, and country kitchen. The accommodations are enhanced by preserved architectural features such as terra-cotta floors and exposed-beam ceilings, and typical Umbrian handicrafts such as wrought-iron beds, renovated antiques, and Deruta ceramics. On the assumption that guests may find it difficult to leave this haven, the hosts offer half board plus lunch and snacks, along with a beautiful swimming pool (heated outside the summer months), tennis, hiking, horseback riding, fishing, and biking. Signora Gabriella, with a passion for cooking, gets all the richly deserved credit for the marvelous meals served either poolside or on the panoramic terrace. Two houses are also available for rent. *Directions:* From either Todi or Orvieto follow route S448 until the turnoff for Vibio at the sign for Prodo-Quadro and follow the well-marked dirt road for 10 km up to the farmhouse.

FATTORIA DI VIBIO
Hosts: Giuseppe & Filippo Saladini
Localita: Buchella-Doglio, Montecastello di Vibio (PG) 06057, Italy
Tel: (075) 8749607, Cellphone: (335) 6594076
Fax: (075) 8780014
2 houses: €770–€1,260 weekly, 14 rooms, Double: €140–€180*
*Includes breakfast & dinner,
Minimum nights required: 2, 7 in Aug
Open: Mar to Dec, Credit cards: all major
Other languages: good English, Region: Umbria
www.karenbrown.com/italy/fattoriadivibio.html

Surprisingly, one of the least visited regions in Italy is the Marches, an area rich in culture, nature, and history bordering on the Adriatic. Just 7 kilometers from the coast in the heart of this gentle, hilly countryside you find the Campana farm, run by ten families of professionals and artists who came here from Milan in search of an alternative lifestyle. The farm, made up of four pale-peach stone houses dating from 1700, has been restored with great care and taste, making space for private quarters, a refined restaurant, wine cellar, studio, music room, and, for guests, eleven rooms, a few large enough for a family of four. Some have lovely terraces looking across vineyard-covered hills to the distant sea, and are decorated with a combination of old and new furnishings. Others are situated within a separate two-story, recently renovated farmhouse. Drawing on the considerable pool of available talent, an unusual variety of activities is offered, including workshops in crafting leather and silk, and wool dyeing with plant extracts. Guests have the use of a swimming pool and tennis courts, as well as bikes for local touring. *Directions:* From Ancona go south on the A14 autostrada, exit at Pedaso, continue south to Cupramarittima, then turn right at the sign for Carassai. After 6 km, turn right for Montefiore, then left after 1.5 km at the small sign for La Campana.

LA CAMPANA
Host: Co-op Agricola
Via Menocchia 39
Montefiore dell'Aso (AP) 63010, Italy
Tel: (0734) 939012, Fax: (0734) 938229
11 rooms, Double: €86–€140
Open: Mar to Dec, Credit cards: MC, VS
Other languages: good English
Region: Marches, Michelin Map: 430
www.karenbrown.com/italy/lacampana.html

La Loggia, built in 1427, was one of the Medici estates during the centuries of their rule. Owner Giulio Baruffaldi, weary of urban life in Milan, transplanted himself and his wife here and succeeded in reviving the wine estate's splendor while respecting its past, enhancing its architectural beauty while giving utmost attention to the preservation of the historic property. Their informal yet refined hospitality is reflected in the care given to retaining the rustic ambiance of the former farmers' homes, each containing one to three bedrooms, living room, and kitchen, some with fireplace, and adorned with country antiques and original paintings from the Baruffaldis' own art collection. In fact, many important bronze and ceramic sculptures by international artists are displayed throughout the gardens of the villa. Four double rooms have been added, some having a fireplace or hydro-massage bath and steam room. Apart from just basking in the pure romance and tranquillity of this place, you can enjoy a heated seawater swimming pool, horseback riding, and nearby tennis and golf facilities. Other activities include the occasional cooking or wine-tasting lesson, and impromptu dinners in the cellar. The charming hostess Ivana personally takes care of guests' needs. *Directions:* Leave the Florence-Siena autostrada after San Casciano at Bargino. Turn right at the end of the ramp, then left for Montefiridolfi (3.5 km). La Loggia is just before town.

FATTORIA LA LOGGIA
Hosts: Giulio Baruffaldi & Cuca Roaldi
Via Collina, Montefiridolfi
San Casciano Val di Pesa (FI) 50020, Italy
Tel: (055) 8244288, Fax: (055) 8244283
4 rooms, Double: €90–€150
10 apartments: €130–€180 daily
Open: all year, Credit cards: MC, VS
Other languages: some English, French, Spanish
Region: Tuscany, Michelin Map: 430
www.karenbrown.com/italy/laloggia.html

Just opposite the lovely Fattoria La Loggia is a bed and breakfast that was actually one of the farmhouses belonging to the vast vineyard property. Gracious Signora Nadia fell in love with the ancient house and decided to retire here after having the entire place restored, leaving the ground floor for herself and the guests' breakfast room while the upstairs provides apartments of flexible configurations for travelers. The two adjoining apartments to the right (yellow and blue color schemes) can become a three-bedroom apartment with three colourful bathrooms, living room, kitchen, and large fireplace. The two one-bedroom apartments in green hues can be rented separately or adjoined as well. Rooms have a clean, country feeling to them with antique armoires, simple wrought-iron beds blending in nicely with stone walls, wood-beamed mansard ceilings and brick floors so typical in Tuscany. A lovely swimming pool sits close to the house overlooking the soft valley. This is a very easy base from which to visit most of the region's highlights besides being only 20 minutes from Florence and 30 from Siena. *Directions:* Exit at Bargino from the Florence-Siena highway and turn right and then immediately left at the sign for Montefiridolfi. After 3 km look for a stone house with large arched windows on the left side of the road before town.

MACINELLO
Host: Nadia Ciuffetti
Via Collina 9
Montefiridolfi, San Casciano Val di Pesa (FI) 50020, Italy
Tel & fax: (055) 8244459
4 apartments: €210–€225 daily
Minimum nights required: 3, 7 Jun to Aug
Open: all year
Region: Tuscany, Michelin Map: 430
www.karenbrown.com/italy/macinello.html

Poggio Miravalle is a peaceful and panoramic haven located atop a hill between the regions of Umbria and Tuscany. Reserved hostesses Rita and Mara have developed the hospitality end of their farm business (organic olive oil and wine) over the past years and today offer accommodation within six apartments, all but two inside the main restored stone farmhouse. Firm believers in the healing benefits of country living, they wish to offer an oasis of silence for true lovers of nature, defined as "ecotourists." Each apartment (among them four named Sun, Moon, Earth, and Sky) has an independent entrance through French doors overlooking the garden and can comfortably accommodate from two to five guests. Pleasantly decorated with a mix of old and new country-style furniture, they include a living area and kitchenette. The barn has been transformed into a common area where breakfast and an occasional dinner are served and nearby is a swimming pool taking advantage of the most scenic and breezy spot overlooking the sweeping valley. Rita and Mara are full of interesting itinerary suggestions following gastronomic, cultural, recreational, or nature themes. *Directions:* Exit from the A1 autostrada at Fabro and travel towards Monteleone. After S. Lorenzo turn right for Miravalle (1.5 km).

POGGIO MIRAVALLE
Hosts: Rita Trincia & Mara Romer Casarotto
Localita: Cornieto 2
Monteleone d'Orvieto (TR) 05017, Italy
Tel & fax: (0763) 835309
Cellphone: (333) 5254620 or (340) 7736315
6 apartments: €594–€723 weekly
Open: Mar 15 to Oct 30, Credit cards: all major
Region: Umbria, Michelin Map: 430
www.karenbrown.com/italy/miravalle.html

One result of increasing interest in the singular attractions of the Maremma, or southern Tuscany, is the opening or expansion of several noteworthy places to stay. The Villa Acquaviva, once owned by nobility and a small family hotel for some years, was extensively remodeled to include eight guestrooms named for and painted in the colors of local wildflowers. The bedrooms all have private baths and are decorated with country antiques and wrought-iron beds. Breakfast of homemade cakes, breads, and jams can be eaten in the breakfast room near the enoteca. The charming breakfast room with its large windows overlooks the lovely swimming pool and a lush flower garden and on to the gently rolling landscape up to the quaint medieval village of Montemerano with its artisan shops. There are ten newer rooms in a stone farmhouse on the property plus eight in another, joined together by a glassed-in reception area. These are our favorites, with beautiful local antiques and colorful matching fabrics adorning beds and windows. Tennis courts and a swimming pool with bar service are attractive features of the complex. In the centre of the park, in a scenic position by the swimming pool, the restaurant presents typical Maremman dishes made with fresh products from the farm. *Directions:* From Rome, take the Aurelia coastal road, exiting at Vulci. Follow signs for Manciano, then Montemerano. Acquaviva is well marked just outside the village.

VILLA ACQUAVIVA
Hosts: Valentina di Virginio & Serafino d'Ascenzi
Localita: Acquaviva, Montemerano (GR) 58050, Italy
Tel: (0564) 602890, Cellphone: (335) 7509100
Fax: (0564) 602895
26 rooms, Double: €103–€130
Minimum nights required: 3 in high season
Open: all year, Credit cards: all major
Other languages: French, good English
Region: Tuscany, Michelin Map: 430
www.karenbrown.com/italy/acquaviva.html

Le Fontanelle country house sits in the heart of the Maremma area of Tuscany where, besides being pleasant and well run, it fills a need for the growing interest in this off-the-beaten-track destination. Signor Perna and his two lovely daughters, originally from Rome, searched and found this peaceful haven from the stress of city life, promptly transferring themselves and undertaking major restoration work. Looking over a soft green valley up to the nearby village of Montemerano, the stone farmhouse with its rusty-red shutters offers four comfortable rooms with spotless private bathrooms. The converted barn houses five rooms while the last room is in a separate cottage set in the woods. Sunlight pours into the front veranda-like breakfast room where coffee and cakes are taken together with other guests at one large table. The Pernas assist guests in planning local itineraries including visits to artisan workshops. With due notice, guests can find a wonderfully prepared dinner awaiting them under the ivy-covered pergola in the rose garden. The property is part of a reserve with deer, wild boar, and various types of wildlife, where Porcini mushrooms, wild asparagus, and berries are found in season. *Directions:* From Rome, take the A12 autostrada. Continue north on Aurelia route 1, turning off at Vulci after Montalto. Follow signs for Manciano then Montemerano. Turn left at the bed-and-breakfast sign before town and follow the dirt road for 1 km.

LE FONTANELLE
Hosts: Daniela & Cristina Perna
Localita: Poderi di Montemerano
Montemerano (GR) 58050, Italy
Tel & fax: (0564) 602762
Cellphone: (335) 6559699 or (338) 9205641
10 rooms, Double: €82
Open: all year, Credit cards: MC, VS
Other languages: some English
Region: Tuscany, Michelin Map: 430
www.karenbrown.com/italy/fontanelle.html

A pleasant alternative to a countryside bed and breakfast is one right in the historical center of the marvelously preserved medieval town of Montepulciano. Most famous for its prized Rosso di Montepulciano wines, its striking charm of the past rivals that of its hilltop neighbors, Pienza and Montalcino. Here Cinzia Caroti offers bed and breakfast on the first floor of a 16th-century palazzo on the main street of town, which is lined with shops and restaurants and is off limits to cars, which adds much to its medieval aura. One flight of wide stairs takes you up to L'Agnolo's reception area. There are three bedrooms off this area and another two off the frescoed dining room with wrought-iron chandelier. The spacious, high-ceilinged rooms have a subdued ambiance, with wrought-iron beds, family antiques, and new white-tiled bathrooms. Better lighting could be used to show off lovely original frescoed ceilings and painted borders. A classic breakfast of cappuccino and fresh croissants is served in the coffee shop below the home, making one feel like a true local resident. Cinzia lives two doors down and is present throughout the day to assist guests and make suggestions from the many sightseeing possibilities in this rich area of Tuscany, bordering Umbria. *Directions:* Park your car in a nearby lot (north or east lot) outside the village walls and follow Via di Gracciano running north-south to the middle. There is a small gold name plaque at the door.

L'AGNOLO
Host: Cinzia Caroti
Via di Gracciano nel Corso 63
Montepulciano (SI) 53045, Italy
Tel: (0578) 717070, Cellphone: (339) 2254813
Fax: (0578) 757095
5 rooms, Double: €83
Open: all year, Credit cards: MC
Other languages: very little English
Region: Tuscany, Michelin Map: 430
www.karenbrown.com/italy/agnolo.html

After years of working in a hotel in Siena, then owning a wine bar, Marcello and his wife Maria Pia decided to put their hospitality experience into practice and opened the charming Bolsinina bed and breakfast. This is a perfect location for travelers, being so close to Siena (18 km) and having easy access to the main road, which passes through the magical Crete Senesi landscapes with their low, rolling clay hills punctuated by an occasional cypress tree against the horizon, to the hilltowns of Montalcino, Pienza, and Montepulciano. The 18th-century brick house has a courtyard where meals are served in season. To one side are the apartments of varying sizes, and to the other is the large house where the beamed guestrooms are located upstairs, along with a large common living room and loggia terrace with splendid views. Downstairs is an open multi-use space rotating around the center staircase with billiard table, cozy living room with fireplace and two large brick arches, and dining room. Guests reserve in the morning for dinner accompanied by excellent local wines. The house and rooms are filled with local antique country furniture and armoires and there is an immediate "at-home," informal air about the place. An inviting swimming pool is an added bonus. *Directions:* From Siena on the S.R.2, pass Monteroni d'Arbia, Lucignano, and before Buonconvento turn left at Casale-Gaggiolo (km 209). Take the gravel road up to the house.

CASA BOLSININA
Hosts: Marcello & Maria Pia Mazzotta
Localita: Casale, Monteroni d'Arbia (SI) 53014, Italy
Tel & fax: (0577) 718477, Cellphone: (338) 2705153
8 rooms, Double: €80–€145, 4 apartments: €410–€950 weekly
Cleaning & heating extra for apartments
Minimum nights required: 3
Closed: Jan 15 to Mar 15, Credit cards: all major
Other languages: good English
Region: Tuscany, Michelin Map: 430
www.karenbrown.com/italy/bolsinina.html

Signora Novella and her family, warm and gregarious hosts, have been welcoming guests for over 17 years, ever since they moved to Emilia-Romagna from the south. Having agricultural experience, they were able to set up a farm, with Novella, a retired schoolteacher, overseeing the kitchen. She is an excellent cook and guests return time and time again for her handmade pasta, joining the family at the long wooden table in their rustic dining room with its hanging brass pots and ox harnesses. Guest accommodations have been transferred from upstairs in the white 18th-century farmhouse (one room remains) to the horse stalls, which have been converted into simple double rooms with private baths all on one level. The rooms are immaculate, if rather plain, with basic modern furnishings. Guests tend to their own rooms and are even apt to help clear the table in the very informal en famille atmosphere at Le Radici. The sea, just 15 kilometers away, can be seen in the distance, and several medieval towns and castles dot the hills in the surrounding countryside. "Must-sees" include Ravenna, Ferrara, and ceramic center, Faenza. A unique experience, best enjoyed if you speak some Italian. *Directions:* On route 9 from Rimini to Cesena, follow signs for Calisese and right in town turn right for Casale-Sorrivoli. Go straight then left at the sign for Le Radici-Via Golano. (Total of 12 km from Cesena.)

LE RADICI
Hosts: Alessandra & Novella Piangatelli
Localita: Montenovo, Via Golano 808
Montiano (FO) 47020, Italy
Tel & fax: (0547) 327001
7 rooms, Double: €92*
*Includes breakfast & dinner
Open: all year
Other languages: good English, French, Spanish
Region: Emilia-Romagna, Michelin Map: 429
www.karenbrown.com/italy/leradici-itb.html

In the northern Piedmont region, leading into the foothills of the Alps, is the peaceful countryside where Piercarlo Novarese, Il Mompolino's cordial host, decided to establish his inn and equestrian center. Run more like a small hotel, the Mompolino has twenty guestrooms divided between two mustard-color buildings. Each room has a private bath and balcony, and is complemented with rustic furnishings. The four larger suites feature sitting rooms and are the nicest accommodations, furnished with the occasional antique. Four small apartments for two to four persons are located in the restored house on the property. A large, open dining room serves breakfast, lunch, and dinner, and boasts delectable regional dishes skillfully prepared by local women. Il Mompolino makes a convenient stopover on the way to the Alps, the lake region, or Milan. It also provides an appealing spot to relax for a few days between more demanding tourist destinations. Sports activities abound, including horseback riding, tennis, swimming, and a gym with sauna. A variety of horseback-riding lessons is offered at the equestrian center, as are mounted excursions into the adjacent national park. *Directions:* Take the Carisio exit from the Milan-Turin A4 autostrada. Mompolino is 7 km from Carisio and well marked.

IL MOMPOLINO
Host: Piercarlo Novarese
Localita: Mompolino
Mottalciata (VC) 13030, Italy
Tel: (0161) 857667, Fax: (0161) 857667
20 rooms, Double: €54–€69, 4 apartments
Restaurant closed Mon
Open: all year, Credit cards: all major
Other languages: very little English
Region: Piedmont, Michelin Map: 428
www.karenbrown.com/italy/mompolino.html

Hostess Silvana's claim to fame is her innate ability to please guests at the dining table and she did this for years in her own restaurant in Alba, which was written up in many culinary guides. Now she concentrates on her privileged guests who can sample her regional specialties right at home. Gracious Silvana and her journalist husband, Gianni, have recently transformed the grandparents' farmhouse, a group of three attached wings forming a U, into an intimate bed and breakfast with just two rooms. Their idea was to offer couples maximum space and privacy in junior suites (Rosa and Azzurra). Each room has its own entrance from the garden, sitting area, bedroom, and bathroom and Azzurra also has a small loft with two extra beds. The most extraordinary feature here is the soul-soothing panoramic views encompassing layers and layers of unspoilt landscapes dotted with villages and farmhouses all the way to the distant Alps on the horizon. All this accompanied by silence or the occasional chirping of birds. At sunset the only thing that can possibly tear guests away from the patio with its huge pots of hydrangeas overlooking the deep-green countryside is the call to dinner for another one of Silvana's fabulous meals served on the veranda. *Directions:* From Murazzano follow signs for Dogliani. After 1 km turn left at a small chapel on the road marked Cichetti and follow it to the end. 35 km from Alba, 70 km from Turin.

❄ ☕ ♨ 🅒 ⛺ 🚶 🐴 🍷 P 🚭 🏠 ⛵ 🌿

CASCINA CICHETTI   New
Hosts: Silvana Faggio & Gianni Galli
Frazione Mellea 69
Murazzano (CN) 12060, Italy
Tel: (0173) 798501, Fax: (0173) 798921
2 rooms, Double: €95
Minimum nights required: 2
Open: all year, Credit cards: VS
Other languages: fluent English
Region: Piedmont
www.karenbrown.com/italy/cichetti.html

In a small pocket of land in the southernmost point of Umbria is the Podere Costa Romana property, immersed in the green hillsides south of ancient Narni. Dynamic hostess Anna Maria left her native Naples for the peace and quiet of the Umbrian hills and meticulously restored the stone 18th-century farmhouse where she now hosts guests within six well-appointed apartments. Rooms have been thoughtfully decorated with antique country furnishings, which harmonize perfectly with the rustic quality of the original farmhouse. Each individual apartment (named for women) can accommodate from two (Giovanna is an adorable love nest) to five guests (Paola has two bedrooms) and is equipped with a kitchenette. Soft-peach and pale-yellow walls highlight exposed stones, beamed ceilings, and brick floors. The large main living room with fireplace and double arches opens out to the surrounding garden and swimming pool overlooking the hills. Travelers can easily reach many lesser-known Umbrian villages as well as the cities and from Orte frequent trains depart for either Rome or Florence. *Directions:* Exit the A1 autostrada at Magliano Sabina and turn right for Otricoli. 8 km after Otricoli turn right at the Narni-Testaccio-Itieli sign and then right again for the Podere Costa Romana.

PODERE COSTA ROMANA   ***New***
Host: Anna Maria Giordano
S.S. Flaminia, Strada per Itieli, Narni (TR) 05035, Italy
Tel: (0744) 722495, Cellphone:(335) 5738210
Fax: (0823) 797118
6 apartments: €100–€200 daily
Minimum nights required: 2
Open: all year
Other languages: some English
Region: Umbria, Michelin Map: 430
www.karenbrown.com/italy/romana.html

La Magioca is a wonderful discovery in the wine country of Valpolicella, close to Lake Garda and historic Verona. The elegant 17th-century country home of the Merighi family was transformed into a luxurious bed and breakfast under the direction of the family's youngest son, Matteo, who runs the operation with flair and efficiency. No detail has been overlooked in this ivy-covered home where many decorating ideas were inspired by innumerable trips to the French countryside. A golden-yellow hue prevails, giving common areas luminosity and warmth. A large living room with enormous arched windows gives access to the surrounding garden and extended lawns, which lead to a private 13th-century chapel and a hidden hydrojet pool for six people. Three double bedrooms, two junior suites, and a suite, all very individually appointed with fine antiques and each more delightful than the other, are divided among the top floors. Rich fabrics, carpets, and paintings harmonize perfectly with wood-beamed mansard ceilings and parquet floors. Matteo's mother, Signora Marisa, is on hand as well and oversees the buffet breakfast. Romantic and peaceful and a great splurge. *Directions:* From Milan exit the A4 autostrada at Verona and follow signs for the city center (centro) for 3.5 km. After passing under a highway, turn left at the sign for the Valpolicella area and Negrar just after Pedemonte. From Negrar, follow signs for La Magioca just 1 km away.

LA MAGIOCA
Host: Matteo Merighi
Via Moron 3
Negrar (VR) 37024, Italy
Tel: (045) 6000167, Fax: (045) 6000840
6 rooms, Double: €170–€230
Closed: Jan 9 to Mar 15, Credit cards: all major
Other languages: good English
Region: Veneto, Michelin Map: 429
www.karenbrown.com/italy/magioca.html

Right next door to the Grazia farm is the very similar property of the Lignana family. Again, a long, straight road takes you off the busy coastal Aurelia highway back to the 700-plus-acre farm and hunting reserve looking out to the distant sea and Mount Argentario. Gracious Signora Marcella and husband Giuseppe live in the ivy-covered ancient stone tower and attached villa, while guests reside within seven comfortable self-catering apartments in a converted barn down the road. Spacious apartments have two bedrooms and two bathrooms, living/dining area, and kitchenette. Some apartments have the bedrooms on a second floor, while others have them split between the main floor and an open loft space. They are nicely appointed in a clean and easy style, with fresh white walls, smart plaid cushions on built-in sofas, framed prints, wicker furniture, and wrought-iron beds. An alternative to sea bathing is a dip in the swimming pool, guarded by olive trees. For nature lovers, the area is full of marvelous expeditions on foot or bike, including the National Park of Uccellina, various forts on Mount Argentario, and the islands of Giglio and Giannutri, not to mention the Saturnia thermal spa. *Directions:* From Rome take the Aurelia Highway 1 and turn right at the sign "Piante-Vivaio" (140.5 km after the turnoff for Ansedonia). From the north you must exit at Ansedonia and return to the highway heading towards Grosseto. 140 km from Rome's Fiumicino airport.

IL CASALONE
Hosts: Marcella & Giuseppe Lignana
S.S. Aurelia sud km 140.5
Orbetello Scalo (GR) 58016, Italy
Tel: (0564) 862160, Cellphone: (329) 2167397
Fax: (0564) 866308
7 apartments: €1,050–€1,250 weekly, €150 daily
Minimum nights required: 2, 7 in Jul & Aug
Open: all year, Other languages: good English
Region: Tuscany, Michelin Map: 430
www.karenbrown.com/italy/casalone.html

The expansive Grazia farm is uniquely located at 3 kilometers from the sea. Gracious and warm hostess Signora Maria Grazia divides her time between Rome and the 300-acre property she inherited from her grandfather. The long cypress-lined driveway takes you away from the busy Aurelia road past grazing horses up to the spacious, rust-hued edifice with its arched loggia. The hosts' home, office, guest apartments, farmhands' quarters, and horse stables are all housed within the complex, which is encased by superb country and has peeks of the sea in all directions. From here one can enjoy touring Etruscan territory: Tuscania, Tarquinia, Sovana, Sorano, and the fascinating Roman ruins of Cosa, or stay by the coast on the beaches of Feniglia on the promontory of Argentario. Comfortably modest accommodations, including living area, kitchen, and breakfast basket, pleasantly decorated with homey touches, are offered within four apartments for two to four persons. Maria Grazia can suggest a myriad of local restaurants specializing in seafood or local country fare. Tennis and horseback riding lessons are available. Altogether a delightful combination. *Directions:* Take the coastal Aurelia road from Rome and after the Ansedonia exit turn right into an unmarked driveway immediately after the Pitorsino restaurant.

GRAZIA
Host: Maria Grazia Cantore family
Localita: Provincaccia, 110, S.S. Aurelia sud km 140.1
Orbetello Scalo (GR) 58016, Italy
Tel & fax: (0564) 881182 or (06) 483945
4 apartments: €95–€140 daily B&B
Minimum nights required: 3
Open: all year
Other languages: good English, French
Region: Tuscany, Michelin Map: 430
www.karenbrown.com/italy/grazia.html

The location of La Chiocciola bed and breakfast, minutes from the main tollway from Rome to Florence and on the border of the Lazio and Umbria regions, is ideal. Added bonuses are the warm hospitality, deliciously prepared regional meals (set rate of €21), and lovely country-style bedrooms. Roberto and Maria Cristina from Rome bought the stone farmhouse dating back to 1400 several years ago and began restoration work while living in the newer house next door. The results of their efforts are five perfectly neat and spotless bedrooms and three suites divided between the two houses, a living room area for guests, and a large rustic dining room with outdoor veranda. Obvious care and attention has been put into the decorating of the air-conditioned bedrooms with wrought-iron canopy beds, crisp, white linen curtains, and botanical prints. The 50-acre property with fruit orchards and olive trees is part of the Tiber river valley and woods. Besides a swimming pool for guests, innumerable day trips and itineraries of special interest are offered in the area of Umbria and Lazio and it's a 40-minute train ride to Rome. *Directions:* From Rome or Florence on the A1 autostrada, exit at Orte and turn immediately left for Orte, passing under the tollway. Continuing towards Orte, turn again for Amelia and repass over the tollway, taking the first left towards Penna in Teverina. La Chiocciola is 5 km along this road.

LA CHIOCCIOLA
Hosts: Roberto & Maria Cristina de Fonseca Pimentel
Localita: Seripola
Orte (VT) 01028, Italy
Tel: (0761) 402734, Cellphone: (348) 5108309
Fax: (0761) 490254
8 rooms, Double: €94–€104
Open: all year, Credit cards: MC, VS
Other languages: good English, French
Region: Lazio, Michelin Map: 430
www.karenbrown.com/italy/lachiocciola.html

A convenient stopover while heading either north or south along the main artery—the A1 autostrada—is the Villa Ciconia inn. Located below the historical center of Orvieto, in the newer commercial outskirts, the property maintains its tranquil setting thanks to the fortress of trees protecting the 16th-century stone villa. The first floor includes reception area, breakfast room, and two large high-ceilinged dining rooms. These latter, with their somber gray-stone fireplaces, tapestries, heavy dark-wood beams, and subdued-color frescoes depicting allegorical motifs and landscapes, give the place a medieval castle's air. The 12 air-conditioned bedrooms on the second floor are appointed either in appropriate style, with antique chests and wrought-iron beds, or with more contemporary furnishings (lower rates) and all the amenities of the four-star hotel that this is. Most rooms are quiet and look out onto the 8 acres of woods behind the villa. There are also two enormous beamed sitting rooms on this floor for guests. The restaurant has a solid reputation for creating excellent Umbrian specialties. Manager Luigi Falcone is always on hand to assist guests. *Directions:* Exiting from the autostrada, turn right towards Orvieto and right again where marked Arezzo, Perugia, passing under the tollway. The Ciconia is just after the river on the left-hand side of the road.

❄ ☕ ⚬ ▦ ☎ ☗ Y P ⟊ 🖼 🔔

VILLA CICONIA
Host: Petrangeli family
Via dei Tigli 69
Orvieto (TR) 05019, Italy
Tel: (0763) 305582, Fax: (0763) 302077
12 rooms, Double: €130–€155
No dinner Mon
Open: all year, Credit cards: all major
Other languages: French, good English
Region: Umbria, Michelin Map: 430
www.karenbrown.com/italy/villaciconia.html

A very high rating goes to the Locanda Rosati on the border of Umbria and Lazio, and just steps away from Tuscany. Giampiero and sister, Alba, with their respective spouses, Luisa and Paolo, sold their cheese production business in Lucca and returned to Orvieto to transform the family farmhouse into a bed and breakfast. The results are splendid and guests, taking priority over the agricultural activity in this instance, are treated with extra-special care. The downstairs common areas include two cozy living rooms with fireplace and a large stone-walled dining room divided by a brick archway leading down to the "tufo" stone cellar. Seven bedrooms upstairs (one with access and bathroom for the handicapped) have been decorated with an animal theme evident in the carvings on bedboards and lamps. Three more bedrooms were added for guests on the top floor with mansard ceilings, leaving the entire home to the bed and breakfast business. Although the house is right on the road, most rooms face the countryside to the back where a large open lawn space leads to the inviting swimming pool. Paolo produces appetizing pastas, soups, and other specialties all written up in a recipe book for guests. *Directions:* Exit from the A1 autostrada at Orvieto and follow signs for Viterbo-Bolsena. Skirt town and continue towards Bolsena for about 8 km on route 71. After a series of sharp curves, the locanda comes up on the right.

LOCANDA ROSATI
Host: Rosati family
Localita: Buonviaggio 22
Orvieto (TR) 05018, Italy
Tel & fax: (0763) 217314
10 rooms, Double: €105–€120
Closed: Jan & Feb, Credit cards: MC, VS
Other languages: good English
Region: Umbria, Michelin Map: 430
www.karenbrown.com/italy/locandarosati.html

Claudia Spatola does a great job of running single-handedly a bed and breakfast in the complex of stone houses known as Borgo Spante, which dates back to the 15th century and has been in her family since 1752. Consisting of a main villa, connecting farmers' houses, chapel, barns, swimming pool, and garden, it is isolated in 500 acres of woods and hills, yet is located only 16 kilometers from Orvieto and not far from Assisi, Todi, and Perugia. Guests stay in a combination of rooms and apartments in the former farmers' quarters with their irregular-sized rooms, sloping worn-brick floors, and rustic country furnishings—very charming in its way. Authentically Umbrian meals, prepared by local women, are served in the dining room with long wooden tables and fireplace. A larger dining area has been added in the former barn, along with four additional mini-apartments, simply and characteristically decorated. Memorable evenings are spent in the garden or poolside conversing with other guests or listening to an impromptu concert. *Directions:* From the A1 autostrada exit at Orvieto and follow signs for Arezzo on route 71. After 7 km, turn right at Morrano and proceed for 12 km to the sign for Spante. Turn left and continue for 2 km.

BORGO SPANTE
Host: Claudia Spatola
Localita: Ospedaletto
San Venanzo (TR) 05010, Italy
Tel: (075) 8709134, Fax: (075) 8709201
5 rooms, Double: €124, 8 apartments*
**Includes breakfast & dinner*
Minimum nights required: 2
Open: all year, Other languages: some English
Region: Umbria, Michelin Map: 430
www.karenbrown.com/italy/borgospante.html

The Belfiore farm property certainly stands out among a very bland choice of bed and breakfasts in the area between the well-preserved Renaissance city of Ferrara and Ravenna with its extraordinary mosaics. The flat countryside is characterized by marshland and the National Delta del Po Park, a paradise for birdwatchers and bikers, where many excursions are organized. The Bertelli sisters, Fiorenza and Daniela, from Ferrara, transformed their farm into a country restaurant with 18 bedrooms on the upper two floors. They are identically appointed with rustic wooden beds painted with a floral motif and matching armoires. Guests can feel right at home in the spacious living room with antiques and enormous open fireplace. The restaurant, where locals come for excellent local fare based on organically produced fruits and vegetables, is divided among several beamed dining rooms and guests are invited into the kitchen for a demonstration of making various types of pastas and breads. Italian lessons are also offered free of charge. A neat garden surrounds the simple rectangular-shaped house with burgundy shutters and a swimming pool sits invitingly in one corner. A mini-spa center includes facial and body treatments, sauna, and massage. *Directions:* Exit from the Ferrara-Comacchio highway at Ostellato and pass through the rather nondescript town to the tall bell tower at the corner of Via Pioppa, following signs to Belfiore.

BELFIORE
Host: Tullio Bertelli family
Via Pioppa 27, Ostellato (FE) 44020, Italy
Tel: (0533) 681164, Cellphone: (335) 275702
Fax: (0533) 681172
18 rooms, Double: €80–€85
Restaurant open Thu to Sun
Open: all year, Credit cards: all major
Other languages: some English
Region: Emilia-Romagna, Michelin Map: 429
www.karenbrown.com/italy/belfiore.html

Armando and Rosalba left behind a coporate life in order to bring this 72-acre property back to its original state as a self-sufficient farm where they could offer very special hospitality. Numerous articles written about this magical spot and a guestbook overflowing with happy travelers' praise testify to the success of their labor of love. Eight lovely bedrooms, a large dining room, living room, game room, library, bird sanctuary, lemon grove, chapel, and agricultural museum are all part of the ancient whitewashed masseria complex. Outside the walls are horse stables, farm animals, fruit orchards, and a vegetable garden, then acres and acres of olive trees divided by rows of low stone walls, so typical of Apulia. No detail has been overlooked in the decor of the bedrooms, which are appointed with selected antiques, wrought-iron beds, fine linens and lace, and paintings. Many have an adjoining room for families and there is an extra kitchen for guests. Dinner, either out in the candlelit courtyard or by the fire, is a very special time and requires full sensory attention. Courses after course of unique culinary combinations are served and explained with anecdotes, poetry, or stories by Armando while Rosalba guides her team of local women in the kitchen. Enchanting! *Directions:* Three km from the sea and close to Alberobello, Castellana Locorotondo, and Martina Franca. Il Frantoio is well marked at km 874 on S.S.16 between Fasano and Ostuni.

IL FRANTOIO
Hosts: Armando & Rosalba Balestrazzi
S.S.16, km 874
Ostuni (BR) 72017, Italy
Tel & fax: (0831) 330276
8 rooms, Double: €156–€176
Open: all year, Credit cards: MC, VS
Other languages: good English
Region: Apulia, Michelin Map: 431
www.karenbrown.com/italy/frantoio.html

With her children grown and traveling around the world, Christine, an expatriate from England, decided to offer hospitality to travelers in her country home. Situated an hour north of Rome by train or car, the pretty countryside home made of typical local tufo brick is a short distance from the ancient village of Otricoli with its ancient Roman origins. It is one of many villages centered in the Tiber river valley, historically an important area for trade and commerce with Rome. A long wing off the main house, reserved for guests, offers three beamed bedrooms decorated with country furniture and overlooking the garden and hills. An order-as-you-like breakfast is served either in the kitchen or out on the patio. The cozy living room with open fireplace invites guests to relax after a day in the city. Being at the edge of Umbria and Lazio, she can suggest a myriad of local itineraries and destinations, known and not so well known, as well as town festivals throughout the region and concentrated in the months of May and June. This is a very informal, at-home accommodation just 7 kilometers from the main Rome-Florence autostrada. *Directions:* Exit at Magliano Sabina and turn left for Otricoli-Terni. Turn off for Otricoli and take the first road to the right-Strada Crepafico. Gates to Casa Spence are on the corner.

CASA SPENCE
Host: Christine Spence
Strada Crepafico 29
Otricoli (TR) 05030, Italy
Tel & fax: (0744) 719758, Cellphone: (329) 0832886
3 rooms, Double: €75
€70 without private bath
Open: all year
Other languages: fluent English
Region: Umbria, Michelin Map: 430
www.karenbrown.com/italy/casaspence.html

Paciano, situated on the border of Umbria and Tuscany, south of Lake Trasimeno, is a perfectly intact medieval village, once named the most ideal village in Italy. It is here that enterprising Luigi Buitoni, of the famous pasta-producing family, decided to put to use his refined culinary skills and international restaurant experience, organizing daily cooking lessons. The old olive-oil press building, part of the family's 12th-century residence in town, now serves as a restaurant with bed and breakfast accommodation upstairs. Seven charming bedrooms and one suite are decorated in country style, each with its own color scheme noted in the rich fabrics of the bedspreads and curtains. (Ask for one of the larger ones.) The palazzo was ingeniously restored preserving all original architectural features while adding an extra floor and converting arched doorways to closets. The upstairs sitting room is inviting with a collection of eclectic antiques, floral tapestry armchairs, fresh flowers, and crystal bottles lining shelves. A full buffet breakfast is served and a swimming pool is available just across the way. A large part of the marvelous attached medieval tower has been transformed into a fully equipped apartment for six to ten persons, which is rented weekly. *Directions:* Leave the A1 autostrada at Chiusi-Chianciano; take the road towards Trasimeno and Perugia and turn right to Paciano where indicated. The locanda is at the edge of town and is well marked.

LOCANDA DELLA ROCCA BUITONI
Host: Luigi Buitoni
Viale Roma 4, Paciano (PG) 06060, Italy
Tel: (075) 830236, Cellphone: (348) 2824863
Fax: (075) 830155
8 rooms, Double: €99–€217
1 apartment: €2,500–€3,000 weekly
No dinner Tue, Open: Mar to Dec, Credit cards: MC, VS
Other languages: good English
Region: Umbria, Michelin Map: 430
www.karenbrown.com/italy/locandadellarocca.html

45 kilometers south of the Amalfi coast is the archaeological site of Paestum with its three well-preserved Greek temples. The area is surrounded by unattractive commercial strips and much new construction, although farther south are the lovely Cilento National Park and the coast. Here the Seliano farm provides an oasis of peace and tranquillity very near the sea. Baroness Cecilia, her two sons, Ettore and Massimino, and manager, Nicola, are wonderful hosts and make the managing of this busy farm, the horseback riding center, restaurant, and bed and breakfast look like a delightful game. The emphasis here is on the preparation of meals using local recipes and their own produce, including fresh mozzarella, most famous in this area. In fact, the Baroness conducts week-long cooking classes including excursions to local cultural and gastronomic highlights. Pleasantly decorated rooms with tiled floors and family antiques are situated in the farmhouse or adjacent yellow house, with two comfortable living rooms for guests. Truly delectable meals are served out on the covered terrace or in the long dining/living room with fireplace and historic paintings. There is an inviting swimming pool for guests. *Directions:* Leave the A3 at Eboli (less traffic than Battipaglia) and head for Paestum. Turn right off the main road (S.S.18) at Paestum and after 1 km turn into the driveway marked Seliano. Pass the main villa (uninhabited) to the main gate.

SELIANO
Host: Baroness Cecilia Bellelli Baratta
Localita: Seliano
Paestum (SA) 84063, Italy
Tel: (0828) 724544, Cellphone: (335) 6674200
Fax: (0828) 723634
13 rooms, Double: €73–€114
Closed: Jan & Feb, Credit cards: MC, VS
Other languages: good English
Region: Campania, Michelin Map: 431
www.karenbrown.com/italy/seliano.html

We look all over for bed and breakfasts that radiate a natural charm like that of Fagiolari, just outside Panzano. Cordial hostess Giulietta has seemingly unintentionally created a haven for travelers just by letting her home be a home. The unique stone farmhouse on three levels is brimming with character and has been restored with total respect for its innate simplicity using stone, terra-cotta brick, and chestnut-wood beams. Entering the front door into the cozy living room with large fireplace, I was impressed by the refreshingly authentic ambiance of this Tuscan home. Two bedrooms are just off this room, the larger having an en-suite bathroom of stone and travertine. The main house and former barn, where you find two other good-sized bedrooms, are united by a connecting roof, left open in the middle to allow for an enormous fig tree. Bedrooms hold lovely antiques, book-lined shelves, collections of framed drawings and artwork, embroidered linens, and views of the delightful garden and cypress-lined paths. Overlooking the swimming pool, an adorable one-bedroom house on the property with a bookcase dividing the kitchen and living area is rented out weekly. Giulietta also teaches cooking classes lasting from one to four days. *Directions:* From the piazza in Panzano follow signs to centro and take the left fork for Mercatale. At .6 km from the piazza turn left after a pale-green building and follow the gravel road downhill to the end.

FAGIOLARI
Host: Giulietta Giovanonni
Case Sparse 25
Panzano in Chianti (FI) 50020, Italy
Tel & fax: (055) 852351, Cellphone: (335) 6124988
4 rooms, Double: €100
1 cottage: €840 weekly
Open: all year, Credit cards: all major
Other languages: some English
Region: Tuscany, Michelin Map: 430
www.karenbrown.com/italy/fagiolari.html

As you wind your way up a steep unpaved road through thick woods, you will no doubt wonder as we did how English couple Sonia and Edward ever found the secluded 70-acre property set above the Sieve river valley to the east of Florence. Upon arrival you will be greeted and rewarded with a glass of fresh spring water from the fountain "shower" (la doccia). It is understandable that long ago the farmhouse was originally a farm for the monks of the local abbey—the views are inspirational and the positions of both the house and the swimming pool take full advantage of the expansive panorama encompassing the Rufina wine valley nature reserve. Original features remain intact after a complete restoration of the house that created a variety of high-level accommodation in the form of four bedrooms, three suites with individual kitchenettes, and two attached houses with two bedrooms each for weekly stays. The perfectly charming home is filled with lovely antiques (local and imported from England), queen- or king-sized beds, and beautiful linens and tiled bathrooms. Guests can wander about the many common rooms and have a glass of wine in front of a spectacular sunset while Edward works Mediterranean wonders in the kitchen. Prepare to be pampered. *Directions:* 40 minutes from Florence, 5 km from Pelago. Detailed directions are supplied at the time of reservation.

LA DOCCIA
Hosts: Sonia & Edward Mayhew
Localita: Paterno, Ristonchi 19/20
Pelago (FI) 50060, Italy
Tel: (055) 8361387, Fax: (055) 8361388
7 rooms, Double: €137–€250, 2 apartments
Minimum nights required: 3
Open: all year, Credit cards: all major
Other languages: fluent English
Region: Tuscany, Michelin Map: 430
www.karenbrown.com/italy/doccia.html

Ideally located at the edge of Chianti and just 20 minutes from the main A1 autostrada, the Fattoria Montelucci property is made up of over 1200 acres of woods, olive groves, vineyards, and pastures. In the heart of this working farm sits the pale-yellow villa with its 12 guestrooms, each decorated in simple country style with eyelet curtains, wrought-iron beds, and antique chests. Downstairs are several common sitting rooms including billiard and music rooms. A luminous, beamed dining room, where a buffet breakfast is served, opens out to a large terrace looking over the breathtaking wooded hills. Other meals are served next door in the converted olive mill, with its original press, stone fireplace, and arched windows looking out over the same spectacular view. A typical Tuscan meal in this marvelous setting is alone worth the visit. Five apartments are located in two separate restored farmhouses a short distance from the main house. There are also riding stables with 30 horses, indoor/outdoor rings, and jumping course, offering lessons and country outings. A lovely swimming pool is available for further recreation. Nearby are the two must-see ancient cities of Arezzo and Cortona, plus many other excursions as suggested by hosts Claudio and Samantha. *Directions:* Exit the A1 autostrada at Valdarno, following signs for Montevarchi-Arezzo. Follow route 69 for Arezzo as far as Pergine Valdarno where there are signs for the fattoria (5 km).

FATTORIA MONTELUCCI
Host: Claudio Chiavolleli
Localita: Le Ville, Via Montelucci 24
Pergine Valdarno (AR) 52020, Italy
Tel: (0575) 896525, Fax: (0575) 896315
12 rooms, Double: €90–€120, 5 apartments: €550–€1,400 weekly
Per person half board: €70–€90
Open: Mar to Oct, Credit cards: all major
Other languages: some English
Region: Tuscany, Michelin Map: 430
www.karenbrown.com/italy/montelucci.html

The southernmost, "heel-side" of Italy's boot-shaped peninsula, known as Puglia, presents another facet of the country's many-sided culture. It is a land with spectacular coastlines, villages with distinct Greek and Turkish influence, endless lines of olive groves, fields of wildflowers, and a rich history of art including baroque (Bari's Santa Nicola church is exquisite). All of this plus delectable cuisine and a warm and open people await in Puglia (Apulia), as does the Masseria Salamina, a 16th-century fortified farmhouse between Bari and Brindisi covering 100 acres of land and producing primarily olive oil. The long driveway leads to the sand-colored castle with turreted tower with expansive vistas over olive groves to the sea. The seven rooms, each with a separate courtyard entrance, are decorated with basic reproductions and wicker furniture, and are a notch up in level but not as luminous as the upstairs apartments. These eight one-bedroom apartments are available for longer stays and are "childproof," with sparse and practical furnishings. Host Gianvincenzo and family live in the main wing and run their masseria like a small hotel. A lofty, vaulted restaurant with terra-cotta floors provides all meals for guests. In the low season a week-long stay including Mediterranean cooking lessons and local excursions for small groups is arranged. *Directions:* From the S.S.16 exit at Pezze di Greco. Just before town take the first right for 1 km to the masseria.

MASSERIA SALAMINA
Host: Gianvincenzo de Miccolis Angelini
Pezze di Greco (BR) 72010, Italy
Tel: (080) 4897307, Fax: (080) 4898582
7 rooms, Double: €78–€98, 8 apartments: €110–€330 daily
Per person half board: €55–€65
Minimum nights required: 7 in Jul & Aug
Open: all year, Credit cards: MC, VS
Other languages: some English
Region: Apulia, Michelin Map: 431
www.karenbrown.com/italy/salamina.html

Located in the Abruzzo region—often a destination of Americans in search of their ancestors—Le Georgiche, a restored 18th-century grain mill near Pescara, is a sweet bed and breakfast for those seeking simplicity, peace, and closeness to nature. These were hostess Teresa's three main objectives when she stumbled upon the old mill and decided to leave her former profession and dedicate her energy to organic farming, herbal treatments, natural therapies, and providing a peaceful haven for travelers. Authentic simplicity reigns in the two bedrooms in the main house off the lofty living space with its beamed ceilings, large fireplace, and original brick floors. The decor is purposefully minimalist, with whitewashed walls and a few country antiques. Two more bedrooms are found downstairs while the remaining and most original one is in the detached grain silo with its bathroom dividing the circular space. Guests enjoy a fresh country breakfast overlooking the swimming pool and tennis courts or in the large living room where candlelit dinners are also served, perhaps accompanied by a little Bach or Chopin played by Teresa herself. Besides the historical cities of Atri, Teramo, Chieti, and Loreto Aprutino, the sea and national parks are all nearby. *Directions:* Exit the A25 at Pescara-Chieti and head towards Cepagatti-Penne. At Cepagatti, turn right on S.S.602 for Catignagno then after 3 km turn right at Micarone and follow signs to Le Georgiche.

LE GEORGICHE
Hosts: Teresa Colavincenzo & Vito Valenzano
Manager: Claudia Cognolato
Contrada di S. Maria
Pianella (PE) 65019, Italy
Tel & fax: (085) 412500, Cellphone: (338) 4545861
5 rooms, Double: €60–€70
Minimum nights required: 3
Open: Apr to Oct, Other languages: some English
Region: Abruzzo, Michelin Map: 430
www.karenbrown.com/italy/georgiche.html

Right along the road connecting the hilltowns of Pienza and Montepulciano is the conveniently positioned farm of Felice and Giulia, transplanted from their hometowns in the regions of Marches and Campania respectively. The 18th-century stone farmhouse forms a U with inner courtyard from which you gain access to the breakfast room/bar, stone-walled restaurant with large dividing arch, living room, and upstairs bedrooms divided on both sides. Bedrooms are luminous and spacious, with immaculate bathrooms, pretty bedspreads, and country furniture. The bedrooms on the right side overlook the hilly countryside, swimming pool, and the 100-acre property of woods and fields, which produces its own wine and olive oil. Ancient Pienza can be seen at a distance. The real treat here is Giulia's cooking using the farm's own fresh produce. She has a flair for combining local traditional recipes with her own personal inventions, having homemade pastas as her base. Hard-working Felice relaxes and jokes with guests, often ending the evening playing the guitar. This is an easy-access touring base for the endless itineraries available, including Siena Montalcino and tours of the d'Orcia wine valley, and a great value. *Directions:* Exit from the autostrada at Chiusi and follow signs for Montepulciano, then Pienza. After a total of 25 km, well before Pienza, the iron gates of the Santo Pietro are on the left.

SANTO PIETRO
Hosts: Felice d'Angelo & Giulia Scala
Strada Statale 126, No. 29, Pienza (SI) 53026, Italy
Tel & fax: (0578) 748410, Cellphone: (347) 0185601
11 rooms, Double: €93
Per person half board: €67
Minimum nights required: 3
Open: Mar to Dec, Credit cards: all major
Other languages: some English
Region: Tuscany, Michelin Map: 430
www.karenbrown.com/italy/santopietro.html

The most striking images of southern Tuscany are in the Orcia Valley—enchanting landscapes with soft, rolling hills topped with rows of cypress trees silhouetted against the sky. This alternating with the area called Le Crete Senesi—barren hills made of clay and resembling moon craters—makes for fascinating scenery. Le Traverse, at 4 kilometers from Pienza, is submersed in this peaceful countryside to which your gracious hosts, Pinuccia and Enrico, retired from Milan. Their charming home has been very tastefully restored and all the right touches (such as terry bathrobes and the finest-quality bedlinens) added to make guests feel right at home. The stone farmhouse with front courtyard is divided between the couple's own quarters, rooms for their visiting children, and an apartment for guests with independent entrance. The other two bedrooms are situated in the one-level converted barn nearby and are enhanced with the family's country antiques and prints. Huge terra-cotta vases overflowing with geraniums, trailing roses, and azalea plants dot the 50-acre property, which includes a swimming pool. Olive oil is produced as well as jams using homegrown fruit. The intimacy of the place with its three rooms makes you feel like a true houseguest and the area is full of delightful day trips. *Directions:* Follow signs for Monticchiello from Pienza (circular piazza). After 3.3 km turn left on an unpaved road up to a group of cypress trees and the house.

LE TRAVERSE
Host: Pinuccia Barbier Meroni
Localita: Le Traverse, Pienza (SI) 53026, Italy
Tel: (0578) 748198, Fax: (0578) 748949
Cellphone: (360) 575158 or (333) 4708789
3 rooms, Double: €155
Minimum nights required: 2
Closed: Jan 22 to 30, Credit cards: all major
Other languages: good English, French
Region: Tuscany, Michelin Map: 430
www.karenbrown.com/italy/traverse.html

La Piccola Pieve lies several kilometers south of the ancient fortified town of Colle Val d'Elsa with its many crystal factories. The ancient house of owner Cristina Grassi, dating back to 1200, is actually the core of a cluster of attached stone houses. Stairs overflowing with cascading geraniums lead up to the front door of her cozy home, which the warm and gracious hostess practically hands over to her guests. A large, antique-filled living room with open stone staircase, fireplace, paintings, Oriental carpets, silver collection, and family photographs puts one immediately at ease. Two lovely bedrooms with one bathroom (perfect for families or two couples) are found down a small corridor to the left of this room, while the other two rooms upstairs are at opposite ends of another comfortable beamed sitting room. The air-conditioned bedrooms as well as bathrooms are quite spacious and elegantly appointed with parquet floors and antique beds. Breakfast of homemade cakes is served at the dining table in the inviting open kitchen with hanging brass pots and exposed brick arches. A wonderful surprise is the expansive garden and lawn with gazebo backdropped by hills. The advantages—location, ambiance, rate—are many in Cristina's warm and charming home in central Tuscany. *Directions:* From Colle take 541 south to Gracciano and right after the playground, take the small gravel road to a group of houses, taking the first right at the driveway.

※ ▭ ✄ 🕴 👫 🏇 P 🚭 🍇

LA PICCOLA PIEVE
Host: Cristina Grassi
Localita: Pieve a Elsa 92
Pieve a Elsa (SI) 53034, Italy
Tel & fax: (0577) 929745, Cellphone: (340) 4084197
4 rooms, Double: €110
Open: Mar to Nov
Other languages: some English, Spanish, French
Region: Tuscany, Michelin Map: 430
www.karenbrown.com/italy/piccola.html

The San Teodoro Nuovo property offers the "way-off-the-beaten-track" traveler a delightful base for exploring the southernmost reaches of Italy. In the Basilicata region, just 5 kilometers from the beaches of the Gulf of Taranto, this 400-acre farm specializing in citrus fruits and olive oil has been in the noble Xenia Doria family for generations and the family from Milan now resides here all year, offering guest accommodation in a variety of renovated buildings. Two apartments appointed with the house's original furniture are found in a wing of the large main brick villa covered with bougainvillea vines, while another five, simpler in decor, are just below on the ground floor facing out to the back orchards. These can accommodate from two to four persons and have a kitchen. The remaining four very pleasant apartments, for two to four people, are in the same building as the restaurant on the property and and are appointed with the family's own pieces, with accents of color from the fresh country fabrics used. Meals at the restaurant are based on local traditional recipes and the farm's own products. In the vicinity are the highlights of Apulia and many Greek archaeological ruins, as well as two 18-hole golf courses and horse riding. *Directions:* From Taranto take the S.S.106 coastal highway and after passing the S.S.407 for Potenza, continue for 7 km and exit at Pisticci. Turn right at the sign for San Teodoro Nuovo.

SAN TEODORO NUOVO
Host: Maria Xenia Doria family
Manager: Claudia Cognolato
Localita: Marconia, Pisticci (MT) 47004, Italy
Tel & fax: (0835) 47004, Cellphone: (338) 5698116
11 apartments: €610–€2,400 weekly, €86–€94 double B&B
Minimum nights required: 3
Open: all year, Credit cards: MC, VS
Other languages: some English
Region: Basilicata, Michelin Map: 431
www.karenbrown.com/italy/teodoro.html

As more and more Italians reclaim family property in the countryside or buy and restore their own abandoned castles, people such as the Baccheschi family are moving into more affordable, lesser-known areas. They left behind a successful fashion business to come to the quiet southern part of Tuscany where they bought the ruins of a 13th-century stone castle/ex-convent and have almost completed putting its pieces back together to form their own private residence and rooms for guests. Two adjacent stunning stone guesthouses are available, plus three suites in the main castle. The smaller house, I Sassi, has one bedroom, a large bathroom, and glassed-in living room taking in the sumptuous view of virgin territory. La Chiesina has a kitchen and spacious living room with intarsia parquet flooring, two bedrooms, and two bathrooms. They are appointed sophisticatedly with family antiques and colonial pieces from Indonesia, and are worthy of an article in Architectural Digest. The suites, decorated in the same vein, share a large kitchen and living room. The travertine swimming pool hangs on the edge of the manicured garden, which drops down into untamed landscapes. *Directions:* From the Grosseto-Siena highway 223, exit at Paganico. After 3 km turn right for Sasso d'Ombrone, and right again for Poggi del Sasso. In town watch for street sign Via de Vicarello on the right and follow the dirt road, keeping left at the fork for 7.5 km to the gray iron gate on the right.

CASTELLO DI VICARELLO
Hosts: Aurora & Carlo Baccheschi Berti
Via di Vicarello 1
Poggi del Sasso (SI) 58043, Italy
Tel & fax: (0564) 990718, Cellphone: (328) 8720670
3 rooms, Double: €190–€220
2 houses: €190–€403 daily
Minimum nights required: 3, 7 in Jul & Aug
Open: all year
Region: Tuscany, Michelin Map: 430
www.karenbrown.com/italy/vicarello.html

The picturesque countryside dotted with medieval hilltowns north of Rome called Sabina is finally getting some recognition after centuries of being just a sleepy rural area. Bed and breakfasts are springing up right and left and at long last the tourist, inexplicably foreign to this lovely area so close to the capital city, has the opportunity to explore this virgin territory with its ancient traditions still in practice. Maria Vittoria, the warm and enthusiastic hostess of "Wonderland," as her bed and breakfast translates, is another newcomer to Sabina. She offers a very comfortable level of accommodation in her own home set down below the main road outside of town and facing out to an impressive panorama of hills covered with olive groves and distant mountains. Four bedrooms are found in the main house, elegantly appointed with precious antiques, paintings, and various collections from Maria Vittoria's worldwide travels. Some have terraces from which you can watch sunsets over the magnificent valley. Two other independent suites have been built into the hillside in front of the home. These are both adorable "nests," one having a loft bedroom with sitting area and kitchenette below. A homemade breakfast is served on the front patio. *Directions:* From the Rome-Rieti Via Salaria (route 4), turn off left for Poggio Nativo and continue on the main road 42 for 5 km. There is an iron gate to the house on the right-hand side before Santa Maria.

PAESE DELLE MERAVIGLIE
Host: Maria Vittoria Toniolo
Via Mirtense km 5
Poggio Nativo (RI) 02030, Italy
Tel & fax: (0765) 872599, Cellphone: (328) 6642954
6 rooms, Double: €78–€96
1 apartment: €468–€576 weekly
Minimum nights required: 2
Open: all year, Other languages: good English
Region: Lazio, Michelin Map: 430
www.karenbrown.com/italy/paese.html

Forty-five kilometers northeast of Florence, in a beautiful, hilly area of Tuscany, lies the Rufina Valley, famous for its robust red wine. Crowning a wooded slope is one of the many residences of the noble Galeotti-Ottieri family. The interior of the 15th-century main villa reveals spacious high-ceilinged halls with frescoes depicting family history. The family has also restored several stone farmhouses on the vast property, one of which is the Locanda Praticino whose upper floor contains lovely, simple double rooms with countryside views down one long hall, each named after its color scheme. Downstairs is a large rustic dining and living room with vaulted ceiling, enormous stone fireplace, worn brick floors, and casual country furniture. Full country-fresh Tuscan meals are only €15. A swimming pool and tennis courts, plus the enchanting landscape, make it difficult to tear oneself away for touring. In order to retain the characteristic flavor of farmers' quarters, the properties have an intentionally unrestored, natural air to them. Available for longer stays are three very tastefully decorated apartments. The Petrognano is a tranquil spot where guests may enjoy the gracious hospitality of this historically important Florentine family. *Directions:* From Florence head toward Pontassieve. Continue to Rufina, turning right at Castiglioni-Pomino. Follow the winding road to the property, marked just before Pomino (12 km from Pontassieve).

FATTORIA DI PETROGNANO
Host: Cecilia Galeotti-Ottieri family
Localita: Pomino
Pomino, Rufina (FI) 50060, Italy
Tel: (055) 2001429 or 8318867, Fax: (055) 2264488
8 rooms, Double: €73–€83
3 apartments: €350–€750 weekly
Open: Apr 15 to Oct, Credit cards: all major
Other languages: good English, French
Region: Tuscany, Michelin Map: 430
www.karenbrown.com/italy/petrognano.html

In the undiscovered valley of Champorcher, Mauro and his wife Piera took over the ancient town grain mill and have reopened its doors as a bed and breakfast. The plain exterior on the road gives no clue to the fascinating interior where enormous dining-room windows look right out over the rushing torrents of Ayasse, which cut directly through this lush valley. In the middle of this spacious room is an antique carpenter's sawing machine, once part of the mill. Restoration work on the stone mill, just off the dining room, is being completed with the hopes of continuing the grain production activity using original methods. A loft living room with fireplace and burgundy sofas looks over the main room. Piera prepares the nightly meal for guests using traditional recipes from this mountain area. The Gontiers' agriculture activity produces various vegetables, berries, and chestnuts. The four sweetly decorated new bedrooms are located on the same floor and all have water views (and sounds!), brand-new bathrooms, lace curtains, and carved pinewood beds. Hiking trails in the valley take you up to the many waterfalls. This is a perfect spot for nature lovers wanting to explore. *Directions:* Exit at Verres from the A5 from the north, heading for Verres, then Bard. At Bard turn right for Hone, Champorcher. After 7 km, just after Pontboset, Le Moulin is located just before the stone bridge on the left-hand side of the road.

LE MOULIN DES ARAVIS   New
Hosts: Mauro Gontier & Piera Chanoux
Fraz. Savin 55, Pontboset (AO) 11020, Italy
Tel: (0125) 809831, Cellphone: (329) 8013184
Fax: (0125) 834982
4 rooms, Double: €42–€46
Per person half board: €30–€37
Open: all year
Other languages: very little English, French
Region: Aosta Valley, Michelin Map: 428
www.karenbrown.com/italy/pontboset.html

Annabella and Cesare Taticchi, daughters, and 11 grandchildren warmly welcome guests to their corn, sunflower, and horse-breeding farm above Perugia, a rambling villa owned by the family since 1600. The former farmer's quarters near the main house contain a breakfast room and guestrooms with wood-beamed ceilings and brick floors, furnished in simple country style. Additional rooms are within the villa. Ceramic bathroom tiles (and lamps), handmade by their talented daughter, depict horses, ducks, roses, butterflies, and the like, for which the rooms are named. The main villa's dramatic entrance foyer with arched stairway leads up to a glassed-in veranda overlooking a neglected garden and woods through which the River Tiber flows. Annabella serves her specialties in the old-style dining room with chandelier and frescoes. Time stands still in the original library/billiard room and the two living rooms with piano, Oriental carpets, and period paintings. Horses are available for lessons in the indoor/outdoor ring or excursions in the area. Weeklong courses with special all-inclusive rates are available in cooking, ceramics, and riding. Il Covone is a busy and informal place for families. *Directions:* Take route E45 from Perugia, exiting at Ponte Pattoli. Turn right at the T-junction and continue for 1 km. The farm is just after the tennis/sport complex.

IL COVONE
Hosts: Annabella & Cesare Taticchi
Strada della Fratticiola 2
Ponte Pattoli (PG) 06085, Italy
Tel: (075) 694140, Fax: (075) 694503
10 rooms, Double: €75–€85
Per person half board: €52–€62
Minimum nights required: 2
Open: all year, Credit cards: all major
Region: Umbria, Michelin Map: 430
www.karenbrown.com/italy/ilcovone.html

Gennarino a Mare is primarily a restaurant—one of the best known in Ponza both for its seafood specialties and its prime location right on the waterfront. It even has a large deck that stretches out over the water, built upon wooden pilings. Gennarino a Mare is a favorite place to dine, especially in summer when boats of all shapes and sizes dock at the adjacent pier and the merry yacht set comes to eat and drink. The restaurant has hosted many of the world's rich and famous, so there's no telling who might be sitting at the next table. It is no wonder the restaurant is so popular: as you enjoy dinner, you can watch the reflection of the fishing boats shimmering in the water and, behind them, the gaily painted houses of Ponza stepping up the hill like brightly painted blocks. Owner Francesco Silvestri was born in the same house where the restaurant now stands. The 12 simple bedrooms, located on the floors above the restaurant, are all decorated similarly with colorful matching drapes and bedspreads setting off white walls. Although small, each room has its own little step-out balcony with a romantic view. Remember, Gennarino a Mare is basically a restaurant, but a real winner for a simple, reasonably priced place to stay in Ponza. *Directions:* Take either the ferry or hydrofoil from Anzio to Ponza. The hotel is on the opposite side of the port, so it is best to take a taxi.

GENNARINO A MARE
Hosts: Tilla & Francesco Silvestri
Via Dante, 64
Ponza, Isola di (LT) 04027, Italy
Tel: (0771) 80071, Fax: (0771) 80140
12 rooms, Double: €114–€216
Open: all year, Credit cards: all major
Other languages: good English
Region: Lazio, Michelin Map: 430
www.karenbrown.com/italy/gennarino.html

Just north of Spoleto is the tiny 14th-century village of Poreta and farther up on the hillside are the remains of the walls of the castle that once dominated the valley. It is here that a group of friends, Luca and American Pam being the omnipresent, genial hosts, restored what was left of the ancient castle and transformed it into a country bed and breakfast. Their idea was to provide not only accommodation but also a special place offering a variety of cultural events such as classical concerts, art shows, poetry reading, and dinners with particular local food themes. The cluster of stone houses where the eight bedrooms are located includes a church restored in the baroque period with original frescoes and faux-marble borders. The small restaurant is made up of two cozy rooms with beamed ceilings, fireplace, and cheery yellow walls. Light meals accompanied by music can be had 4 kilometers away in their new wine bar. A clean and pleasant country style pervades the bedrooms with their soothingly soft beige tones and occasional country antiques. They need no elaborate paintings for decoration as the views out the windows suffice. The buildings are united by an expansive brick terrace overlooking olive groves and sweeping views of the valley—a wonderful spot for watching the spectacular sunsets while enjoying a pre-dinner drink. *Directions:* From the N3 Spoleto-Perugia road turn right after 8 km at Poreta and follow signs up to the castle.

IL CASTELLO DI PORETA
Hosts: Luca Saint Amour di Chanaz & Pam Moskow
Localita: Poreta
Poreta–Spoleto (PG) 06049, Italy
Tel: (0743) 275810, Cellphone: (335) 7371838
Fax: (0743) 270175
8 rooms, Double: €99–€114
Open: all year, Credit cards: all major
Other languages: good English
Region: Umbria, Michelin Map: 430
www.karenbrown.com/italy/poreta.html

The Vecchio Convento is a real gem, offering quality accommodation for a moderate price. Its several dining rooms are brimming with rustic country charm and serve delicious meals prepared from local produce. There are 15 guestrooms tastefully decorated with antiques. The town of Portico di Romagna is like the inn, inviting yet unpretentious—an old village surrounded by wooded hills and clear mountain streams. A stroll through medieval pathways, which twist down between the weathered stone houses, leads you to an ancient stone bridge gracefully arching over a rushing stream. The inn, too, is old, but was not (as you might expect from its name) originally a convent. According to its gracious owner, Marisa Raggi, it was named for a restaurant located in a convent that she and her husband Giovanni (the chef) used to operate—when they moved here they kept the original name. The restaurant is still their primary focus, as its fine, fresh cuisine reflects. Italian lessons are also organized. *Directions:* Because of the winding, two-lane mountain highway that leads to the village, it takes about two hours to drive the 75 km from Florence. The inn is located 34 km southwest of the town of Forli.

ALBERGO AL VECCHIO CONVENTO
Hosts: Marisa Raggi & Giovanni Cameli
Via Roma, 7
Portico di Romagna (FO) 47010, Italy
Tel: (0543) 967053, Fax: (0543) 967157
15 rooms, Double: €90
Closed: Jan 12 to Feb 12, Credit cards: all major
Other languages: some English
Region: Emilia-Romagna, Michelin Map: 429
www.karenbrown.com/italy/vecchioconvento.html

On the outskirts of historical Mantova sits the Villa Schiarino Lena, one of the magnificent estates formerly belonging to the Gonzaga family, once among the most powerful nobility in Lombardy. The very cordial Lena Eliseo family, the present owners, have taken on the enormous task of restoring the 15th-century palace room by room. With high vaulted ceilings, completely frescoed rooms, wrought-iron chandeliers, and original terra-cotta floors, the seemingly endless parade of rooms reveals one delight after another. Besides being a museum, the villa is used for large parties, weddings, and business meetings, and guestrooms are also available. Surrounding the villa are small houses, once inhabited by farmhands, which are now offered to travelers on a daily or weekly basis. The three modest but spacious and comfortable apartments are appointed with a mixture of antique and contemporary furniture and can accommodate up to four persons. Each apartment has its own living area and one includes a kitchenette. This location is the ideal spot to base yourself while exploring less-touristy Ferrara, Cremona, Verona, and Mantua, which are filled with medieval and Renaissance buildings (Palazzo del Te and Palazzo Ducale are "must sees"). *Directions:* From Mantova take route N62 north past the church and turn left on Via Gramsci. Follow it for 1 km to the villa.

VILLA SCHIARINO LENA
Host: Giuseppe Lena Eliseo family
Via Santa Maddalena 7, Porto Mantovano (MN) 46047, Italy
Tel: (0376) 398238, Cellphone: (347) 6097784
Fax: (0376) 393238
2 rooms, Double: €100–€110
3 apartments: €100–€110 daily B&B
Minimum nights required: 2
Open: mid-Mar to Oct, Credit cards: MC, VS
Other languages: good English, Region: Lombardy
www.karenbrown.com/italy/schiarino.html

Accommodation of all levels is available in Positano's many hotels: from five-star luxury to simple bed and breakfasts like Casa Cosenza, with its sunny yellow façade. Sitting snug against the cliff side, halfway down to the beach, it is reached by descending one of the variety of stairways found in this unique seaside town. The front arched entranceway, lined with terra-cotta pots overflowing with colorful local flora, leads to an enormous tiled terrace overlooking the pastel-color houses of Positano and the dramatic coastline. Seven guestrooms on the second floor, each with a balcony and air conditioning, enjoy the same breathtaking panorama. The residence dates back 200 years, as evidenced by the typical cupola ceilings, originally designed to keep rooms cool and airy. Guestrooms have bright, tiled floors and are simply and sweetly decorated with old-fashioned armoires, desks, and beds. Room 7 (at a slightly higher rate), although smaller and with an older bathroom, has a lovely large terrace, as do two suites behind the main house that can accommodate three to four persons. Two apartments located in the back and above the B&B also have lovely views. A Continental breakfast is served on the terrace. The helpful Cosenza family assures visitors of a pleasant stay. *Directions:* Park your car in a garage in town and ask for directions for the scalinatella stairway where there are signs to Casa Cosenza. Remember to pack light!

CASA COSENZA
Host: Salvatore Cosenza family
Via Trara Genoino 18, Positano (SA) 84017, Italy
Tel: (089) 875063, Fax: (089) 8122365
9 rooms, Double: €120–€190
2 apartments: €1,450–€1,650 weekly
Minimum nights required: 3 in high season
Open: all year, Credit cards: all major
Other languages: very little English
Region: Campania, Michelin Map: 431
www.karenbrown.com/italy/casacosenza.html

The spectacular Amalfi coast offers a wide variety of accommodation, yet few as special as La Fenice—as fantastic as the mythological bird for which it is named. Guests leave their cars on the main road and climb the arbored steps to discover the white villa hidden amid lush Mediterranean vegetation. Costantino and Angela heartily welcome new arrivals on the shady front terrace, where a basic Continental breakfast is served each clement morning. Seven luminous bedrooms, three with terrace and marvelous sea views, the others with lateral sea or no sea view, are simply and sparsely furnished with an occasional antique armoire or bureau in a wing off the family's home. Eight more rooms of varying dimensions, most with terraces, reached by many steps down from the road, are built separately into the side of the cliff and have colorful, tiled floors and similar furnishings. Descending yet more steps, you'll come to the curved seawater pool and Jacuzzi carved against the rock (open June to October), where an occasional salad or sandwich is served during summer months (at an extra cost). A coastal boat tour (pick-up at La Fenice's beach) including a stop for lunch can be arranged. This property has few or no amenities in the rooms, but is a natural wonder, cascading down to the sea and a small private beach. *Directions:* Located on the coastal highway south of Positano towards Amalfi. Two curves after town, watch for gates on both sides of the road.

⚓ ☕ 🍴 ⛺ 🚶 🐎 P 🚭 ≈ ♨ 💃

LA FENICE
Hosts: Angela & Costantino Mandara
Via Marconi 4
Positano (SA) 84017, Italy
Tel: (089) 875513, Fax: (089) 811309
15 rooms, Double: €125
Open: all year
Other languages: some English
Region: Campania, Michelin Map: 431
www.karenbrown.com/italy/lafenice.html

Villa Rosa opened its doors six years ago after restoration work by local couple Virginia and Franco who own a clothing store and ceramic store in town (the house has always been in Virginia's family). The 150-year-old villa, built into the cliffside and hidden behind bougainvillea vines high above the road right in town, is on three levels. Taking the stairs up to the middle level, you find the reception area and large common living room where guests are greeted. The twelve bedrooms are spread over all three floors, each having access to the large front terraces which are divided by plants and grapevine-covered pergolas for privacy. Picturesque views of Positano's colorful houses and the spectacular coastline are enjoyed from any point. Breakfast is served either in rooms or out on individual terraces adorned with large terra-cotta vases laden with cascading pink and red geraniums, in sharp contrast to pure white walls. Bedrooms maintain original tiles and vaulted ceilings and are furnished with simple antiques, while bathrooms display typical yellow and blue hand-painted tiles from Vietri. Air conditioning is an exceptional amenity offered along with satellite TV, mini bar, telephone, and safe. Easy day trips include Amalfi, Ravello, and the ruins of Pompeii, Paestum, or Herculum. *Directions:* Following the main road through town, you find Villa Rosa almost at the end just before the famous Sirenuse Hotel. Parking is possible in a nearby public garage only.

❄ ⚓ ☕ ✂ 💳 ☎ 🚶 🍸 🖼 🏄

VILLA ROSA
Hosts: Virginia & Franco Caldiero
Via C. Colombo 127
Positano (SA) 84017, Italy
Tel: (089) 811955, Fax: (089) 812112
12 rooms, Double: €130–€140
Open: Mar to Oct, Credit cards: all major
Other languages: some English
Region: Campania, Michelin Map: 431
www.karenbrown.com/italy/rosa.html

From the moment you enter the grand foyer looking out over the classical Italian Renaissance garden of this 16th-century country villa, all sense of time and place is lost. The Rucellais' devotion to their estate (in the family since 1759) is apparent, as is their warm hospitality. Guests are given the run of the rambling old home, from the cozy bedrooms, varying in size and decor; antique-filled library; and spacious living room with fireplace, worn floral sofas, and family portraits to a gracious buffet breakfast room where guests are served en famille at a long table. At the entrance is a duck pond, a large shady area with tables and a 15th-century swimming pool backed by a stone wall of the actual house. The four children and their families all live on the wine- and olive-oil-producing estate and Francesca and Frank enjoy suggesting itineraries for their guests, as well as cultural events such as art courses, concerts, and art exhibits. Villa Rucellai serves as an excellent base for visiting Florence, Siena, Lucca, and Pisa. The town of Prato with its many restaurant choices is conveniently just a ten-minute walk away. *Directions:* From Florence take the A11 autostrada, exiting at Prato Est towards Vaiano-Vernio. Circle left onto Borgo Valsugana, keeping the river and railroad to the left. Follow signs all the way to the Trattoria La Fontana, then go another 1.5 km on the very narrow Via di Canneto up to the marked villa on the hillside.

VILLA RUCELLAI DI CANNETO
Host: Rucellai Piqué family
Via di Canneto 16
Prato (FI) 59100, Italy
Tel & fax: (0574) 460392, Cellphone: (347) 7745073
11 rooms, Double: €90
Open: all year
Other languages: fluent English
Region: Tuscany, Michelin Map: 430
www.karenbrown.com/italy/rucellai.html

The fascinating Castello di Proceno in the Lazio region bordering Tuscany and Umbria is a unique accommodation and combines some of the main features that make agritourism accommodation popular—historical context, authentic ambiance, unspoiled landscapes, regional foods and wines, and congenial hosts. The Cecchini Bisoni family, owners of this 12th-century hilltop fortress for many generations, have done an outstanding job of restoring some of the farmers' quarters that make up part of the village grouped around the tower. They modernized plumbing, electricity, and heating systems without disturbing the innate quaintness of these stone dwellings. In addition, Signora Cecilia is a passionate decorator and has found very clever ways of displaying many of the family's antique collections and restored furniture throughout the comfortable apartments. The restaurant, complete with cantina and fireplace, leads to a labyrinth of tunnels and stairways connecting to four of the apartments, while the remaining three are located in the fortress attached to the ancient pentagonal walls of the tower and castle, in a wooded area leading down to the swimming pool. All apartments have one or two bedrooms and a kitchenette and all feature both a fireplace and garden area or terrace. *Directions:* The castello is in the village of Proceno, 16 km north of Lake Bolsena. Follow S.S.2 from the lake to Acquapendente and after 3 km turn left for Proceno.

CASTELLO DI PROCENO
Host: Cecilia Cecchini Bisoni family
Corso Regina Margherita 155
Proceno (VT) 01020, Italy
Tel & fax: (0763) 710072, Cellphone: (335) 373394
7 apartments: €100–€135 daily
No dinner Mon & Tue, Minimum nights required: 2
Open: all year, Credit cards: MC, VS
Other languages: good English
Region: Lazio, Michelin Map: 430
www.karenbrown.com/italy/proceno.html

One option (among at least 20 possibilities) for in-home accommodations in the Radda area is at the home of a gregarious Florentine couple, Giuliana and Enis Vergelli, whose stone house sits on a long, winding road, just before the castle/village of Volpaia. The guest quarters are actually found in another stone house a few steps away in the quaint 14th-century village. The wood-shuttered residence can be rented entirely or as two separate apartments. One apartment, just like a doll house, is comprised of a mini living area with minuscule fireplace, kitchenette, and a ladder staircase leading up to the bedroom and bath—an absolutely adorable love nest for two. The other apartment, also on two floors, has a good-sized living room with kitchen, bathroom, and two bedrooms, simply and very comfortably furnished. Giuliana also offers accommodation in a bedroom with bathroom, garden, and separate entrance in her own home. Guests are welcome to wander through the Vergellis' garden and enjoy the terrace with sweeping views over Chianti country. Giuliana adores pampering her guests and appears now and then with jams, honey, or a freshly made soup. *Directions:* Driving through the town of Radda, turn right at signs for Volpaia castle. Go uphill for several kilometers to the first house before entering town, marked Vergelli.

AZIENDA AGRICOLA VERGELLI
Hosts: Enis & Giuliana Vergelli
Localita: Volpaia
Radda in Chianti (SI) 53017, Italy
Tel & fax: (0577) 738382
1 room, Double: €68
2 apartments: €78 daily (2 people), €120 daily (4 people)
Open: all year
Other languages: none
Region: Tuscany, Michelin Map: 430
www.karenbrown.com/italy/aziendaagricolavergelli.html

Weary of life in the intense financial world of Milan, Guido and Martina packed up and headed for the hills of Chianti and the "good life" that attracts so many there. After a long search they chose the scenic property where La Locanda now stands, primarily for its magnificent position facing out to medieval Volpaia and an endless panorama filled with layers of virgin hills. The results of their meticulous restoration of three simple stone farmhouses are formidable and today fortunate guests can share in their dream. Its remote location among woods and olive groves guarantees total silence and tranquillity and the comfortable, decorator-perfect common rooms and luminous colors harmonize divinely with this idyllic setting. An understated elegance permeates the six bedrooms and suite divided among one of the two-story farmhouses. They are tastefully appointed with antiques and smart plaid curtains, and four have the advantage of the views. Breakfast and dinner (except Mondays and Thursdays) are served out on the terrace above the swimming pool whose borderless edge spills into the landscape. Guido and Martina, natural and gregarious hosts, exude a contagious enthusiasm for their new surroundings. *Directions:* From Radda follow signs for Florence and turn right for Volpaia. Continue on the unpaved road for another 3.8 km after Volpaia village, following signs to La Locanda/Montanino.

LA LOCANDA
Hosts: Guido & Martina Bevilacqua
Localita: Montanino
Radda in Chianti (SI) 53017, Italy
Tel: (0577) 738833, Fax: (0577) 739263
7 rooms, Double: €180–€270
Minimum nights required: 2
Open: Apr to Nov, Credit cards: all major
Other languages: good English
Region: Tuscany, Michelin Map: 430
www.karenbrown.com/italy/lalocanda.html

Podere Terreno combines idyllic location and authentic, charming ambiance with delightful hosts Sylvie and Roberto, a Franco-Italian couple, and son, Francesco. The 400-year-old rustic stone farmhouse is surrounded by terra-cotta flower vases, a grapevine-covered pergola, a small lake, and sweeping panoramas of the Chianti countryside. Inside are seven sweet double bedrooms with very small bathrooms, each decorated differently with country antiques and the family's personal possessions, which make the feeling very informal and homelike. Guests convene in the main room of the house around the massive stone fireplace on floral sofas for a glass of house wine before sitting down to a sumptuous candlelit dinner prepared by your hosts. This is a cozy, stone-walled room, filled with country antiques, brass pots, dried-flower bouquets hanging from the exposed beams, and shelves lined with bottles of the proprietors' own Chianti Classico wine. Wine tastings take place within the new cantina. The hosts are experts at suggesting local itineraries and directing guests to the many quaint villages waiting to be explored. *Directions:* From Greve follow signs to Panzano, then go left for Radda and on to Lucarelli. After 3 km turn right at Volpaia and after 5 km turn right at the sign for Podere Terreno.

PODERE TERRENO
Hosts: Marie Sylvie Haniez, Roberto Melosi
& Pier Francesco Rapisarda-Haniez
Via della Volpaia, Radda in Chianti (SI) 53017, Italy
Tel: (0577) 738312, Fax: (0577) 738400
7 rooms, Double: €190*
*Includes breakfast & dinner, Minimum nights required: 2
Open: all year, Credit cards: all major
Other languages: good English
Region: Tuscany, Michelin Map: 430
www.karenbrown.com/italy/podereterreno.html

Both Radda and Greve are excellent bases from which to explore the scenic Chianti wine country with its regal castles and stone villages, in addition to Siena, Florence, and San Gimignano. Radda in particular offers a myriad of possibilities for accommodation, including many private homes with rooms or apartments. The Val delle Corti is the home and vineyard property of gracious hostess Eli Bianchi and her son Roberto where they produce a high-quality Chianti Classico wine. The cozy pale-stone house with white shutters tops a hill overlooking the quaint town. The hosts, who moved here over 27 years ago from Milan, are extremely active in community affairs and are a superb source for area information. The guest accommodation is a lovely separate little house called il Fienile (hay barn), simply appointed with family antiques and newer pieces, which has a large open kitchen and living space looking out to the vineyards, and two bedrooms and one bathroom on the first floor. Meals can be taken at one of the excellent restaurants right in nearby Radda. *Directions:* Equidistant from Florence and Siena off the N222 Chianti road. Before entering Radda, turn right toward Lecchi-San Sano, then take the first left at Val delle Corti.

PODERE VAL DELLE CORTI
Hosts: Eli & Roberto Bianchi
Localita: La Croce
Radda in Chianti (SI) 53017, Italy
Tel: (0577) 738215, Fax: (0577) 739521
1 apartment: €700–€800 weekly, €110 daily (heating extra)
Minimum nights required: 3
Open: all year, Credit cards: MC, VS
Other languages: good English
Region: Tuscany, Michelin Map: 430
www.karenbrown.com/italy/poderevaldellecorti.html

In the very heart of Chianti between Radda, Castellina, and Vagliagli sits the Pornanino farm surrounded by 90 acres of wooded hills and olive groves. Hosts Franco and Lia have carefully restored the main house for themselves plus two stone barns for guests, appointed with the same warm country style as their own home, with antique furniture enhancing beamed ceilings and cotto floors. Il Capannino is completely refurbished and offers a large central room with open kitchen at an upper level, dining room/living room with open fireplace, and two bedrooms with two bathrooms. A large arched glass door opens onto the pergola-covered terrace for outside meals. Il Leccino is similar but has just one bedroom. Guests can also take advantage of the lovely swimming pool overlooking the olive groves. Franco and Lia are part of the increasing breed of "neo-farmers" migrating from major cities in search of a slower-paced lifestyle where the basic values of life are emphasized in everyday living. Franco has become a passionate producer of top-quality olive oil and even conducts small seminars and tastings on the subject. The Lombardis are part of a group of family and friends (called Casa Spante) offering similar rentals in the area. *Directions:* The farm is located 9 km south of Radda, 5 km from Castellina, and 4 km north of Vagliagli on route 102 but the turnoff is not marked, so it is best to call ahead. Located: 18 km from Siena and 54 km from Florence.

PORNANINO
Hosts: Lia & Franco Lombardi
Localita: Pornanino 72
Radda in Chianti (SI) 53017, Italy
Tel: (0577) 738658, Cellphone: (347) 7980012
Fax: (0577) 738794
2 houses: €725–€1,100 weekly (2 to 4 persons, heating extra)
Open: all year, Credit cards: MC, VS
Other languages: good English, French
Region: Tuscany, Michelin Map: 430
www.karenbrown.com/italy/pornanino.html

On the opposite side of town from the Podere Val delle Corti live relatives Lele Bianchi Vitali and her family, who offer a two-bedroom apartment in a stone tower dating from 1832. This unique accommodation, perfect for a family of four, has an enchanting view of Radda and the countryside. The three-story tower has terra-cotta floors and beamed ceilings, a living room/kitchenette on the ground floor, one bedroom and a bath on the second floor, and a second bedroom on top. Furnishings are simple and in keeping with the tower's rustic features. A small olive grove separates the tower from the Vitalis' Tuscan farmhouse, where a swimming pool bordered by lavender plants awaits road-weary guests and a double bedroom with bathroom is offered. Lele is a vivacious hostess who divides her time between guests, her three sons and grandchildren, and cooking lessons with several other bed and breakfast owners in the area whose success has brought them to the States to teach as well. *Directions:* From either Siena or Florence, follow signs for Radda off the spectacular Strada del Chianti N222. Go through town until you reach the hotel/restaurant Villa Miranda (not recommended), after which turn right at the sign for Canvalle and follow the dirt road up to the tower.

TORRE CANVALLE
Hosts: General Enrico & Lele Bianchi Vitali
Localita: La Villa
Radda in Chianti (SI) 53017, Italy
Tel & fax: (0577) 738321
1 room, Double: €108
1 tower apartment: €759 weekly
Open: all year
Other languages: good English
Region: Tuscany, Michelin Map: 430
www.karenbrown.com/italy/torrecanvalle.html

Nicoletta Innocenti is the delightful owner and hostess of La Palazzina, one of our favorite bed and breakfasts. The stately 18th-century villa has 11 lovely guestrooms appointed with antiques, each having its own cool pastel color scheme. The large dining room with checked black-and-white tiled floors looks out to the garden and expansive lawns. A swimming pool hugs the side of the hill overlooking sweeping panoramas. Two of the three apartments within a 17th-century stone farmhouse, Colombaio, have two double bedrooms each, living area with kitchenette, fireplace, and bathroom. The third is a studio apartment for two persons. They are rustically furnished with local antiques and offer gorgeous valley views. The lovely Villa Fonte Emerosa, appointed with period antiques, has three bedrooms, three bathrooms, large living rooms with fireplace, garden, and swimming pool and faces out to the mountains. The 18th-century farmhouse, Casa di Terra, is set among the vineyards and includes three bedrooms, two bathrooms, kitchen, living room, and dining room. This southeast corner of Tuscany offers a rich variety of sites to explore, including the Amiata Mountains and the hilltowns of Montepulciano, Pienza, and Montalcino. *Directions:* From Florence on the A1 autostrada, exit at Chiusi and drive towards Sarteano on route 478, turning left for Radicofani. After 14 km turn left for Celle Sul Rigo then right at the sign for La Palazzina.

LA PALAZZINA
Host: Innocenti family
Localita: Le Vigne, Radicofani (SI) 53040, Italy
Tel: (0578) 55771, Cellphone: (335) 8253937
Fax: (0578) 53553
11 rooms, Double: €119–€129
3 apartments: €450–€620 weekly
2 houses: €414–€2,582 weekly, Minimum nights required: 2
Open: all year, Credit cards: all major
Other languages: good English, Region: Tuscany
www.karenbrown.com/italy/palazzina.html

The Villa Maria is perhaps best known for its absolutely delightful terrace restaurant, which has a bird's-eye view of the magnificent coast. Whereas most of Ravello's hotels capture the southern view, the Villa Maria features the equally lovely vista to the north. The hotel is easy to locate, being on the same walking path that winds its way from the main square to the Villa Cimbrone gardens. After parking a level below the main square (or at the owner's other hotel, Giordano, where porters can handle your luggage and a heated pool can be used), look for signs for the Villa Maria, perched on the cliffs to your right. The building is a romantic old villa with a garden stretching to the side where tables and chairs are set, a favorite place to dine while enjoying the superb view. Inside, there is a cozy dining room overlooking the garden. The bedrooms are air-conditioned and furnished with antique pieces including brass beds. The bathrooms have been freshly remodeled and some have Jacuzzi tubs. Ingredients for excellent Mediterranean dishes come directly from the property's organic vegetable garden and for those wishing to know more about this regions's fine cuisine, weekly cooking courses have become very popular here. A private garden down the road is another relaxing spot for guests who fill the comments book with appreciation of the warm hospitality. *Directions:* Ravello is about 6 km north of Amalfi on a small road heading north from the highway.

VILLA MARIA
Host: Vincenzo Palumbo
Via San Chiara 2
Ravello (SA) 84010, Italy
Tel: (089) 857255, Cellphone: (338) 6764540
Fax: (089) 857071
22 rooms, Double: €210–€265, 1 apartment: €300–€420 daily
Open: all year, Credit cards: all major
Other languages: good English
Region: Campania, Michelin Map: 431
www.karenbrown.com/italy/maria.html

Ravenna is a splendid small city boasting one of the world's most prized collections of Byzantine mosaics housed within eight of its churches, basilicas, and mausoleums. The city comes alive in the summer months with a full program of theater, opera, and outdoor concerts, and even evening opening hours of churches to view the mosaics by night. There are lovely shops and the historical center of Ravenna is quiet since most residents get around by bicycle. Since we found bed and breakfast possibilities in the surrounding area to be much too spartan, the Hotel Diana with its yellow façade, in the center of Ravenna, is the best accommodation choice. A very friendly staff welcomes you into the luminous reception area with various sofas and armchairs arranged around a faux-marble fireplace, and a small patio outside. A buffet breakfast is served downstairs and an elevator takes you up to the second and third floors where the renovated bedrooms are located. These are rather standard but pleasant, with cream-colored walls and bedspreads, carpeting, and reproduction furniture. All have satellite television, air conditioning, and nice new bathrooms. The recommended superior doubles afford more space and have hydromassage tubs. Within a drive of an hour or less are Venice, Padua, Ferrara, Bologna, and the ancient ceramic center of Faenza. *Directions:* Follow signs for city center (Centro) then follow yellow hotel signs. Near the San Vitale Basilica.

HOTEL DIANA
Manager: Filippo Donati
Via G. Rossi 47
Ravenna 48100, Italy
Tel: (0544) 39119 or 39009, Fax: (0544) 30001
33 rooms, Double: €107
Open: all year, Credit cards: all major
Other languages: good English
Region: Emilia-Romagna, Michelin Map: 429
www.karenbrown.com/italy/diana.html

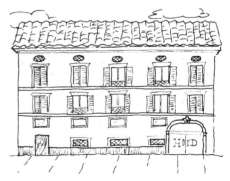

Highly recommended for those desiring to roam around a lesser-known part of Italy is the central section of the Marches region, an enchanting area offering something for every possible interest. The ancient town of Recanati with its redbrick houses and monumental main square was home to one of Italy's most famous poets, Giacomo Leopardi. Today the palazzo where the 18th-century poet lived is a museum incorporating a library with over 20,000 volumes, 15th-century wine cellars, and an exhibit highlighting his biography. Descendents of Leopardi, the Count Vanni and his daughter, Olimpia, currently live on the palazzo's upper floors, besides owning over 300 acres of farmland in the immediate vicinity. Across the street from the palazzo is a small two-story brick home where at one time artisans used to weave fabrics and where four comfortable independent apartments are now offered to guests. Apartments have a bedroom, bathroom, and living room with kitchenette (concealed in furniture), and one has a small rooftop terrace. In stages of restoration are several farmhouses on the family's surrounding property including Tre Ulivi, a typical farmhouse of the area with four bedrooms. For more independent travelers (no breakfast served), this is an ideal base rich with history from which to explore. *Directions:* Exit the A14 at Loreto and drive towards Recanati center, then follow signs for Casa Leopardi.

IL TELAIO   New
Hosts: Vanni & Olimpia Leopardi di San Leopardo
Piazzuola Sabato del Villaggio 5
Recanati (AN) 62019, Italy
Tel & fax: (071) 7573380, Cellphone: (338) 2274634
4 apartments: €80–€110 daily
Open: all year
Other languages: good English, French
Region: Marches, Michelin Map: 430
www.karenbrown.com/italy/telaio.html

With passion and determination, Daniela and her architect husband, Piero, brought back to life the family's ancient property with total respect for its 9th-century origins. This very special place has a rich historical past and a Romanesque church within the home where concerts are held. A nature lover's paradise, the complex of stone houses is surrounded by lush vegetation, vineyards, woods, and olive groves from which the family's prestigious olive oil comes. Hospitality is offered within six apartments attached to the main house accommodating from two to five persons, impeccably decorated with the family's refined antiques, which live harmoniously with their perfectly preserved centuries-old environment. The dwellings feature living room with fireplace, balconies taking in either the sweeping countryside views down to the sea or out to the woods and a 200-year-old oak tree, wrought-iron beds, and original paintings by Daniela's father, a renowned fresco painter. Daniela, a world traveler, is a hostess par excellence and her contagious enthusiasm makes a stay at Caminino splendidly memorable. Besides Siena and Montalcino, there are plenty of off-the-beaten-track sights to see and bikes can be rented. *Directions:* From Grosseto take Aurelia route 1 north and exit at Braccagni. Continue towards Montemassi and before town turn right for Caminino (on most maps) and Roccatederighi. After 1 km turn right at the gate for Caminino.

❄ ⚓ ☕ ✂ ☕ CREDIT 🏔 🏃 👫 🐎 🍷 P ⊘ ♿ ♿ 🍇

FATTORIA DI CAMININO
Hosts: Daniela Locatelli & Piero Marrucchi
Via Provinciale di Peruzzo, Roccatederighi (GR) 58028, Italy
Tel: (0564) 569737 or (055) 214898
Cellphone: (335) 6095183, Fax: (055) 2675819
6 apartments: €580–€1,050 weekly, €100–€200 daily
Minimum nights required: 2, 7 Jun to Sep
Open: all year, Credit cards: all major
Other languages: good English
Region: Tuscany, Michelin Map: 430
www.karenbrown.com/italy/caminino.html

Tuscany is the most visited region in Italy—mostly between Siena and Florence—but it nonetheless contains many other treasures off the beaten track. Heading west from Florence toward the coast you find the lovely towns of Lucca and Pisa, and just north of them is the beautifully scenic area known as Garfagnana, which features two nature reserves and the Apuan Alps. Here in the northernmost tip of Tuscany is evidence of how Italian culture varies not only from one region to another, but within a region itself. In the heart of these mountains, the genial Coletti family runs a lively local restaurant in the village and cultivates cereals, wild berries, and chestnuts on the farm. Hospitality is offered within seven very simple double rooms with a mountain-cabin feeling, having pinewood floors and ceilings, in a restored three-story building within the stone village of Roggio. Most have a balcony and all have modern bathrooms. Meals, including breakfast, are taken around the corner at the family restaurant where Gemma Coletti prepares her special lasagna and polenta with porcini mushrooms, among other local specialties. A budget choice for nature lovers and climbers, and a way to see a slice of village life. *Directions:* From Lucca, take route 445 toward Castelnuovo and on to Vagli di Sotto then right for Roggio. Take a winding road up to Roggio, where a sign indicates the Coletti restaurant in the village.

LA FONTANELLA
Hosts: Gemma & Severino Coletti
Localita: Vagli Sotto
Roggio (LU) 55100, Italy
Tel: (0583) 649163 or 649179, Fax: none
7 rooms, Double: €45
Open: all year
Other languages: very little English
Region: Tuscany, Michelin Map: 430
www.karenbrown.com/italy/lafontanella.html

With the momentous occasion of the Millenium combined with the Holy Year celebration at the Vatican, a myriad of bed and breakfasts popped up in Rome, among them Villa Delros. Offering hospitality to foreigners is nothing new to Rosemarie Diletti, whose daughter, Patrizia, took over the family's Hotel Venezia in Rome (see listing). With the children grown and busy with their own careers, and because she misses the daily contact with international guests, Rosemarie decided to offer accommodation in the family home on the outskirts of the city. The sprawling, very modern home built in the sixties is located on a small road with other large estates and the property extends to the back overlooking lush green countryside. Two spacious air-conditioned guest suites on the upper floor each have a double bedroom, bathroom, corner kitchenette, sitting room, and large terrace. A third suite is located at garden level. With Rosemarie being a collector of antiques, the house is filled to the brim with pieces from the baroque period, as seen in the common rooms downstairs as well as in guestrooms. Breakfast is served out on the terrace looking out to the garden and a swimming pool. Transportation to the local train station is provided and the center of Rome is just 15 minutes away. *Directions:* North of Rome 4 km from the GRA ring highway, Via Livigno is just off the Via Flaminia. Call in advance to arrange pickup at a nearby meeting point.

VILLA DELROS
Host: Rosemarie Truninger Diletti
Via Livigno 166
Rome 00188, Italy
Tel: (06) 33679837, Cellphone: (340) 9295488
Fax: (06) 33678402
3 rooms, Double: €160
Minimum nights required: 3, Open: Mar to Dec
Other languages: good English
Region: Lazio, Michelin Map: 430
www.karenbrown.com/italy/delros.html

The Due Torri, a small and charming city hotel, dates to the early 1800s and is tucked away on a tiny, narrow cobblestone street in the historical heart of Rome very near the Navona Square with its Bernini fountains. The 26 rather petite bedrooms, decorated with period antiques and matching burgundy drapes and bedspreads, are accompanied by newly tiled bathrooms. Amenities include an elevator and air conditioning, which provides welcome relief on hot Roman summer days. The contained reception and sitting area have Oriental carpets, pieced marble floors, brocaded draperies, gilt-framed mirrors and paintings, and red-velvet chairs accenting the cream-colored walls. The fifth-floor mansard rooms (even smaller size) have small terraces and fourth-floor rooms have balconies with enchanting views over typical tiled rooftops and terraces. A buffet breakfast is served in a windowless room made cheery with painted borders and paintings. Super hostess Cinzia (owner as well of the newer Fontanella Borghese, also featured in this book) and her courteous staff are very helpful at arranging everything from advance ticketing for museums to transfers and restaurant and itinerary suggestions. *Directions:* Use a detailed city map to locate the hotel, north of Navona Square in a maze of winding streets.

HOTEL DUE TORRI
Owner: Cinzia Pighini Giordani
Vicolo del Leonetto 23
Rome 00186, Italy
Tel: (06) 6876983 or 6875765, Fax: (06) 6865442
26 rooms, Double: €170–€220
Open: all year, Credit cards: all major
Other languages: good English
Region: Lazio, Michelin Map: 430
www.karenbrown.com/italy/duetorri.html

Many hotels in Rome can boast panoramic views over the city, but few have such a close-up view of a world-famous monument as the Hotel Fontana. Located directly on the square containing the magnificent Trevi Fountain, the Fontana's windows look out on to its gushing waters—you can practically toss a coin from your room. The sleek black-and-white breakfast room with wrought-iron chairs and tables is situated on the top floor of the 14th-century building, giving a bird's-eye view over the square from an enormous picture window. The small bedrooms are sweetly done with pastel-floral wallpaper, bedspreads, and white curtains and vary in size and decor. Bathrooms were incorporated into each room later, and are quite small. Narrow, vaulted-ceilinged halls leading to the guestrooms are adorned with antique prints of Rome. Signora Elena and her staff at the desk attend to guests' every need. The noise commonly associated with a city hotel is not a problem here as the square is closed to traffic, although loud voices of tourists lingering into the early hours can be a problem in the summer. There is a supplement for air conditioning in rooms without a fountain view. *Directions:* Use a detailed city map to locate the hotel in the Piazza di Trevi off the Via Tritone.

HOTEL FONTANA
Host: Elena Daneo
Piazza di Trevi 96
Rome 00187, Italy
Tel: (06) 6786113 or 6791056, Fax: (06) 6790024
25 rooms, Double: €260
Open: all year, Credit cards: all major
Other languages: good English
Region: Lazio, Michelin Map: 430
www.karenbrown.com/italy/fontana.html

The many travelers who have enjoyed staying at the Due Torri can also experience the same charismatic hospitality offered by Cinzia in her other hotel very close by. The hotel has the same name as the triangular-shaped piazza where it is located, directly in front of the imposing Palazzo Borghese leading to the Spanish Steps. The enormous doors of the 17th-century building open up to a courtyard where you take the elevator up to the second floor. The small lobby has a sitting corner and a sweeping spiral staircase up to additional rooms on the next floor. Guestrooms have sparkling new bathrooms and modern amenities such as satellite TV and air conditioning, and are appointed with either an antique desk or armoire, green or blue matching bedspreads and draperies, and prints of Rome. An effort was made to preserve the original gray-marble floors in some rooms, while parquet flooring was put in the others. Most have a view on a narrow and very characteristic cobblestone street, or on the inner courtyard, offering rare silence. The reception area leads to the breakfast room with marble floors and matching faux-marble doorways. Cinzia oversees every detail in both hotels and the secret to her success is that she obviously has guests' comfort foremost in mind. Even extra assistance such as securing advance reservations to certain museums is offered. *Directions:* Consult a detailed city map.

HOTEL FONTANELLA BORGHESE
Owner: Cinzia Pighini Giordani
Largo Fontanella Borghese 84
Rome 00186, Italy
Tel: (06) 68809504, Fax: (06) 6861295
29 rooms, Double: €175–€217
Open: all year, Credit cards: all major
Other languages: good English
Region: Lazio, Michelin Map: 430
www.karenbrown.com/italy/fontanellaborghese.html

The Hotel Locarno is centrally located on the corner of a rather busy street, only two blocks from bustling Popolo Square. Its downtown location makes noise unavoidable, so it is advisable to request a room away from the street, even though the installation of thermal windows has helped. Even with the extensive renovations it has undergone, the hotel, dating from 1925, retains the art-deco flavor it originally had. The red-carpeted reception area leads to a cozy bar and long, mirrored sitting room lined with cushioned banquettes and café tables. There is also a side patio with shady canvas umbrellas where guests can have breakfast in warm weather, if not in the cheery breakfast room looking out to the patio. A very special feature of the hotel is the rooftop garden where you can gaze over Rome's tiled roofs and terraces to St. Peter's dome and the Villa Borghese Park. The comfortable rooms (regular and superior doubles), decorated with antiques, gold-framed mirrors, and pretty floral wallpaper, are air-conditioned. Two two-bedroom apartments (no kitchen) are offered to guests in the building directly across the street. The Locarno offers such extras as a parking garage and free use of bicycles with which you might tour the Villa Borghese Park. It is no wonder that this has always been a favorite among artists and writers. Reserve well in advance. *Directions:* Use a detailed city map to locate the hotel one block east of the River Tiber at the Flaminia Square sign.

※ ⚓ ☕ ✏ 💳 ☎ 🛗 🚶 👫 🐎 🍸 P 🖼 ⛷ ♿ 🍇

HOTEL LOCARNO
Host: Caterina Valente
Via della Penna 22
Rome 00186, Italy
Tel: (06) 3610841 or 3610842, Fax: (06) 3215249
66 rooms, Double: €200–€310
2 apartments: €510 weekly B&B
Open: all year, Credit cards: all major
Region: Lazio, Michelin Map: 430
www.karenbrown.com/italy/hotellocarno.html

Marco and Giulia Di Tillo are young and enterprising hosts who have adopted the family hotel tradition with their Hotel Modigliani. Leaving their careers as musician and writer (Marco just wrote a guide on seven romantic itineraries in Rome), they totally renovated a centuries-old building with the goal of offering comfortable and practical, no-nonsense accommodation with many amenities (air conditioning, satellite TV, mini bar, laundry service, motorbike and car rental, city tour excursions, nearby garage), topped off with an efficient but friendly staff. With its unbeatable central location close to Via Veneto and the Spanish Steps, they have all the elements for success. The front desk, sitting area, and breakfast room make up the ground-floor common spaces and have a clean, contemporary ambiance. A personalized touch has been given to the breakfast room with framed black-and-white photos of the couple's children hanging throughout and they hope to eventually display the artwork of friends. Bedrooms on the three upper floors, reached by an elevator, are decorated along the same clean lines with wood floors and olive-green-striped spreads and drapes. Most desirable are the top-floor rooms with balconies and views over rooftops including St. Peter's cupola while others face the inner courtyard or quiet street. Being next door to a convent, quiet is guaranteed! *Directions:* Via della Purificazione is a side street just north of the Piazza Barberini.

HOTEL MODIGLIANI
Hosts: Marco & Giulia Di Tillo
Via della Purificazione 42
Rome 00187, Italy
Tel: (06) 42815226 or 42027931
Cellphone: (338) 9269528, Fax: (06) 42814791
24 rooms, Double: €190–€233
Open: all year, Credit cards: all major
Other languages: good English
Region: Lazio, Michelin Map: 430
www.karenbrown.com/italy/modigliani.html

Trastevere, literally translated as "across the Tiber," is the most delightful and authentically Roman neighborhood of the city's historic center. Tourists flock here to stroll down the narrow cobblestone streets, visit artisans' shops, dine in one of the many excellent sidewalk trattorias, or just watch the daily life of locals. What pleasure to have discovered the new Hotel Santa Maria, the first accommodation to speak of in the area, which has proved already to be a true winner. Native Romans Paolo and Valentina had the ingenious idea of transforming a plot of open land between the jumble of ancient apartment buildings into a unique one-story hotel with rooms looking out to two courtyards with orange trees. Paolo designed the complex himself then supervised the four-year construction. The couple welcomes travelers as private houseguests, serving a buffet breakfast with freshly baked cakes either out in the courtyard or in the breakfast room/wine bar. Before going out for dinner in one of many nearby favorite restaurants, guests enjoy a glass of wine with nibbles from a nearby bakery. Bedrooms, each with its own entrance to the outside, are identically decorated in pale yellow, with a splash of color on matching bedspreads and curtains, and enjoy amenities such as air conditioning, mini bar, and TV. *Directions:* In the heart of Trastevere just behind the famous Piazza Santa Maria, on the tiny Vicolo del Piede. Garage parking is available.

✻ ⌄ ▥ ⚒ 💳 ☎ 🍴 🐎 ☥ P ⊘ 🖼 ⚓ ♿ 🍷

HOTEL SANTA MARIA
Hosts: Paolo & Valentina Vetere
Vicolo del Piede 2
Rome 00153, Italy
Tel: (06) 5894626, Cellphone: (338) 6672861
Fax: (06) 5894815
19 rooms, Double: €145–€205
Open: all year, Credit cards: all major
Other languages: good English
Region: Lazio, Michelin Map: 430
www.karenbrown.com/italy/santamaria.html

Rome — Casa Stefazio — Map: 10d

A delightful alternative to our other accommodations in Rome is Casa Stefazio, the only true in-home bed and breakfast. The location and setting are as perfect as the dedication and warm hospitality offered by Stefania and Orazio in their large, ivy-covered suburban home, just 16 kilometers from the very center of the city, surrounded by several acres of manicured garden and utter silence. On the lower level, with a separate entrance, are one bedroom and two spacious suites (with sauna) accommodating a family of four, each with its own immaculate bathroom, satellite TV, air conditioning, and mini bar. The main areas include living room, large American-style kitchen, where the Azzolas work wonders, and eating area overlooking the expansive lawn and distant woods. Dinner is served on request under the pergola. Their style, in both decorating and easy entertaining, has obviously been influenced by their yearly winter sojourn in the States, which they adore. Sports activities such as horseback riding, tennis, golf, and swimming are easily arranged. The hosts also organize excursions for groups of friends throughout Italy. Highly recommended by readers. *Directions:* Located north of Rome just outside the circular highway around the city (GRA), close to the tollway north to Florence and south to Naples. Call one day ahead for detailed directions.

CASA STEFAZIO
Hosts: Stefania & Orazio Azzola
Via della Marcigliana 553
Rome 00138, Italy
Tel: (06) 87120042, Cellphone: (338) 2180612
Fax: (06) 87120012
3 rooms, Double: €220–€275
Open: Apr to Nov
Other languages: good English
Region: Lazio, Michelin Map: 430
www.karenbrown.com/italy/casastefazio.html

Hotel Venezia is part of the group of select family-run city hotels, efficiently run and owned by brother-and-sister team, Patrizia and Francesco. Although hotels near train stations are generally less desirable, the area around Rome's Termini station has experienced dramatically positive changes—there is a high concentration of hotels and offices within refurbished turn-of-the-century-style buildings. Even though the Venezia has 61 rooms, it has the feeling of a small and friendly place the moment you enter its doors. Patrizia and Francesco inherited the hotel from their parents and their mother's passion for collecting antiques such as Orientals rugs and rich period paintings is evident throughout the spacious sitting rooms. A complimentary buffet breakfast is served in a room with peach tablecloths and fresh flowers topping tables. Upstairs the spotless rooms are decorated uniformly in white and rose hues with Venetian glass chandeliers, and offer all modern amenities, including Internet access. Patrizia has purposely decorated predominantly with white so that any sign of dirt can be spotted immediately. The corner rooms are the most spacious and those on the top floor have small balconies. Centrally located, the hotel is a 15-minute walk to Rome's historical center. In the exact same style is the family's nearby 45-room Hotel Columbia with its lovely rooftop terrace. *Directions:* Consult a detailed city map—the hotel is to the right of the station.

❋ ⚓ ☕ ⚕ 💳 ☎ ♿ 🚶 👥 🐎 🍸 P 🚭 🖼 🍇

HOTEL VENEZIA
Hosts: Patrizia & Francesco Diletti
Via Varese 18
Rome 00185, Italy
Tel: (06) 4457101, Fax: (06) 4957687
60 rooms, Double: €133–€149
Open: all year, Credit cards: all major
Other languages: good English
Region: Lazio, Michelin Map: 430
www.karenbrown.com/italy/venezia.html

Beyond the city gates of Porta Pia, whose ancient walls lead from the Via Veneto, is tranquil, tree-lined Via Nomentana, once a luxurious residential street. Many elegant pastel-colored villas remain (including that of Mussolini), but most have been converted into embassy-owned apartments over the years, while the Villa del Parco has been transformed into a lovely, quiet hotel with a bed-and-breakfast feel to it. A flower-edged driveway leads to the villa, passing by tables set up for breakfast in the small front garden. When you enter the pleasant lobby scattered with antiques and comfy sofas, you feel that you've arrived home. Three cozy sitting rooms invite guests to sit and relax. All of the 30 guestrooms, each with private bath, have been renovated and vary greatly in size and decor, which tends to be a mixture of old and new furnishings. The very cordial Elisabetta Bernardini and her friendly staff are happy to make restaurant and itinerary suggestions. Special features are an elevator, central air, and five nice new bedrooms on the top floor with beamed mansard ceilings. A 24-hour snack bar service is available. *Directions:* Rely on a detailed city map to locate the hotel in a residential district, a 15-minute walk from the city center.

※ ⬆ ☕ ⚑ CREDIT ☎ ♟ 🜊 Y P 🖼 ♿

HOTEL VILLA DEL PARCO
Host: Bernardini family
Via Nomentana 110
Rome 00161, Italy
Tel: (06) 44237773, Fax: (06) 44237572
30 rooms, Double: €155–€180
Open: all year, Credit cards: all major
Other languages: some English
Region: Lazio, Michelin Map: 430
www.karenbrown.com/italy/villadelparco.html

The spectacular 2,500-acre hilltop farm property of Montestigliano is a rich combination of woods, cultivated fields, olive groves, and open meadows all surrounding the hamlet dating from 1730. British-born hostess Susan makes sure guests are comfortable in one of the ten independent apartments within the various houses scattered about the property. All retain their original Tuscan character in furnishings and have a combination of two or three bedrooms, kitchen, living room (some with fireplace), and essential modern amenities like washing machines and telephones. The granary has been restored and converted into a farm shop, recreation room, and dining room where meals are served upon request from Monday to Friday. Groups of up to 12 persons have the opportunity to reside in the main villa. Two swimming pools are at guests' disposal, plus many paths and trails. Montestigliano is a marvelous base for getting to know in depth a part of Tuscany whose traditions and lifestyles have remained intact, while still having Siena, San Gimignano, Pienza, Montalcino, and the Chianti area at one's fingertips. Plenty of places to dine are available in Rosia and Sovicille. Susan has also recently arranged weddings in this idyllic setting for groups staying at Montestigliano. *Directions:* From Siena (12 km) take S.S.223 (towards Grosseto). After 12 km, just after a gas station, turn right and after 2 km turn left for Brenna and drive up the unpaved road to the end.

MONTESTIGLIANO
Host: Susan Pennington
Rosia (SI) 53010, Italy
Tel: (0577) 342189, Cellphone: (347) 7778761
Fax: (0577) 342100
10 apartments: €454–€1,622 weekly
1 villa: €1,382–€2,957 weekly
Minimum nights required: 5, Open: all year
Other languages: fluent English
Region: Tuscany, Michelin Map: 430
www.karenbrown.com/italy/montestigliano.html

The climb up to L'Abri is worth the trip just for the spectacular view over the valley and for the warm welcome given by amiable hostess Antonella, a young, enterprising woman who opened her sweet and simple bed and breakfast within her grandmother's home in order to be able to live in her native area. The typical stone house with slate roof is part of a miniature village with just a few other houses, restaurant, church, and school. A collection of grandmother's lace and domestic work adorns the entrance to the left of a small breakfast room. Six small bedrooms are dispersed about this compact home's upper three floors, including the attic. Three have small balconies decorated with cascading geraniums and all are identically appointed using local pine for beds and wall paneling, accented with colorful Provençal curtains. A nice extra is the possibility of sampling local fare at the family's trattoria next door. For two generations traditional dishes such as polenta with meat, rice (no pasta served in this region!), soups, crêpes, and scrumptious desserts made with apples from their own orchards have been served in the cozy dining room covered with black-and-white photos of decades past. Enthusiastic Antonella is an expert on local tourism and can suggest many interesting itineraries for the area. *Directions:* Exit the A5 at Aosta-Ovest and follow signs for Saint Pierre (1 km) and then up to Vetan where L'Abri is located (15 km).

L'ABRI   New
Host: Antonella Montrosset
Fraz. Vetan Dessous 83
Saint Pierre (AO) 11010, Italy
Tel: (0165) 908830, Cellphone: (333) 2095679
Fax: (0165) 908228
6 rooms, Double: €50–€58
Open: all year, Credit cards: MC, VS
Other languages: some English, French
Region: Aosta Valley, Michelin Map: 428
www.karenbrown.com/italy/labri.html

The Aosta mountain valley has just recently joined the agritourism trend in Italy, with 40 farms in the region currently offering hospitality. Les Ecureuils was one of the first to open, well ahead of the trend, and is the most established of the group. The Gontiers' large property—a cheese farm—overlooks the valley surrounding the capital city of the region, Aosta. The main chalet, which dates to the mid-1800s, houses five double bedrooms and a characteristic dining room adorned with ceramic plates, brass pots, and locally fashioned sabots. A modern barn for the goats and three typical stone houses make up the farm complex. The three front bedrooms have small balconies and valley views, while the remaining two look into the pine woods. The individually decorated, homelike rooms have floral wallpaper and carpeted or wood floors. Each room is equipped with a shower and sink and has a private toilet just outside. Plans to renovate and add full bathrooms are projected for the next season. Half board is required here and meals are based for the most part on fresh products from the farm including various salamis, vegetables, poultry, and their primary production of high-quality goat cheeses. The Gontiers organize half- and full-day nature walks and picnics in the back woods accompanied by the family mule. *Directions:* After the A5 autostrada ends at Aosta, continue 6 km to Sarre and turn right, following the winding road for 6 km up to the end.

🍵 ☕ 🚶 👫 🐴 P 🍽 🎿 🚭 🍇

LES ECUREUILS   New
Hosts: Pepe & Glori Gontier Ballauri
Fraz. Homené Dessus 8
Saint Pierre (AO) 11010, Italy
Tel: (0165) 903831, Fax: (0165) 909849
5 rooms, Double: €70–€78*
*Includes breakfast and dinner
Closed: Jan & Dec
Other languages: good English, French
Region: Aosta Valley, Michelin Map: 428
www.karenbrown.com/italy/ecureuils.html

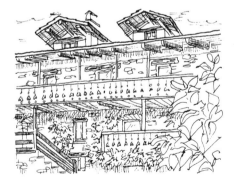

Parma is without doubt the city internationally most known for its Parmesan cheese and prosciutto ham, which you should not fail to sample while you're in the region. Thirty kilometers from Parma are found the curative thermal waters of Salsomaggiore and just beyond town is the Antica Torre, the ancient 13th-century tower that majestically crowns a hilltop overlooking the soft green countryside. The Pavesi family, proprietors of the surrounding farm, offer warm hospitality to its guests within the tower where one bedroom with bath is located on each of the four floors. In addition, there are five suites available in the main stone residence, including a large two-bedroom suite, which is ideal for a family. Rooms are simply decorated and have lovely views over the valley. The barn has been converted into a pleasant dining room where fortunate guests sit down together to a hearty, homemade, Emiliana-style meal, including fresh pastas, vegetables, meat, and poultry direct from the farm (drinks not included in half-board rate). Amenities include a swimming pool, bicycles, and horses. *Directions:* From Salsomaggiore, go through town, following signs for Cangelasio and then Antica Torre, 3.5 km from Salsomaggiore.

ANTICA TORRE
Host: Francesco Pavesi family
Localita: Cangelasio-Case Bussandri 197
Salsomaggiore Terme (PR) 43039, Italy
Tel & fax: (0524) 575425
9 rooms, Double: €80–€100
Per person half board: €60–€70
Minimum nights required: 2, 7 in Jul & Aug
Open: Mar to Nov, Other languages: some English
Region: Emilia-Romagna, Michelin Map: 429
www.karenbrown.com/italy/anticatorre.html

In the southeastern corner of Tuscany is a delightful, yet-undiscovered pocket of absolutely stunning countryside. It was only natural that Andrea, with his expert culinary skills, and his lovely wife, Cristina, a born hostess, should open a bed and breakfast close to their vast 1,000-acre countryside property producing olive oil, wine, cereals and vegetables. La Crocetta sits at the crossroads leading up to the charming town of San Casciano, offering eight guestrooms above the restaurant. You enter the small restaurant by way of a front porch, where meals are also served outdoors, into the cozy reception area set around a large sit-in fireplace. Here within the two dining rooms with soft-pink-colored walls Andrea presents his delectable creations featuring homemade pastas with vegetable fillings and other regional dishes using the best local ingredients available. His success has been noted in several restaurant guides as well as articles. Small guestrooms with varying color schemes, each with a new bathroom, are pleasantly appointed with canopy beds and fresh country fabrics used for bedspreads and curtains. Thermal hot springs with spa treatments and horse-riding facilities are located in the vicinity. Orvieto, Perugia, Siena, and the hilltowns of Montepulciano and Montalcino are all at easy touring distance. *Directions:* From the A1 autostrada, exit at Fabro from the south or Chiusi from the north, traveling towards Sarteano-Cetona, then San Casciano.

LA CROCETTA
Hosts: Cristina & Andrea Leotti
Localita: La Crocetta, San Casciano dei Bagni (SI) 53040, Italy
Tel: (0578) 58360, Cellphone: (339) 6366336
Fax: (0578) 58353
8 rooms, Double: €90–€95, Per person half board: €72
Minimum nights required: 2
Open: Mar 30 to Nov 12, Credit cards: MC, VS
Other languages: good English
Region: Tuscany, Michelin Map: 430
www.karenbrown.com/italy/lacrocetta.html

Perched atop a hill and enjoying a 360-degree view of perfectly unspoiled landscape, including a stunning medieval castle, sits the Le Radici farmhouse. Partners and ex-urbanites Marcello and Alfredo carefully chose this peaceful spot in order to offer accommodation to those who truly appreciate nature and the sense of well-being it inspires. The two farmhouses have been restored, maintaining most of the original rustic flavor, and divided into seven double rooms, three suites, and two apartments. The apartments include one or two bedrooms, living room with fireplace, kitchenette, and bathroom. The tastefully appointed rooms in muted colours are adorned by wrought-iron beds and antique furnishings, complemented by wood-beam and brick ceilings. Special attention has been given to landscaping around the immediate property, which includes vineyards and olive groves. The real treat is the absolutely gorgeous "borderless" swimming pool with cascading water, which fits harmoniously into its surroundings. A romantic candelit dinner showing off Alfredo's passion for cooking is served in the dining room or out on the terrace, using fresh ingredients from the property. The hosts suggest many interesting itineraries in this area, which borders Umbria. One can relax in the thermal waters of San Casciano or venture out to the towns of Orvieto, Todi, or Pienza, among others. *Directions:* From San Casciano follow signs for Le Radici (4 km).

LE RADICI
Hosts: Alfredo Ferrari & Marcello Mancini
San Casciano dei Bagni (SI) 53040, Italy
Tel: (0578) 56033, Cellphone: (338) 5856890
Fax: (0578) 56038
10 rooms, Double: €108–€186
2 apartments: €110–€178 daily (utilities extra)
Minimum nights required: 2, Open: all year, Credit cards: MC, VS
Other languages: good English
Region: Tuscany, Michelin Map: 430
www.karenbrown.com/italy/leradici.html

Agritourism and bed-and-breakfast-type accommodations are virtually nonexistent in the northern lake district, so coming across the enchanting Villa Simplicitas was a special treat. The pale-yellow country house of Milanese family Castelli, run by sister-in-law Ulla, sits isolated high up in the hills between Lakes Como and Lugano and is surrounded by thick woods. There is a wonderful old-fashioned charm to the place, enhanced by many heirloom turn-of-the-century antiques scattered about the cozy living and dining rooms. Pretty floral fabrics cover sofas and armchairs, in perfect harmony with the soft-yellow walls bordered with stenciled designs. The same warmth is spread among the ten guest bedrooms with their pinewood floors and trompe l'oeil paneled walls, antique beds, and lace doilies adorning dressers. Innovative meals prepared by local chef Maurizio are served either inside or out on the veranda with green-and-white-striped awnings and matching director's chairs. In the evening, impeccably set tables are candlelit for a romantic dinner for two—simply heavenly. *Directions:* From Como head north to Argegno. Turn left, passing through S. Fedele, then just after town at the first bus station, turn left—it is just 2 km up to the house.

VILLA SIMPLICITAS
Host: Curzio Castelli family
Localita: Simplicitas
San Fedele d'Intelvi (CO) 22028, Italy
Tel: (031) 831132 or (02) 460421, Fax: (02) 460407
10 rooms, Double: €94–€120
Open: May to Oct, Credit cards: all major
Other languages: good English
Region: Lombardy
www.karenbrown.com/italy/simplicitas.html

Il Casale is a highly efficient and very popular bed and breakfast, thanks to warm and dedicated host, Alessandro, who has combined his extensive hospitality experience with a desire to see his great-grandfather's lovely country property restored properly. Six double rooms and two small apartments including bedroom, kitchen/eating area, and bathroom are all housed within the extended stone farmhouse. Another section is reserved for Alessandro and the family who looks after the wine estate. Access to the guest entrance is through a well-kept garden around the back with a small chapel and lovely views over the soft hills. Main areas include a sitting room and beamed breakfast room with fireplace. The spotless home is appointed with scattered antiques and the very comfortable guestrooms, each with a different color scheme, have new bathrooms and either countryside views or garden or interior patio entrance. Infinite care to details in both the esthetics and service offered is given to guests. The entrepreneurial Alessandro has also restored the stone barn and cantina over in the olive grove, Rocca degli Olivi, creating an apartment, five lovely bedrooms with either mansard or vaulted ceilings and gorgeous views, and a breakfast room. An inviting swimming pool is hidden among the olive trees. Plenty of tourist information is on hand. *Directions:* From San Gimignano follow signs for Certaldo for 3 km. Il Casale is on the left and well marked.

IL CASALE DEL COTONE
Host: Alessandro Martelli
Localita: Cellole 59
San Gimignano (SI) 53037, Italy
Tel & fax: (0577) 943236, Cellphone: (348) 3029091
11 rooms, Double: €93–€103
3 apartments: €93–€130 daily
Open: all year, Credit cards: all major
Region: Tuscany, Michelin Map: 430
www.karenbrown.com/italy/casaledelcotone.html

Due to the ever-increasing popularity of the stunning medieval village of San Gimignano, accommodations in the surrounding countryside have flourished. The Casanova is a typical square stone farmhouse with wood shutters and red-tile roof, which you'll grow accustomed to seeing throughout Tuscany. The bed and breakfast's exceptional feature is that it enjoys a privileged view of the towers of San Gimignano, an ancient town referred to as the "Manhattan" of the year 1000. Roberto and his wife Monica, who aim to offer quality accommodation at competitive rates, have the bed and breakfast, adding amenities in rooms such as air conditioning, satellite TV, and telephone, and have also installed a swimming pool. Breakfast is served on the outside patio where guests are immersed in breathtaking scenery, before heading out to visit intriguing San Gimignano and the many surrounding villages. This is an authentic wine-producing farm with eight double rooms with private baths and one apartment for two persons. Country furniture characteristic of the region decorates the rooms, whose original architectural features have been preserved. *Directions:* From San Gimignano take the road toward Volterra. After 2 km, turn left at the sign for Casanova, not Hotel Pescille.

CASANOVA DI PESCILLE
Hosts: Monica & Roberto Fanciullini
Localita: Pescille
San Gimignano (SI) 53037, Italy
Tel & fax: (0577) 941902
8 rooms, Double: €80–€90
1 apartment: €104 daily
Open: Mar to Dec, Credit cards: all major
Other languages: very little English
Region: Tuscany, Michelin Map: 430
www.karenbrown.com/italy/casanovadipescille.html

Accidentally coming upon the Casolare, tucked away in the unpopulated hills 8 kilometers past medieval San Gimignano, was a delightful surprise. Just before reaching the bed and breakfast, you'll see a half-abandoned stone convent dating back to 1100. The attractive renovated farmhouse, hosted by Andrea, a former art and antiques dealer, and his Spanish wife, Berta, retains all the features characteristic of the original structure. The five double rooms are extremely comfortable and tastefully appointed. Rooms are divided between the two floors of the house, with one being an independent structure poolside. The suites for two to four persons with terrace and living room have been decorated with refined antiques as well. Original watercolor paintings by a local artist adorn an entire wall in the inviting double living room. An extra bonus is the breathtaking swimming pool, with sweeping countryside panorama, surrounded by a manicured lawn, fruit trees, and terra-cotta pots overflowing with pink geraniums. It provides refreshment after a hot day of sightseeing, while you anticipate another appetizing candlelit meal at dusk under the pergola. Berta is an excellent cook and prepares very special Tuscan menus accompanied by an impressive wine list. This is a truly tranquil haven. *Directions:* From San Gimignano follow signs for Montaione. Staying left at the fork, turn left for Libbiano and take the dirt road to the end.

CASOLARE DI LIBBIANO
Hosts: Berta & Andrea Bucciarelli
Localita: Libbiano 3, San Gimignano (SI) 53037, Italy
Tel & fax: (0577) 946002
Cellphone: (349) 8706933 or (347) 4760138
8 rooms, Double: €162–€204*
*Includes breakfast & dinner
Open: Apr to Nov, Credit cards: all major
Other languages: good English
Region: Tuscany, Michelin Map: 430
www.karenbrown.com/italy/casolaredilibbiano.html

The increasing popularity of this perfectly intact medieval town and the resulting availability of accommodations have made San Gimignano a hub from which tourists fan out to visit nearby, lesser-known treasures such as Volterra, Colle Val d'Elsa, and Monteriggioni. A pleasant, informal stay can be had at the Podere Villuzza, run by friendly young Sandra and Gianni Dei who opened the doors of their 150-year-old stone farmhouse to guests after extensive modification. Chairs are set up in front where visitors can enjoy the view of vineyard-covered hills leading up to the impressive multi-towered town. Common areas include the rustic living room with ceramic-tiled tables and fireplace where guests convene after a day of touring. While gregarious Sandra pampers guests, Gianni occupies himself with the production of top-quality olive oil. Six double rooms on ground and first floors accessed by several different entrances are furnished in true country style with a mix of wrought-iron beds and antique armoires, complemented by mansard beamed ceilings and stone walls. Rooms have views out over the countryside and town or over back hills. Also available for weekly stays are three small apartments within the house that include a living area and kitchen. A swimming pool just to the left of the farmhouse is a great bonus for guests. *Directions:* Go through town and follow signs for Certaldo. After 2 km turn right and follow signs for Villuzza.

PODERE VILLUZZA
Hosts: Sandra & Gianni Dei
Strada 25, San Gimignano (SI) 53037, Italy
Tel: (0577) 940585, Cellphone: (335) 7118172
Fax: (0577) 942247
6 rooms, Double: €93–€99
3 apartments: €730– €835 weekly double B&B
Open: all year, Credit cards: MC, VS
Other languages: good English
Region: Tuscany, Michelin Map: 430
www.karenbrown.com/italy/poderevilluzza.html

The countryside around San Gimignano is becoming like the Alto Adige mountain area where practically every house offers some kind of accommodation, and the competition has created bed and breakfasts with high standards of quality and service. Among these, Il Rosolaccio (the local name for the poppies that cover the hill in springtime) is an 18th-century typical Tuscan farmhouse perched high above the road between Certaldo and San Gimignano. As expected, the view over the vineyards and hillsides is absolutely breathtaking. After a 30-year career running a hotel in Rome, Ingrid Music, with her son Steven and his Russian wife, Natalie, bought and very carefully restored the house which, by tradition, was added on to each time someone in the family got married. All the right ingredients are included for a perfectly delightful stay, with tastefully decorated bedrooms and apartments perfectly in tune with the simple beauty of the preserved farmhouse, warm and discreet hospitality, and marvelous views to be enjoyed either poolside or at sunset with a glass of wine. Common areas include the vaulted dining room and cozy upstairs living room with huge open fireplace and family antiques. *Directions:* From San Gimignano follow signs for Certaldo and after 7 km, turn right at the sign up to Il Rosolaccio. From Certaldo drive in the direction of San Gimignano for 5 km and turn left at Rosolaccio.

IL ROSOLACCIO
Hosts: Ingrid, Natalie & Steven Music
Localita: Capezzano Basso
San Gimignano (SI) 53037, Italy
Tel: (0577) 944465, Fax: (0577) 944467
6 rooms, Double: €88–€96, No dinner Mon
6 apartments: €650–€1,084 weekly
Open: Mar to Oct, Credit cards: all major
Other languages: fluent English, French, German
Region: Tuscany, Michelin Map: 430
www.karenbrown.com/italy/rosolaccio.html

After her parents left their native England to settle into life in Tuscany—a dream shared by many—Maria followed suit, leaving behind a career in marketing. Her parents have been offering hospitality for years in four apartments all within one large house next door to their own called La Fonte. Maria bought her own property nearby and opened a bed and breakfast five years ago. Turning off the main road, you immediately find a cluster of small houses, one attached to the other, belonging to several different owners. Her own home is next to the guesthouse (originally the priest's quarters, as the name Vicario indicates) and chapel with front courtyard. The five double bedrooms upstairs off one long hall all have an en-suite bathroom except one, and are decorated with simple country furniture and wooden beds to complement the worn terra-cotta brick floors. A few of the rooms look out to woods at the back and the rest look to the front. A Continental breakfast is served either in a little room downstairs off the living room or out on the front patio. Just above Maria's quarters is a one-bedroom apartment with kitchenette/sitting room with nice views to both sides of the property. A new swimming pool in the vineyard overlooks the valley. *Directions:* From San Gimignano, take the first possible right turn north towards Ulignano and after 3 km, instead of turning right for Ulignano, turn left towards San Benedetto then turn at the sign for Il Vicario.

IL VICARIO
Host: Maria Bergamasco
Localita: San Andrea 1, San Gimignano (SI) 53037, Italy
Tel: (0577) 941599, Fax: (0577) 945635
5 rooms, Double: €80
1 apartment: €75 daily
Minimum nights required: 2
Open: mid-Mar to Oct
Other languages: fluent English
Region: Tuscany, Michelin Map: 430
www.karenbrown.com/italy/vicario.html

The lesser-known area of Tuscany south of Siena makes a delightful discovery and the variety of landscapes within an 8-kilometer drive provides one of the most fascinating excursions in the region. Besides the charming hilltowns of Montepulciano, Pienza, and Montalcino, there are the abbeys of Monte Oliveto and Sant'Antimo, plus the thermal baths of Bagno Vignoni. A perfect base in this richly historical and natural area is the magnificent castle of the Aluffi Pentini family, theirs for the past 400 years or so and practically a village in itself. The family resides in the upper reaches of the castle while guests are accommodated in several separate farmers' houses divided into a combination of apartments with one or two bedrooms, living room, and kitchenette, plus six simply and characteristically appointed bedrooms with country furniture. Rooms facing out have absolutely breathtaking views over the virgin valley. Downstairs is the dining room with wood tables covered with cheery checked cloths, where breakfast and dinner are served using homegrown products. A common space for guests is the old granary, converted into a large cozy reading room with fireplace. This is truly like a place out of a fairy-tale. *Directions:* The castle is well marked at 5 km from San Quirico d'Orcia. Ripa d'Orcia is marked on most maps.

CASTELLO DI RIPA D'ORCIA
Host: Aluffi Pentini family
Via della Contea 1/16
San Quirico d'Orcia (SI) 53023, Italy
Tel: (0577) 897376, Fax: (0577) 898038
6 rooms, Double: €99–€125
7 apartments: €465–€770 weekly
No dinner Mon, Minimum nights required: 2
Open: Mar to Nov, Credit cards: MC, VS
Region: Tuscany, Michelin Map: 430
www.karenbrown.com/italy/castellodiripadorcia.html

Bagno Vignoni is a charming little village whose unique piazza is actually an ancient stone pool with thermal water. In medieval times the large bath was divided for men and women who came to soak in the rejuvenating waters, hoping to cure such ailments as arthritis and rheumatism. Today, tourists come to view this remarkable place and take advantage of these same curative properties in the nearby falls or modern pool facilities. With the success of their wine bar (enoteca) here, it was only natural that the young Marinis should open a bed and breakfast for travelers. The stone building dates to the 1300s and was thoughtfully restored after having been abandoned for more than 30 years. The eight double bedrooms and large living room with loft and grand piano are very cozy and purposely old-fashioned in feeling. The beamed guestrooms and pretty new bathrooms each have their own theme and corresponding soft pastel color schemes and are romantically appointed with lace curtains and pillows, antique beds and armoires, and painted stencil borders. Breakfast is served across the way in the historic enoteca, which was once part of the Capuchin friars' monastery. With its informal and warm hospitality, it is no wonder that the bar is a favorite place for artists and writers. *Directions:* Bagno Vignoni is 5 km south of San Quirico. Park in the town lot and walk the short distance to the locanda.

LA LOCANDA DEL LOGGIATO
Hosts: Sabrina & Barbara Marini
Piazza del Moretto 30
San Quirico d'Orcia–Bagno Vignoni (SI) 53023, Italy
Tel & fax: (0577) 888925, Cellphone: (335) 430427
8 rooms, Double: €130
Open: all year, Credit cards: MC, VS
Other languages: some English, French
Region: Tuscany, Michelin Map: 430
www.karenbrown.com/italy/loggiato.html

The beautiful countryside surrounding the hilltown of Montalcino unfortunately does not offer much in the way of accommodation. Descending from Montalcino towards the Amiata Mountains and Grosseto, one comes across the picturesque hilltop town of S. Angelo in Colle, still undiscovered by tourists, and just below is the scenic 5-acre vineyard property and stone farmhouse where the Girardi family offer bed and breakfast hospitality within six double rooms. Four bedrooms decorated identically with wooden country furniture are upstairs while the other two are on the ground floor, with their own exterior entrances, next to the breakfast room. The large windows of this room look out over a small manicured lawn and lavender-lined garden. Just about everything about the property is impeccable, and for this reason and the fact that return clients come for the peacefulness and privacy of this haven, it is not ideal for small children. To the back of the house is a covered terrace with spectacular valley views, while to the front, through the olive groves, you find a lovely secluded swimming pool. Settle in for a week or so and make this your base for visiting Sant'Antimo Abbey, San Galgano, Montalcino, Pienza, and Siena (50 km). *Directions:* 10 km south of Montalcino. From Grosseto on the S.S.223 to Siena, exit at Paganico and follow signs for Montalcino. After 16 km, Il Poderuccio is on the right-hand side of the road before the town of S. Angelo in Colle.

⊥ ➡ 桥 Y P ≈ ❦

IL PODERUCCIO
Host: Giorgio Girardi family
Sant'Angelo in Colle, SI 53024, Italy
Tel: (0577) 844052, Fax: (0577) 844150
6 rooms, Double: €85
Minimum nights required: 4
Open: Easter to Nov
Other languages: good English
Region: Tuscany, Michelin Map: 430
www.karenbrown.com/italy/poderuccio.html

During the 18th century under the rule of Leopoldo II, the flat plains to the south of Cortona were divided into equal farm lots, each having a rectangular-shaped farmhouse topped with pigeon loft, called "case Leopoliane". Diletta and Dimitri found the Agrisalotto property already restored with the former stables trasformed into an elegant restaurant below and five guest apartments on the floor above. The comfortable apartments for two to six persons are of varying dimensions and include either one or two bedrooms, bathroom, and living room with kitchenette. Each is decorated individually with a mix of family antiques and newer reproductions. A garden lined with overflowing terra-cotta vases of flowers leads to an enclosed swimming pool. Agrisalotto prides itself also on refined Tuscan cuisine, rich in tradition and naturally fresh flavors, accompanied by vintage wines. The Jacomoni family selects and produces the grapes and personally follows the production and bottling of wine sold at the farm. Cooking and wine lessons along with organized daily itineraries are arranged for groups of six or more. An excellently located base for both Umbria and parts of Tuscany. *Directions:* Exit from autostrada A1 at Valchiana and head towards Perugia. Leave this highway at Foiano-Cortona and follow signs to Agrisalotto.

AGRISALOTTO
Hosts: Diletta & Dimitri Jacomoni
Localita: Burcinella 88
Santa Caterina di Cortona (AR) 52040, Italy
Tel & fax: (0575) 617417, Cellphone: (338) 7378393
5 apartments: €748–€955 weekly (Jul & Aug),
€142–€180 daily
Closed: Nov, Credit cards: MC, VS
Other languages: some English, French
Region: Tuscany, Michelin Map: 430
www.karenbrown.com/italy/agrisalotto.html

Right in the heart of the chic (and expensive) Italian Riviera is a small jewel of a bed and breakfast hugging the hillside high above the ports of Portofino and Santa Margherita. The young host, Roberto, has restored almost single-handedly the two small stone farmhouses on a piece of his grandfather's property. Nine tastefully decorated double rooms are divided between the two houses, each with private bath, scattered antiques, and lovely panoramic views over the olive trees and fruit orchards and down to the sea. A cozy living room, inviting one to curl up with a book or to converse, gives visitors the feeling of being at the home of friends. The ambiance is intimate and welcoming. In the small, beamed dining room or out in the panoramic terraced garden, breakfast and dinner (featuring local specialties such as the famous fresh pesto sauce) are served and prepared by Roberto himself while his darling wife, Simona, serves and attends to guests. From Genoa to the marvels of Cinque Terre, the Ligurian coast holds some very special treasures, and the Gnocchi makes a perfect and very reasonable place from which to discover them. Arrival accepted before 1:30 pm or after 5 pm. *Directions:* From Santa Margherita follow signs to Genova/S. Lorenzo uphill for about 4 km to a blue sign indicating an intersection. Just after the sign, about 90 meters before the intersection, take the narrow, winding road on the left with the red-and-white gate down to the end.

VILLA GNOCCHI
Hosts: Simona & Roberto Gnocchi
Via Romana 53
Santa Margherita (GE) 16038, Italy
Tel & fax: (0185) 283431, Cellphone: (333) 6191898
9 rooms, Double: €94
Per person half board: €65
Open: mid-Apr to mid-Oct
Other languages: good English
Region: Liguria, Michelin Map: 428
www.karenbrown.com/italy/villagnocchi.html

Il Muto di Gallura, named after a legendary bandit of this wild west area of Sardinia, is the region's most integral agritourism farm property, offering a gamut of services from accommodation, meals, sale of local products, horseback-riding lessons, hiking excursions, and even hunting in the winter months. All farm products (grains, vegetables, and fruit) are organically grown and farm animals include sheep, cows, pigs, goats, and donkeys. As with most of the agritourism properties in Sardinia, the business opened as a country restaurant open to the public and rooms were added later. The busy and informal ranch-style farm offers accommodation within rather small but cozy guestrooms in the main house (above the restaurant) or in four separate wood bungalows for two persons adjacent to the house. Rooms are decorated with the family's country antiques and the rustic dining room with hanging brass pots and stone fireplace is divided between two floors. The area of Aggius is most famous for its dramatic granite rock formations referred to as the "moon valley" for its variety of rock shapes (a free climbers' paradise). Easy day trips include Tempio Pausania and outlying Nuraghi archaeological sites, and Calangianus, the center of the cork industry (Sardinia is a major producer of bottle corks). *Directions:* From Tempio Pausania take the road north for Aggius and after 4 km turn left at the sign. 1 km before Aggius on the road.

IL MUTO DI GALLURA   *New*
Hosts: Gianfranco & Francesca Serra
Localita: Fraiga
Aggius (SS) 07020, Italy
Tel & fax: (079) 620559 or 620353
8 rooms, Double: €62, 4 bungalows
Minimum nights required: 2
Open: all year
Other languages: some English
Region: Sardinia, Michelin Map: 433
www.karenbrown.com/italy/gallura.html

On the island's west coast you find the ancient port town of Alghero, Sardinia's lobster and coral capital. With origins dating back as far as 1100, the walled seaside village still preserves evidence of a strong Spanish influence. The road bordering the coast takes you past the archaeological site of Palmavera with its typical Nuraghi construction from the Bronze Age; the bay of Porto Conte with its nature park; and the Capo Caccia scenic point with the fascinating Nettuno cave. In the near vicinity is the Porticciolo agritourism farm, named after the ancient watchtower on the coast. The flat property made up of cultivated fields surrounds the family's simple white rectangular house and new restaurant. Like most farms in Sardinia, buildings are all of recent construction as the agritourism activity is in its beginning stages. Just behind the building that houses the restaurant are six separate guesthouses for four persons each with a bedroom, bathroom, loft bed, and living area with kitchenette, nicely appointed with wood furnishings and wrought-iron beds. The enormous glassed-in dining room with fireplace where fish and meats are grilled is where Maria and her entire family work together presenting delectable Sardinian specialties topped off with the island's myrtle-berry cordial. *Directions:* From Alghero (16 km) take the S.S.127 to Fertilla, go past Porto Conte bay, and turn right for S.M. La Palma. Turn left at the first road to Porticciolo.

PORTICCIOLO   New
Host: Maria Angius family
Localita: Porticciolo
Alghero (SS) 07041, Italy
Tel & fax: (079) 918000, Cellphone: (347) 5231024
6 apartments: €620–€785 weekly
Open: May to Oct, Credit cards: all major
Other languages: very little English
Region: Sardinia, Michelin Map: 433
www.karenbrown.com/italy/porticciolo.html

We recommend the Piccolo Golf hotel in order to offer the less-adventurous traveler a more classic accommodation than the rather spartan agritourism choices of the region. It is also a more reasonable alternative to the expensive hotels for which the Emerald Coast is so famous. Beautifully positioned, the peach-colored stone hotel immersed in Mediterranean vegetation overlooks the Pevero Golf Club to one side and the bay of Cala di Volpe to the other. This is a more secluded and peaceful area of the Emerald Coast, with small, hidden coves and rocky beaches, between the more famous towns of Porto Cervo and Porto Rotondo. The large reception and bar area have wicker furnishings and lead out to the surrounding garden and swimming pool. To the right of the entrance is a simple veranda dining room where regional meals are served. Bedrooms are practical and basic, with light-blue bedspreads and trimmings accenting cream-colored walls. Rooms have either garden or sea views (slightly higher rate), with the top-floor rooms catching glimpses of the turquoise-blue sea, which is very reminiscent of the Caribbean. This is a perfect location for viewing the coast or exploring the more rugged interior landscapes of the island—the "real" Sardinia. *Directions:* 30 km from Olbia airport. Drive towards Palau and turn off right for Porto Cervo then right again for Capricciolo. Cala di Volpe is 4 km before town and the hotel is opposite the luxurious Hotel Cala di Volpe.

*IL PICCOLO GOLF   **New***
Host: Mario Azzena
Localita: Cala di Volpe
Cala di Volpe, Porto Cervo (SS) 07020, Italy
Tel: (0789) 96520, Fax: (0789) 96565
17 rooms, Double: €77–€204
Open: all year, Credit cards: AX, VS
Other languages: some English
Region: Sardinia, Michelin Map: 433
www.karenbrown.com/italy/piccolo.html

British expatriate Jane Ridd settled in the wild west of Sardinia many years ago and with her husband took over the family cheese farm. The 150-acre property consists of cork woods, vineyards, and pastures where livestock, mostly sheep, roam. Over the years, Jane has gained fame (Michelin star) for her completely homemade local Gallura cuisine using primarily the farm's own products. Below the dining room local women can be seen working away in an enormous kitchen creating gnocchi and a variety of pastas of all shapes, and filling ravioli with a selection of ricotta and cheeses made right on the farm. Two rustic dining rooms, one open-air for summer months, accommodate the many culinary enthusiasts who gather here. Completely immersed in the trees, the four guestrooms are in an attached section of the restaurant almost carved out of the enormous granite rock that backs the property. Their decor is very basic and practical, with white walls, double beds (one is a quadruple), armoires, and new bathrooms. Besides interesting nature hikes and the nearby sea, one can explore inland local towns and follow fascinating archaeological itineraries (there are over 6,000 examples of the prehistoric round stone structures of the Bronze-Age Nuraghi civilization on the island). *Directions:* From Olbia (20 km away) head for Calangianus and after 6 km turn right at Ponte Moroni then turn left at the end of the road. 2 km after Priatu, turn left at the sign.

LI LICCI   *New*
Host: Jane Elizabeth Ridd
Localita: Valentino-Priatu
Calangianus (SS) 07023, Italy
Tel & fax: (079) 665114
4 rooms, Double: €80
Minimum nights required: 2
Open: all year
Other languages: fluent English
Region: Sardinia, Michelin Map: 433
www.karenbrown.com/italy/lilicci.html

Although many think of Sardinia as purely a sailors' paradise (which it is), the development and widespread publicity of the chic Emerald Coast has robbed the island of its true identity. The beauty of ancient Sardinia (dating back to the Neolithic and Bronze Age periods) lies in its stark and rugged windswept landscapes and its relatively simple lifestyle. With the strategic location of Monti Tundu, the traveler can take advantage of both coast and mountain excursions, exploring this corner of the island. Making your way up the steep dirt road, you are rewarded with mountaintop views over the rocky Mediterranean terrain stretching out to the Cugnana Gulf. Meals incorporating local delicacies such as the island's famed Percorino cheeses are served in the simple circular dining room with windows looking out over the striking vistas. A separate one-story L-shaped stone house contains the guestrooms, each with independent entrance from the exterior and more sweeping views. Newly refurbished double rooms (all of which can become triples) and bathrooms have soft pastel color schemes, beige tiled floors, and simple and practical furnishings. Hosts Gianni and Giuseppina offer warm Sardinian hospitality. *Directions:* 10 km from Olbia (airport and ferry port). From Olbia take the S.S.125 regional road towards Arzachena/Palau. Monti Tundu is marked on the right side of the road. Follow the very rough, steep road up to the very end.

MONTI TUNDU   New
Hosts: Gianni Spolittu & Giuseppina Serra
Localita: Casagliana, S.S.125 Olbia-Palau
Postal address: Via Francoforte 4
Casagliana, Olbia (SS) 07026, Italy
Tel & fax: (0789) 613072 or 58001
Cellphone: (336) 9608389
10 rooms, Double: €78, Open: all year
Other languages: French, Spanish
Region: Sardinia, Michelin Map: 433
www.karenbrown.com/italy/tundu.html

For those who wish to become better acquainted with the real Sardinia, head inland where the natives live, the scenery is striking, and the food authentic. Sardinia presents travelers with its own unique scenery, layers of history, artisans' craftwork and folklore, traditional cuisine, and delightfully warm hospitality (not one single place we stopped at neglected to offer us refreshment). The 150-acre property of the Corda Altana family is isolated and completely immersed in the typical Sardinian landscape where huge time-worn granite rocks emerge on the horizon surrounded by cork trees and Mediterranean brush vegetation. Roads are bordered by low stone walls and the base of the family's prim white house was built on the granite foundation. The six bedrooms (two are adjoining for families), all on the first floor and separate from the family's quarters, are new and immaculate like the rest of Maria's house. Breakfast and dinner are served either out on a large granite table or within the spacious dining room, which caters to non-guests as well (Maria is well known for her homemade gnocchetti and soups). Innumerable hiking or horseback-riding excursions are organized from the property. *Directions:* From Olbia head south for San Teodoro and after 10 km turn right for Padru. After Padru drive another 8 km towards Buddusò, turning left for Pedra Bianca-Sas Concas. The house is marked on the right after 3 km.

TONINO CORDA   New
Host: Maria Sabina Altana family
Localita: Sas Concas-Pedra Bianca
Padru (SS) 07020, Italy
Tel & fax: (0789) 49125
6 rooms, Double: €80*
*Includes breakfast & dinner
Minimum nights required: 2
Open: all year, Other languages: none
Region: Sardinia, Michelin Map: 433
www.karenbrown.com/italy/corda.html

Hidden away from the nearby fashionable beaches of the Emerald Coast of Sardinia is the Ca'La Somara farm where warm hosts Laura and Alberto offer alternative hospitality in nine guestrooms. The 20-acre property stretches up a rocky granite mountainside where the rare Sardinian mules bred here are seen grazing. The bougainvillea-covered one-story main house next door to the owners' quarters has a large glassed-in dining room looking out to a walled, untamed garden. Rustically decorated in typical Sardinian style (Mexican in feeling), it has colourful hand-woven rugs on the walls, as well as baskets and saddles for the mules, and an interior wooden balcony along the length of the room. Guest bedrooms are in a separate house, each painted in bright colors, with matching bedspreads and bathrooms (only two en suite). A breakfast of homemade breads and cakes is served outdoors under the portico and a superlative vegetarian dinner can also be arranged upon advance request. The hosts' warm and informal hospitality puts guests immediately at ease. The location allows visitors to see two sides of Sardinia: spectacular seaside and inland villages. Many archaeological sites are in the area and activities such as biking, sailing, diving, horseback riding, and hiking can all be arranged. This is a nature lovers' paradise. *Directions:* From Arzachena head for Porto Cervo and turn right for San Pantaleo. After 1 km, turn left for Ca'La Somara.

CA'LA SOMARA   New
Hosts: Laura & Alberto Lagattolla
San Pantaleo, Arzachena (SS) 07021, Italy
Tel & fax: (0789) 98969
9 rooms, Double: €52–€100
Minimum nights required: 2
Closed: Jan 5 to Feb 15
Other languages: good English
Region: Sardinia, Michelin Map: 433
www.karenbrown.com/italy/cala.html

The remote L'Agnata property is truly unique and mystic. After leaving the main road, you follow a seemingly endless country road dense with cork trees and their curious shaved trunks. Never fear—you are delightfully rewarded at last when you come into the world of silence at L'Agnata. You leave your car parked at the entrance near a lake down a ravine and walk up the arbored path to the main 100-year-old ivy-covered house. Host Piero greets guests at the reception house and shows them to their rooms either upstairs in the main stone house where the owners, the De Andre family, reside during the summer months or in the guesthouse at the back across an expansive green lawn. An inviting swimming pool sits at the side of the house and looks perfectly natural with its surrounding large rocks sitting up straight like sculptures. Rooms are well appointed with antiques and warm colors in the rich fabrics and walls. The manicured lawn spreads around both houses and represents the taming of nature while the rest of the 400-acre property is immersed in the more wild and rugged mountain landscapes so typical of Sardinia. In the corner of the magical garden is a little waterfall creating soothing sounds which break the silence. Excellent dishes of this area called Gallura are served in the muraled dining room. *Directions:* From Tempio, follow the S.S.392 towards Oschiri. After 4.5 km turn right for S. Bachisio and take the unpaved road all the way to the end.

L'AGNATA   New
Host: Piero Angius
Localita: L'Agnata, Tempio Pausania (SS) 07029, Italy
Tel & fax: (079) 671384
10 rooms, Double: €140–€160*
*Includes breakfast & dinner
Minimum nights required: 3
Closed: Nov, Credit cards: all major
Other languages: very little English
Region: Sardinia, Michelin Map: 433
www.karenbrown.com/italy/lagnata.html

The charming home of Cristina Bizzarri, from Milan, is found in a lovely area in the southern part of Tuscany called the Orcia Valley (Val d'Orcia). It is a favorite because of the variety of landscapes, which change dramatically within short driving distances, from the storybook-perfect medieval hilltowns to the Crete Senesi, crater-like gray hills south of Siena up to the Amiata Mountains. The sun-colored La Ghiandaia bed and breakfast is easily accessible, being right on the crossroads, and has a nice surrounding garden with swimming pool. Cristina has reserved five double rooms for her guests on both ground and first floors, all tastefully appointed with the antiques she had in her former home. The soft-peach interior colors of the stenciled walls, set off by that special Tuscany light, give the rooms a warm glow and guests can relax in either of two living rooms and a dining room where a delicious country breakfast is served. Cristina also has a delightful tiled country kitchen with hanging brass pots and can arrange private cooking lessons upon advance request. Dinner can also be arranged upon request—in fact, Cristina enjoys creating meals for special occasions or theme dinners. In addition, she can assist you plan a wide range of cultural or more active itineraries. *Directions:* Exit the A1 at Chiusi, following signs for Sarteano. Pass through Sarteano towards Radicofani and after 6 km take the first left towards Fonte Vetriana. The house is just beyond this crossroads.

LA GHIANDAIA
Host: Cristina Bizzarri
Via della Montagna di Cetona 2
Sarteano (SI) 53047, Italy
Tel & fax: (0578) 265169, Cellphone: (348) 3222399
5 rooms, Double: €82–€90
Minimum nights required: 2
Open: all year, Credit cards: MC, VS
Other languages: good English
Region: Tuscany, Michelin Map: 430
www.karenbrown.com/italy/ghiandaia.html

The stately 16th-century home of Fabio, Italian businessman from Venice, and Yuri, his Japanese wife, a painter and musician, is conveniently situated close to many highlights of Tuscany. Their combination of cultures is reflected throughout the decor of the home, which they have opened as a very comfortable and refined bed and breakfast. Practically the entire house is open to guests who are made to feel at home in any one of the common areas—living room, terrace, veranda breakfast room overlooking a manicured garden, or swimming pool. The distinguished and impeccable home is appointed with selected antiques, white sofas, Oriental carpets, a grand piano, and Yuri's hand-painted porcelain. Four pristine and spacious bedrooms upstairs each have apricot marble bathrooms and elegant touches such as brocaded bedspreads and draperies, wrought-iron fixtures, and gilded mirrors. The suite has a palatial bathroom with Jacuzzi and features a large terrace taking in a sweeping, panoramic view of the unspoiled countryside. From this idyllic location, both Umbria and highlights of southern Tuscan hilltowns are at one's fingertips. *Directions:* From the center of Sarteano follow signs for Chianciano and after 3 km turn right at the sign for Villa Iris. It is the first house on the left.

VILLA IRIS
Hosts: Yuri Hashimoto & Fabio Moretto
Strada Palazzo di Piero 1
Sarteano (SI) 53047, Italy
Tel: (0578) 266111, Fax: (0578) 265993
5 rooms, Double: €155–€240
Minimum nights required: 2
Open: Apr to Oct, Credit cards: all major
Other languages: good English
Region: Tuscany, Michelin Map: 430
www.karenbrown.com/italy/iris.html

As more travelers realize how close together destinations of interest throughout Italy are, weekly house rentals to use as a home base for excursions have become more popular. One such ideal base is La Sovana, bordering Tuscany and Umbria and equidistant to Siena, Perugia, Assisi, Arezzo, and many other smaller hilltowns such as Montepulciano, Pienza, and Montalcino—the area where Italy's finest wines are produced. Two stone farmhouses were carefully restored to provide comfortable suites for two to six people. Tastefully decorated with local antique beds and armoires, matching floral bedspreads and curtains, each has a fully equipped kitchenette and eating and living area. Guests can dine by candlelight in the dining room in the main house, whose enormous arched window takes in the expansive view of vineyards, wheat fields, and impeccable landscaping. Giovannella and Giuseppe Olivi, dedicated and amiable hosts, and their two grown children, Riccardo and Francesca, dine with their guests each evening. Potted flowers abound around the farmhouses and pool, where on Saturday nights a sumptuous barbecue is organized to enable guests to meet one another. Two tennis courts, a small fishing lake, and bikes are available. There are more bi-level suites in a large converted barn in the woods a short walk away from the main farmhouse. *Directions:* Just 2 km from the Chiusi exit of the A1 autostrada. La Sovana is just before Sarteano on the right.

LA SOVANA
Host: Giuseppe Olivi family
Localita: Sovana, Sarteano (SI) 53047, Italy
Tel: (0578) 274086 or (075) 600197
Cellphone: (335) 7258560, Fax: (075) 5158098
15 rooms, Double: €124–€181
Minimum nights required: 3, 7 in Jul & Aug
Open: Mar 16 to Nov 3
Other languages: good English
Region: Tuscany, Michelin Map: 430
www.karenbrown.com/italy/lasovana.html

Tenuta La Bandita is set amid 150 acres of woods, olive groves, orchards, and meadows within a beautifully undisturbed area south of Livorno near the sea. Dino and Daniela, with their former business and hotel experience, bought the estate not too long ago and are in the process of gradually bringing it back to its past splendor. There is certainly plenty to keep them busy since the property includes six additional farmhouses surrounding the 17th-century main villa where most of the guest bedrooms are situated. Their idea was to transform the villa into a bed and breakfast while leaving as much as possible of the original structure and atmosphere of the private residence intact. This was made easier by the fact that the home came with ten furnished bedrooms with bathrooms, situated down one long corridor. The rooms are appointed with original period furniture, chandeliers, and matching drapes and bedspreads. Guests can lounge on the front terrace or in the spacious arched living and dining room downstairs with gray-stone fireplace and framed portraits. Fifteen additional rooms are divided within two adjacent houses, between the villa and swimming pool. *Directions:* Exit from S.S.1 at Donoratico and head for Sassetta/Castagneto for 11 km on a winding mountain road. Take the turnoff left for Laderello/Monteverdi (not Sassetta) for 1 km to the La Bandita property. Pass through the gate and go past the first group of houses to the villa.

TENUTA LA BANDITA
Hosts: Daniela & Dino Filippi
Via Campagna Nord 30
Sassetta (LI) 57020, Italy
Tel: (0565) 794224, Fax: (0565) 794350
25 rooms, Double: €83–€135
Minimum nights required: 2
Open: Mar 24 to Nov, Credit cards: all major
Other languages: some English, German, French
Region: Tuscany, Michelin Map: 430
www.karenbrown.com/italy/tenutalabandita.html

Saturnia's thermal waters have been gushing from an underground volcano for over 2,000 years, yet only recently have it and the enchanting surrounding Maremma area become internationally famous, leading to new accommodations springing up. One such is the charming Villa Clodia, once home to nobility, now run by former restaurateur Giancarlo Ghezzi. The villa is a curiosity, seemingly built out of the limestone rock, one side overlooking the street and the other an expansive valley of grapevines and olive trees. Because of its unusual proportions, each room is unique in size and decor. A small winding stairway takes guests up or down to rooms, some of which have been literally carved out of the rock. All bedrooms feature scattered antiques, new bathrooms, and valley views, and a fortunate few boast a terrace. Amenities include air conditioning, TVs, and mini bars. Breakfast is offered in a sweet, luminous room next to the sitting room. A lush rose garden and fruit orchard surround the inviting star-shaped pool. Advance reservations are a must and weekly stays preferred. *Directions:* From Rome take the Aurelia highway north, turning off to the right at Vulci following signs for Manciano, Montemerano, and Saturnia. Villa Clodia is in the middle of town.

VILLA CLODIA
Host: Giancarlo Ghezzi
Via Italia 43
Saturnia (GR) 58050, Italy
Tel: (0564) 601212, Fax: (0564) 601305
12 rooms, Double: €88–€99
Minimum nights required: 4
Closed: Dec 1 to 20, Credit cards: VS
Other languages: good English
Region: Tuscany, Michelin Map: 430
www.karenbrown.com/italy/clodia.html

North of the beautifully austere ancient city of Bergamo, at the foothills of the Ortighera mountain range right on the River Brembo is the farm property of young local couple, Cinzia and Ferdy Quarteroni. They bought the stone farmhouse at the edge of thick woods, which dates to 1850, and completely restored it to include four guestrooms, their private quarters, dining rooms, and small store where they sell their home-produced goat cheeses. The cabin-like bedrooms on the two upper floors are simply decorated in tune with the natural features of the house: stone walls, wood-beamed ceilings, and brick floors. Downstairs in the cozy, arched, stone-walled dining room with large fireplace, gregarious Cinzia serves excellent local fare and an ample breakfast with freshly baked cakes and breads. This is a nature lover's paradise where Ferdy sees to the goats and organizes itineraries by mountain bike, horse, or foot while nearby there are several ski resorts. This is a perfect vacation spot for families. *Directions:* From the A4 autostrada exit at Dalmine (35 km), heading north for Villa d'Almè, San Pellegrino, San Giovanni, and Scalvino. Ten km after San Pellegrino, the source of the famous mineral water, park on the right-hand side of road at the agriturismo sign and cross over the footbridge up to the house.

FERDY
Hosts: Cinzia & Ferdy Quarteroni
Localita: Scalvino
Scalvino–Lenna (BG) 24010, Italy
Tel & fax: (0345) 82235
4 rooms, Double: €62–€80
Per person half board: €47–€55
Open: all year, Credit cards: MC, VS
Other languages: good English
Region: Lombardy, Michelin Map: 428
www.karenbrown.com/italy/ferdy.html

The Locanda Strada della Marina, another answer to the increasing request for charming accommodation in this infrequently visited region, is just 20 kilometers north of Ancona in the northern section of the Marches area. In the summer this part of the flat Adriatic coast is normally inundated with Italian and northern European tourists who flock to the shores for sun and entertainment. Gianmarco had the family's house in the nearby countryside restored into a peaceful bed and breakfast with emphasis on excellent dining. The converted tobacco-drying barn is where chef Mariano Faraoni combines traditional cuisine with his own creative approach and has been noted in guides such as Michelin, Veronelli, and Gambero Rosso. Meals are accompanied by a vast choice of wines. The ten bedrooms in the pale-yellow main house have many amenities. Decorated with a fresh country flavor, they have parquet floors and sparkling bathrooms, and some enjoy a loft sitting space or extra bed. Common spaces are found both in the ground-floor living area where breakfast is served and a cozy upstairs corner with fireplace. Surrounding the house is an open lawn space and garden with heated swimming pool. The Beccis are friendly hosts who can suggest many interesting local itineraries. *Directions:* Leave the A14 at Senigallia and drive through the city to the Strada della Marina, which leads to Scapezzano. The Locanda Strada della Marina is on this road before town.

❆ ⚓ ☕ 🛅 ⛟ ☎ 🍴 🐎 ♈ P 🍽 🏊 🖼 🐾 ♿

LOCANDA STRADA DELLA MARINA   **New**
Hosts: Stefania & Gianmarco Becci
Strada della Marina 265
Scapezzano di Senigallia (AN) 60010, Italy
Tel: (071) 6608633, Fax: (071) 6611727
10 rooms, Double: €60–€70
Open: all year, Credit cards: all major
Other languages: good English
Region: Marches, Michelin Map: 430
www.karenbrown.com/italy/dellamarina.html

Luciana and Luigi from Rome are pioneers in offering accommodation in Sabina, bringing back to life a lovely inherited piece of property. Gregarious Luciana is the hostess par excellence: she goes out of her way to see that guests' needs are taken care of and suggests many fascinating local itineraries and events. Accommodation is offered in a variety of apartments divided between the main villa and the well-restored farmhouse with adjacent scenically positioned pool down the hill. Each has one or two bedrooms, bathroom, kitchenette, and eating area, while a double living room with enormous stone fireplace is reserved for all guests. The cozy country decor, with its stenciled borders and mix of family antiques, is the result of Luciana's good taste. Apartments on ground and second floors (some with terraces) take in views of the sweeping valley below. Rooms in the villa are more elegant, with frescoed ceilings, panoramic terraces, and antique furnishings. In addition to producing wine, olive oil, and fruit, Luigi raises thoroughbred horses. Luciana also arranges interesting walking tours and courses in Italian and cooking. *Directions:* From Rome, leave the A1 at Ponzano Romano/Soratte (a new exit and not marked on maps) after the Fiano exit. Drive towards Stimigliano Scalo, turn right after the railroad crossing, and continue until the turnoff left for Forano. Before the church turn right for Selci, then right before town at Via Vallerosa.

VILLA VALLEROSA
Hosts: Luciana Pancera & Luigi Giuseppi
Via di Vallerosa 27
Selci Sabino (RI) 02040, Italy
Tel & fax: (0765) 519179, Cellphone: (339) 1226213
7 apartments: €690–€1,075 weekly, €114–€190 daily
Minimum nights required: 2, 7 in high season
Open: all year
Other languages: good English
Region: Lazio, Michelin Map: 430
www.karenbrown.com/italy/vallerosa.html

Wandering off the main tourist trail in Sicily is recommended for the traveler who truly enjoys contact with local people and their culture (best to have some command of Italian) and is curious and open to new experiences, without being tied to rigid schedules. If you leave yourselves in the hands of the Contes, you will certainly be rewarded with a once-in-a-lifetime stay. Reaching Gangi is an adventure in itself, taking you far away from the main route through the scenic Madonie Mountains, which cut across the mid-northern part of Sicily. Villa Raino is just outside Gangi, with its tightly packed houses covering the tip of a mountaintop. Genuine host, Aldo, left the family hotel business in town and restored this 100-year-old brick house once owned by a noble family, offering an excellent countryside restaurant for local families and city people coming from as far away as Palermo. On the first and second floors there are ten unique guestrooms with mansard ceilings, some having a small balcony. A mix of family antiques is scattered about the rooms, which have Tiffany bedside lamps and walls stenciled using an ancient technique that gives the effect of floral wallpaper. Bathrooms have brightly colored tiles. All in all Villa Raino provides a delightful opportunity to explore. *Directions:* From A19 exit at Tre Monzelli and follow S.S.120 to Gangi for 38 km. A sign before town takes you down a rough, unpaved road to the property.

VILLA RAINO
Hosts: Nina & Aldo Conte
Contrada Raino
Gangi (PA) 90024, Italy
Tel: (0921) 644680, Fax: (0921) 644424
10 rooms, Double: €70
Open: all year, Credit cards: all major
Other languages: some English
Region: Sicily, Michelin Map: 432
www.karenbrown.com/italy/raino.html

On the southwestern coast between the archaeological ruins of Selinunte and Sciacca with its hot springs, lies the anonymous town of Menfi. Menfi was virtually destroyed in the earthquake of 1968, and consequently is a mix of new construction and devastated areas still awaiting government funds. In the very center of all this sits the splendid 18th-century palazzo of the noble Ravida family, which miraculously survived disaster. You enter the front iron gates from the city street to discover a large stone courtyard with palm trees leading to the U-shaped villa with its solid Doric stone columns. Hospitality is offered within the villa and garden house wing in lovely air-conditioned bedrooms which are in perfect harmony with the general feeling of the home. There is a perfume of the past as you wander through the frescoed sitting rooms filled with ancestral paintings and period antiques worn by time. Fortunately for guests, the gracious hosts, the congenial Baron and his wife, are experts in itineraries throughout Sicily. Their large agricultural property at a short distance from town comprises vineyards and vast citrus and olive groves. With hundreds of years of tradition in producing oil, it is no wonder that Ravida has received national and international recognition as the best producer in Sicily. They also host a week-long cooking course combining daily outings. *Directions:* Follow signs to the center of Menfi and ask for Via Roma or Villa Ravida.

VILLA RAVIDA
Hosts: Nicola & Ninni Ravida
Via Roma 173
Menfi (AG) 92013, Italy
Tel: (0925) 71109 or 75836, Fax: (0925) 71180
6 rooms, Double: €105–€130
Minimum nights required: 3
Closed: Aug 5 to 20, Credit cards: VS
Other languages: good English
Region: Sicily, Michelin Map: 432
www.karenbrown.com/italy/ravida.html

The Alcalà farm, made up of citrus and olive groves and a wide variety of fruit trees, extends over 75 acres of fertile plain backdropped by the Etna volcano—a picture-perfect setting. Cordial hostess Anna Sapuppo and her young family have taken over the family's agricultural business and have added hospitality activity as well. The main house is a hundred-year-old masseria, built in several sections, while guests are situated nearby in four different apartment setups (one has handicapped facilities) for two to six persons. Two of them are separate houses and all have terraces of varying dimensions. They include living room areas and kitchenettes and are simply decorated with floral sofas and a mix of modern and old family furniture. Although breakfast is not served, guests can help themselves in season to plenty of oranges, tangerines, and grapefruit. An occasional typically Sicilian dinner is served in the rustic wine cantina with its enormous wooden wine barrels or by request in your apartment. Anna, a native Sicilian, gladly assists her guests with touring suggestions, which include Catania city (important where not to go), Syracuse, Etna National Park, and the temples of Agrigento. *Directions:* Take the Palermo-Catania autostrada A19 and leave at the first exit Motta S. Anastasia. Turn left, backtracking towards Catania on route 192, pass the U.S. army base, then turn left again at the Alcalà sign (milestone 78). Go to the end of the private road.

ALCALÀ
Host: Anna Sappupo family
Casella Postale 100-S.S.192 at km 78
Misterbianco (CT) 95045, Italy
Tel & fax: (095) 713002 or (095) 7130342
Cellphone: (368) 3469206
4 apartments: €44–€53 daily (per person)
Minimum nights required: 3, 7 Jul, Aug, Easter & Christmas
Open: all year, Credit cards: MC, VS
Other languages: good English, Region: Sicily
www.karenbrown.com/italy/alcala.html

The coastal stretch from Messina to Cefalu has special appeal to the off-the-beaten-track traveler who will find the perfect place to stay at Casa Migliaca, a 200-year-old farmhouse nestling in the wooded hills 7 kilometers off the main road. This stone house just outside town, owned by Maria Teresa and Sebastiano, who left the city several years ago in favor of a rural lifestyle, offers a lovely sweeping view over olive and citrus groves down to the sea. The very congenial hosts love to converse with guests around the kitchen table or down in the cool dining room (originally the oil-press room) around the press wheel. A special effort was made to keep everything possible intact, giving the house its own very distinct charm, maintaining all original floors, ceilings, beams, kitchen tiles, and furniture, although new bathrooms have been incorporated in most of the rooms. There are even extra showers out in the garden! Guests are offered a choice of three double bedrooms upstairs or five downstairs. For those who desire direct contact with Sicilian culture, Casa Migliaca is a truly memorable experience. *Directions:* From coastal route 113, just 25 km after Cefalu, turn right at the sign for Pettineo and follow it right past town. Just after a gas station, turn right on a descending gravel road to the house (unmarked) 300 meters from Pettineo.

CASA MIGLIACA
Host: Maria Teresa Allegra
Contrada Migliaca, Pettineo (ME) 98070, Italy
Tel: (0921) 336722, Cellphone: (335) 8430645
Fax: (0921) 391107
8 rooms, Double: €110*
*Includes breakfast & dinner
Open: all year, Credit cards: all major
Other languages: good English
Region: Sicily, Michelin Map: 432
www.karenbrown.com/italy/casamigliaca.html

For those who prefer the intimacy of a small pension, native Salvatore and his amiable Panamanian wife Marisin await you with open arms. The pale-yellow three-story house sits in the quaint town of Scopello with its piazza and three streets. From ancient times this was an important fishing center especially for tuna, and the Tonnara stone fishing station down by the sea still stands as proof. The entrance hall is a combination breakfast and dining room with a sitting area in the corner around the fireplace. A central staircase leads up to guestrooms, a few with balconies facing out to the distant sea. The rooms are simply appointed with light-wood armoires, wrought-iron beds, and crocheted white bedspreads. In the evening after a day at the seaside or touring, you come "home" to a delicious three-course home-cooked meal of fresh fish or meat and vegetables from their garden. Enthusiastic Marisin spends time chatting with her guests and advising them what to visit in this culturally rich area. "Must sees" include the ancient town of Erice, the ruins of Segesta, Selinunte, and Agrigento. Well-marked hiking trails cover the spectacularly beautiful Zingaro Nature Reserve along the northern coast (one of its kind in Sicily). *Directions:* From Palermo, exit from autostrada A29 at Castellammare and follow signs for Scopello. The Tranchina is found just after the bar with outdoor tables.

PENSIONE TRANCHINA
Hosts: Marisin & Salvatore Tranchina
Via A. Diaz 7
Scopello (TP) 91014, Italy
Tel & fax: (0924) 541099
10 rooms, Double: €62–€72
Per person half board: €49–€58
Open: all year, Credit cards: all major
Other languages: fluent English
Region: Sicily, Michelin Map: 432
www.karenbrown.com/italy/pensionetranchina.html

The Limoneto was recommended to us by a reader who raved about the "open arms" hospitality, the excellent meals, comfortable accommodations, and proximity to fascinating Syracuse. We have to agree. At just 10 kilometers from the historical center of Syracuse with its Greek and Roman influences, the orange- and olive-grove farm is a perfectly delightful, safe, and economical base from which to explore Sicily's southeastern corner. Adelina, Alceste, and son, Francesco, make guests part of their family. Guestrooms are split between the refurbished barn and part of the main house, all with individual entrances. Rooms, some for up to four persons, are new with pleasant modern decor and all have spotless bathrooms. Dinner is served either in the spacious dining room where locals come for a Sunday meal, or out in the back garden. You are welcome into Adelina's kitchen to observe and participate in the making of typical regional meals. The warmth exudes and when the evening is just right and the limoncello flowing, she might even read some poetry. Truly unique is the boat tour on the river among the Papiro trees of Egyptian origin. *Directions:* From Catania, take the autostrada to Syracuse and exit at Palazzolo (km 152) after a brown sign for the Limoneto B&B. Drive towards Floridia on the S124 and turn left at the first intersection for Canicattini B. At the T-junction turn right again for Canicattini: the house is on the left after 4 km.

LIMONETO
Hosts: Alceste & Adelina Norcia
Via del Platano 3, Mailing address: Viale Teracati 142
Syracuse (SR) 96100, Italy
Tel: (0931) 717352, Fax: (0931) 717728
8 rooms, Double: €70
Minimum nights required: 3
Closed: Nov, Credit cards: MC, VS
Region: Sicily, Michelin Map: 432
www.karenbrown.com/italy/limoneto.html

Taormina is on what could be referred to as the Amalfi coast of Sicily and, although the town is lovely and rich with history, it is very touristy. This of course means that rates are on the high side but, happily, the Villa Schuler makes it affordable and its location and service are superb. The villa was converted from a private residence to a hotel by the Schuler family a century ago and now grandson Gerardo is the proud owner. The pink façade faces out to the street and has a large raised terrace with potted flowers, palms, and cypresses, where a large suite with two bathrooms, Jacuzzi, kitchenette, and garden area has been added. A Continental or full breakfast is served either here or in the gazebo where you can enjoy open views encompassing the coastline and the peak of the Etna volcano. To the back is an enchanting botanic garden filled with a profusion of jasmine, bougainvillea, and geraniums with several quiet places to sit in the shade. The garden gives directly onto the main street of town and it is just a short walk to the cable car that takes you down to the beach where guests gain free entrance (or you may take the shuttle service). Inside are the luminous bedrooms, some with sea views, and five mansard junior suites that have everything, including air conditioning, satellite TVs, safes, and terraces with sea views. For its efficient service, ideal location, and incredibly low rate, the Villa Schuler is a winner. *Directions:* Follow hotel signs through town.

VILLA SCHULER
Host: Gerardo Schuler family
Via Roma 2
Taormina (ME) 98039, Italy
Tel: (0942) 23481, Fax: (0942) 23522
32 rooms, Double: €110–€220
Minimum nights required: 3
Open: Mar to Nov, Credit cards: all major
Other languages: good English
Region: Sicily, Michelin Map: 433
www.karenbrown.com/italy/villaschuler.html

So very close to Siena, yet having the advantage of countryside tranquillity, is the elegant Villa dei Lecci of the Albuzza sisters from Milan. The enterprising and energetic pair left their city careers to resettle in Tuscany, totally renovating an abandoned 17th-century country home to create an upscale bed and breakfast and an intimate and romantic retreat for couples. The yellow bedroom downstairs is a suite with large bathroom adjacent to the frescoed dining room where a generous breakfast is served. A candlelit dinner can also be had upon request here or out in the garden gazebo. Upstairs, where the noble proprietors once lived, the quarters are more elaborate, with painted, wood-paneled ceilings and a large living room and library filled with fine antiques. The Victorian-style Peach Room has floral wallpaper, lace curtains, and silver-framed family photos, while the Alcove Suite is done in golden tones and rich fabrics. Adding to guests' indulgence are a hot tub, exercise room, and sitting area on a frescoed veranda. A weeklong cooking program is organized in off-season months. An excellent touring base. *Directions:* Exit the A1 at Val di Chiana and take 326 to Siena. Continue straight on to the Siena Est exit, arriving at Due Ponti. Take a sharp right at Bar Due Ponti onto Strada Pieve al Bozone for 2.5 km, turning left at the crucifix onto an unpaved road, Strada di Larniano. Continue 1.8 km to the end of the road and up to the gate of the stone villa.

❄ ☕ ☙ ⛺ 🍴 🚶 🐎 P 🚭 🖼 ♿ 🍇

VILLA DEI LECCI
Hosts: Miki & Marika Albuzza
Strada di Larniano 21/1
Siena 53100, Italy
Tel & fax: (0577) 221126, Cellphone: (339) 1543743
4 rooms, Double: €233
Minimum nights required: 3
Open: mid-Mar to Dec
Other languages: good English
Region: Tuscany, Michelin Map: 432
www.karenbrown.com/italy/lecci.html

The fascinating Marches region has been justifiably receiving great press recently as one of Italy's last undiscovered treasures. Certainly one of the most interesting areas from which to begin exploring is that of Monte Conero, which boasts the most spectacular coastline on the Adriatic, with white cliffs plunging into the sea. Here you find many historic villages and churches in scenic countryside, the highest concentration of historic theatres in Italy, and a summer opera festival in Macerata and Pesaro. Just slightly inland is the 80-acre agritourism property of the noble Nembrini Gonzaga family, producers of top-quality Rosso Conero wine and virgin olive oil. Next to the family's elegant 18th-century villa is a restored grain mill converted into guest apartments. An extensive two-story structure of white stone typical of the area, it contains pleasant, practical accommodation for two to five persons consisting of one or two bedrooms, bathroom, and living room with kitchenette. In the works for spring 2003 is an eight-bedroom bed and breakfast adjacent to the apartments and surrounded by a large garden. A wide variety of sports including sailing, golf, hiking on national-park trails overlooking the sea, and horseback riding can all be arranged. *Directions:* Exit the A14 autostrada at Ancona Sud heading for Sirolo-Numana. In Coppo (on most maps), 2 km before Sirolo, turn right on the road opposite the bar and follow the Via Valcastagno up to the property.

❄ ⚱ ▦ ✄ 💳 ☎ 🏠 🧍 👫 🐎 ▼ P 🖼 🚿 ♿ 🍇

RELAIS IL GRANAIO DI VALCASTAGNO   ***New***
Host: Francesca Nembrini Gonzaga family
Via Valcastagno 10, Sirolo (AN) 60026, Italy
Tel: (071) 7391580, Fax: (071) 7392776
8 rooms, Double: €70–€130
8 apartments: €65–€70 daily
Minimum nights required: 2, 7 in Jul & Aug
Open: all year, Credit cards: MC, VS
Other languages: fluent English, French
Region: Marches, Michelin Map: 430
www.karenbrown.com/italy/granaio.html

There is a beautiful stretch of coastline on the Adriatic Sea just south of Ancona, dramatically different from the more flat, uninteresting shoreline to the north and south with its modern hotels and condos. The 14th-century quaint stone village of Sirolo sits high above the water on a mountainside looking down to the beaches of the Riviera Conero. Delightful seafood restaurants dot the shore, where you might enjoy a plate of pasta with fresh clams while watching the tide come in. Here Isabella and Giorgio offer seven guestrooms above their small, quaint, peach-colored restaurant. The Locanda, dating to 1300, being actually part of the town's walls and arched entryway, is of great architectural and historical importance, so it has taken them many years to acquire permits to restore and renovate rooms. Their patience has paid off and their bed and breakfast, respecting the original structure, is a true charmer. Bedrooms, most with sea views, have exposed stone walls and terra-cotta floors showing off wrought-iron beds and antique armoires. Amenities such as air conditioning, telephones, TVs, mini bars, and hairdryers were added for guests' comfort. They also have two apartments nearby overlooking the park and sea for stays of four nights or more. Isabella's highly praised meals feature seafood dishes. *Directions:* The Rocco sits at the edge of the town of Sirolo, after Portonovo.

LOCANDA ROCCO
Hosts: Isabella & Giorgio Tridenti
Via Torrione 1
Sirolo (AN) 60020, Italy
Tel & fax: (071) 9330558, Cellphone: (339) 5205519
7 rooms, Double: €115–€160
2 apartments: €700–€800 weekly
Open: Apr to Nov, Credit cards: MC, VS
Other languages: some English
Region: Marches, Michelin Map: 430
www.karenbrown.com/italy/locandarocco.html

The real fascination about the gorgeous Val Gardena mountain resort area is that you can actually ski from one connecting valley to the next and finish up at the end of the day over near Cortina. Siusi is a convenient place to set up camp in any season and the Aquila Nera with its excellent restaurant and amenities of a hotel is steps up from the very economical bed and breakfast choices of the region. The very cordial Mutschlechner family, with a long tradition in the hospitality business, renovated most of the former private home whose origins date back to 1518. A second building was added on, creating additional rooms (and an elevator), which are very fresh with light-wood furnishings and cheerful fabrics. Downstairs common rooms include a luminous sitting area, a stube, a breakfast room completely paneled in wood including floor and ceiling, and a large contemporary dining room where five-course dinners are served based on a combination of Italian and southern Tyrolean recipes. A small swimming pool at the back, plus sauna, steam bath, and free shuttle to the lifts are nice added extras. *Directions:* Turn into the main street of town, Via Santner, and take the first right to Via Laurin.

AQUILA NERA
Host: Mutschlechner family
Via Laurin 7
Siusi allo Sciliar (BZ) 39040, Italy
Tel: (0471) 706146, Fax: (0471) 706335
21 rooms, Double: €204–€340*
*Includes breakfast & dinner
Closed: Apr 1 to May 24, Oct 26 to Dec 25
Credit cards: all major, Other languages: some English
Region: Trentino-Alto Adige, Michelin Map: 429
www.karenbrown.com/italy/aquilanera.html

The Kristiania is a typical bed and breakfast (or garni as they are called here) of the Dolomite mountain region west of Cortina where a German dialect is the common language. The area is a favorite among Italians, especially in August when swarms of natives flock here to relax in cooler temperatures, enjoy the scenery, and take advantage of the lower rates. Located in the town of Siusi, near the spectacular Siusi Alps known for its excellent cross-country skiing and hiking trails, the white stucco and wood chalet-style home of the Fill family is surrounded by a garden and looks up to the rocky peaks of the Sciliar. The decor varies minimally from house to house in this area and the Kristiania, as with most of the others, uses wood paneling on walls and ceilings as the basic decor (floors are covered with linoleum). The breakfast room is the common room, with a corner table set around the wood-burning stove heater. All rooms have balconies lined with geranium flowerboxes in the summer and there is also a sauna for guests. The area is truly paradise for nature lovers. *Directions:* Turn into the center of Siusi on Via Santner and turn left at the first street, Via Burgfrieden.

GARNI KRISTIANIA
Host: Josef Fill
Via Burgfrieden 13
Siusi allo Sciliar (BZ) 39040, Italy
Tel: (0471) 706439, Fax: none
10 rooms, Double: €57
Open: all year
Other languages: German
Region: Trentino-Alto Adige, Michelin Map: 429
www.karenbrown.com/italy/kristiania.html

To the west of Cortina, the most fashionable ski area in the Dolomites, is Val Gardena, which is almost too storybook-perfect to be true. The valley, once part of Austria, still preserves its Germanic heritage. Marmsolerhof, a very typical bed and breakfast, is owned and run by a local couple. The crisp-white house with its old stone-and-wood attached barn has been in the same family for over 400 years and has been renovated gradually over time. The entrance foyer walls are adorned with antique farm tools, harnesses, and cowbells. On the same floor is a dining room where guests enjoy breakfast with a view of the velvet green hillside. The five guestrooms, all but one with snug private shower, are basic and comfortable, furnished with pinewood beds and armoires, bright-orange curtains, and fluffy comforters. Stepping out on the balcony reveals a breathtaking panorama of the pine-covered mountains and dramatic peaks of the Sciliar. The Riers are happy to suggest scenic places to explore by car or on foot (although communication is limited) and know the best places for rock climbing up into one of the most spectacular ranges in Europe. *Directions:* Exit at Bolzano Nord from the Verona-Brennero autostrada and follow signs for Siusi. Beyond town, before Castelrotto, turn right for Alpe de Siusi and San Valentino, and after 1 km make a sharp left turn for Marmsolerhof. Use the back door—grandma lives on the ground floor.

MARMSOLERHOF
Host: August Rier family
San Valentino 35
Siusi allo Sciliar (BZ) 39040, Italy
Tel & fax: (0471) 706514
5 rooms, Double: €52
Open: all year
Other languages: very little English, German
Region: Trentino-Alto Adige, Michelin Map: 429
www.karenbrown.com/italy/marmsolerhof.html

In yet another lesser-known pocket of Tuscany halfway between Siena and the sea is the absolutely stunning 1,000-acre property of the Visconti family. Dating back to the 1400s, in its heyday it was a village in itself, complete with the noble family's main villa, farmers' houses, church, nuns' quarters, oil press, and blacksmith and carpenter's shops. These stone buildings are all attached to the villa in a U-shape formation with a beautiful formal garden within. Terra-cotta pots with lemon trees and red geraniums give spots of color among the greenery. Vitaliano and Vittoria, whose home has been in the same family since its origins, welcome guests in the restored part of the villa where nine bedrooms with private bathrooms have been created including three large triples. All with beamed ceilings and brick floors, they are simply appointed with beds and armoires, looking out either to the garden or woods at the back. Common areas are the living room with enormous fireplace, the dining room where delectable Tuscan country meals are served (€20), and an upstairs loggia with a panoramic view over the countryside, which seems to take in all of Tuscany. Three apartments are available for weekly stays. For those who enjoy spectacular scenery in a very special, historical setting, this is the place. *Directions:* From the Florence-Siena highway exit at Colle Val d'Elsa Sud. Follow signs for Grosseto-Radicondoli-Castelnuova Val di Cecina, then Fattoria Solaio.

FATTORIA SOLAIO
Hosts: Vittoria & Vitaliano Visconti
Solaio–Radicondoli (SI) 53030, Italy
Tel: (0577) 791029, Fax: (0577) 791015
9 rooms, Double: €85–€114
3 apartments: €100 daily
Minimum nights required: 2
Open: Mar to Nov, Credit cards: all major
Other languages: good English
Region: Tuscany, Michelin Map: 430
www.karenbrown.com/italy/fattoriasolaio.html

The town of Spoleto has gained international fame thanks to the July Due Mondi festival, a month-long series of cultural events including ballet, theater, opera, and concerts with renowned artists, which attracts a worldwide audience. Accommodations are reserved from one year to the next. For the rest of the year, however, Spoleto holds its own along with nearby Assisi, Spello, Todi, and Perugia as an enchanting medieval stone town, rich in its historical past. The 14th-century Palazzo Dragoni, situated on a quiet little street in the heart of the town near the famous cathedral, was completely renovated by the Diotallevi family and offers charming accommodation within 15 bedrooms. Son Roberto manages the bed and breakfast while his parents reside in a section of the palazzo. The spacious bedrooms (larger ones are considered suites) are spread out among the three floors, reached by elevator, and have new bathrooms and many modern amenities including air conditioning. Everything possible has been done to maintain the original architecture and ambiance of a private home, with vaulted and frescoed high ceilings, antique furnishings, Oriental carpets, and Murano chandeliers. The real treat is breakfast served in the glassed-in loggia, taking in splendid views of the tiled rooftops and bell tower of the Duomo. *Directions:* Follow signs for the center of Spoleto, by way of Via P. Bunilli, passing the football field (campo sportivo). Follow white signs for the hotel.

❄ ☕ ✂ ♨ 💳 ☎ 🐕 ♿ 🚶 🏇 ☿ 𝐏 🏞 🔔 🍇

PALAZZO DRAGONI
Host: Roberto Diotallevi family
Via del Duomo 13
Spoleto (PG) 06049, Italy
Tel: (0743) 222220, Fax: (0743) 222225
15 rooms, Double: €120–€150
Open: all year, Credit cards: MC, VS
Other languages: some English
Region: Umbria, Michelin Map: 430
www.karenbrown.com/italy/dragoni.html

On the border of Liguria and Piedmont and conveniently located near the Genoa-Milan autostrada sits the hillside property of friendly hosts, Domenico and Rosanna, national vice president of the regional agritourism association. The house is immersed in woods at the end of a long gravel road and is barely visible through the ivy and rose vines that conceal it—a true spectacle in late May. This gives just a hint of one of Rosanna's two passions: cooking and gardening, both of which guests can participate in by taking lessons. Two bedrooms are situated in the main farmhouse dating to 1714 and in Rosanna's family since that time. The apartments with exposed beams are located next door in the converted barn and are all decorated in pleasant country style with antiques and family memorabilia. Guests sit down together en famille at a long table to taste one of Rosanna's delectable meals prepared with their own fresh, organically-grown produce from the garden (Domenico's passion). Guests/friends are made to feel right at home in this informal and tranquil atmosphere, where silence and privacy are highly respected and guests become a natural part of the farm's everyday life. A small pool is hidden in lush vegetation just behind the house. *Directions:* Exit the A7 autostrada (Milano-Genova) at Vignole Borbera, following the sign for Stazzano (4 km). Turn right in town at the traffic light and follow the bed and breakfast sign for 2 km on an unpaved road.

LA TRAVERSINA
Hosts: Rosanna & Domenico Varese
Localita: Traversina 109, Stazzano (AL) 15060, Italy
Tel & fax: (0143) 61377, Cellphone: (335) 494295
2 rooms, Double: €82–€98
4 apartments: €105–€168 daily
Per person half board: €60–€80
Open: all year, Credit cards: all major
Other languages: some English
Region: Piedmont, Michelin Map: 428
www.karenbrown.com/italy/traversina.html

The well-preserved medieval village of Stroncone sits on the southernmost edge of Umbria bordering Lazio, 7 kilometers from Terni. It is here that Cristiana from Genoa and her film-producer husband, Massimiliano, whose parents were originally from this area, bought and restored an ancient building in the stone village and opened a charming bed and breakfast. The eight bedrooms are divided among the top three floors of the medieval building, which centuries ago was once the police station. The old wooden doors of the cells remain intact and are part of the small reception and breakfast room where a buffet table holds breads and cakes each morning. Each bedroom is unique in size and pastel color scheme, with stenciled borders, new bathrooms, and variations according to the original architecture, with either brick-vaulted or wood-beamed ceilings. A mansard bedroom on the top floor offers privacy and rooftop views over the village, besides being the only bedroom with air conditioning (the others remain naturally cool with the thick stone walls). The hosts organize a week-long painting course with daily excursions taking advantage of the scenic surrounding landscapes and villages. Attractions in the area include highlights of Umbria as well as the Etruscan territory surrounding Viterbo (Tuscia). *Directions:* Stroncone is 9 km directly south of Terni. The B&B is on Via del Sacramento, the main street of the village.

LA PORTA DEL TEMPO
Hosts: Cristiana & Massimiliano Brunelli
Via del Sacramento 2
Stroncone (TR) 05039, Italy
Tel: (0744) 608190, Fax: (0744) 609034
8 rooms, Double: €80–€110
Open: all year, Credit cards: all major
Other languages: good English
Region: Umbria, Michelin Map: 430
www.karenbrown.com/italy/portadeltempo.html

Nowadays the owners of agritourism operations are increasingly city people rather than local farmers but Il Tondino, by contrast, goes back to tradition, with simple and informal hospitality and board offered on the farmland of a local family. Andrea, his two brothers, and his father divide up the chores on the ranch between them, attending to guests, cooking, caring for the horses, and producing cereal and grains. The property is comprised of three buildings: the family's brick house with attached restaurant in the former barn, the stables with guest living room/game area above, and a small guesthouse with three pleasant air-conditioned bedrooms with quilts, rustic wood furniture, and new bathrooms. Five new rooms have been created out of the barn and have wrought-iron beds and characteristic beamed ceilings. A low-ceilinged apartment on the lower level of the main house is also available, although very dark. All pasta and breads are homemade and served at long tables in the cheery dining room with yellow-sponged walls and brick-vaulted ceilings. In the area famous for the production and worldwide distribution of Parmesan cheese and Parma prosciutto, eating well has never been a problem. The castles of Parma are among the many treasures in the area to explore. *Directions:* Exit from the A1 at Fidenza and head towards Salsamaggiore until the sign for Tabiano. After 3 km turn left at the Il Tondino sign and drive for another 4.5 km to the farm.

※ ♨ ⚒ ♨ 〦 P ⑪ ⚓ ♿ 〒

IL TONDINO
Host: Andrea Bertoletti
Localita: Tabiano 58
Tabiano–Fidenza (PR) 43036, Italy
Tel & fax: (0524) 62106
8 rooms, Double: €75–€80, 1 apartment
Minimum nights required: 2
Open: Mar to Oct
Other languages: some English
Region: Emilia-Romagna, Michelin Map: 429
www.karenbrown.com/italy/tondino.html

Halfway between Florence and Siena in the heart of the Chianti region is the Sovigliano farm, restored by a gracious couple from Verona, Claudio Bicego and his wife, Patrizia, and daughter, Claudia. Guests have an independent entrance to the four bedrooms with kitchenette, each very much in keeping with the pure simplicity of this typical farmhouse. Exposed-beam ceilings and worn terra-cotta floors, antique beds and armoires, and bucolic views make time stand still here. Besides three apartments (two with air conditioning) in a separate farmhouse, there is also a spacious two-bedroom apartment within the house with kitchen and dining area and fireplace. At guests' disposal are a living room, kitchen with country fireplace, TV, large surrounding garden with swimming pool and hydrojet, exercise trail, and outdoor eating area overlooking the characteristic hills of Chianti. Signor Bicego is actively involved in the production of top Tuscan wines in conjunction with several other wine estates, and also coordinates with other area residents to organize lessons in language, history, and culinary arts with local professors. *Directions:* From Siena, exit the superstrada at San Donato in Poggio; from Florence at Tavarnelle Val di Pesa. Drive through the village of Tavarnelle following the directions to Certaldo-Marcialla. At the end of Tavarnelle, at the third traffic circle, veer to the left (blue sign says Magliano), following signs for Sovigliano.

❄ 🍺 ☕ CREDIT 🍕 🚶 🐎 🍷 P 🏊 🏠

SOVIGLIANO
Hosts: Patrizia & Claudio Bicego
Via Magliano 9, Tavarnelle Val di Pesa (FI) 50028, Italy
Tel: (055) 8076217, Fax: (055) 8050770
4 rooms, Double: €120–€140
4 apartments: €840–€1,050 weekly B&B
Minimum nights required: 3
Closed: Jan 15 to 31, Credit cards: MC, VS
Other languages: good English
Region: Tuscany, Michelin Map: 430
www.karenbrown.com/italy/sovigliano.html

With their hearts set on running a bed and breakfast in the Liguria region, the Giani family searched hard and long before finding Giandriale. Set high up in the remote mountains above the coast, the 18th-century stone farmhouse is surrounded by a low range of mountains covered with thick woods as far as the eye can see. Utter silence prevails. There are just two guestrooms within their home and five others plus two apartments in the refurbished stone barn, simply decorated with country-style wooden furniture. Guests can relax in one of two comfortable living rooms. Meals are enjoyed in the downstairs dining room with its old-fashioned country stove, which is used occasionally in winter for making polenta. Lucia prepares coffee cakes and jams for breakfast and uses mostly regional recipes in her cooking, taking advantage of their own organic produce. Classic sightseeing destinations in the area include the Riviera (Portofino, Santa Margherita, Chiavari) and the Cinque Terre, 45 minutes away. Nereo can also suggest several interesting off-the-beaten-track itineraries beyond Giandriale. Hiking trails and mountain bikes are available. *Directions:* From autostrada A14, exit at Sestri Levante and follow signs for Casarza Ligure, Castiglione, then, after 2 km and many curves, Missano. After a long tunnel turn right for Tavarone and just before town follow B&B signs for 2.5 km.

GIANDRIALE
Hosts: Lucia Marelli & Nereo Giani
Localita: Giandriale, Tavarone di Maissana (SP) 19010, Italy
Tel: (0187) 840279, Cellphone: (339) 5324177
Fax: (0187) 840156
7 rooms, Double: €60, 2 apartments: €37 daily (per person)
Minimum nights required: 4 in Jul & Aug
Open: all year, Credit cards: all major
Other languages: some English
Region: Liguria, Michelin Map: 428
www.karenbrown.com/italy/giandriale.html

In order to stand out among the crowd of recently opened bed and breakfasts in Italy, many hosts have begun to specialize according to their own personal interests. This is true for enthusiastic and friendly hosts, Alberto and his Brazilian wife Luzia, who opened a gourmet vegetarian bed and breakfast on their isolated 27-acre farm up on a mountain ridge between Perugia and Lake Trasimeno, the first of its kind in Umbria. A 4-kilometer gravel road ends at the panoramic property with its main house, two stone guesthouses, and cultural center where courses on yoga and meditation and ethnic music concerts are held. Under the direction of Luzia, an architect, a good part of the construction and restoration was done "in house." An informal ambiance prevails and the total respect for nature and tranquillity is evident among guests who take hikes in the surrounding woods or read poolside, enjoying both sunrise and sunset over the opposite valleys. The ten neat rooms with independent outside entrances are comfortably decorated with teak-wood beds and armoires and the paintings of a reputed artist. The sun-filled dining room is where guests convene for Luzia's and Alberto's famed fare based on strictly organic produce from the farm. So unique is this bed and breakfast that the BBC did a special documentary on it. *Directions:* From Perugia follow route 220 for approximately 22 km and turn right before Tavernelle at Colle San Paolo.

MONTALI
Hosts: Luzia & Alberto Musacchio
Via Montali 2, Tavernelle di Panicale (PG) 06068, Italy
Tel: (075) 8350680, Fax: (075) 8350144
10 rooms, Double: €136–€156*
*Includes breakfast & dinner
Minimum nights required: 3
Open: Mar to Oct, Credit cards: MC, VS
Other languages: good English
Region: Umbria, Michelin Map: 430
www.karenbrown.com/italy/montali.html

Another one of Italy's best-kept secrets is the Cinque Terre coastline of southern Liguria bordering Tuscany, though this beautiful and quite unique area is now gaining increasing popularity. Its five quaint stone villages hugging the hillside as it sweeps down to the sea were, until recently, accessible only by boat or by foot and are a delight to explore. Just south of the area right on the Poet's Gulf is the adorable seaside town of Tellaro hugging the rock over the sea, where visitors make a point of stopping to have a memorable meal at the Miranda restaurant. Husband-and-wife team Giovanna and Angelo have their own inimitable and ever-varying style of cooking based exclusively on fresh seafood (no meat), which is present in the inexhaustible series of antipasti and pasta plates. Angelo has received plenty of press and praise (Michelin star) for these extraordinary dishes. Meals are served in one of the newly renovated dining rooms, pleasantly appointed with scattered antiques. In the same vein are the bedrooms, most with gulf view, which Aunt Miranda used to rent out and are now in the capable hands of son, Alessandro. Guests have a cozy living room with fireplace for relaxing. Upon prior request, personalized cooking courses can be arranged. Reserve well in advance. *Directions:* Leave the A12 autostrada at Sarzana, following signs for Lerici on route 331. Tellaro is 4.5 km down the coast and the Miranda is on the main road before town.

LOCANDA MIRANDA
Hosts: Angelo & Giovanna Cabani
Via Fiascherino 92
Tellaro (SP) 19030, Italy
Tel: (0187) 968130 or 964012, Fax: (0187) 964032
7 rooms, Double: €225*
*Includes breakfast & dinner
Closed: Jan, Credit cards: all major
Other languages: good English
Region: Liguria, Michelin Map: 428
www.karenbrown.com/italy/locandamiranda.html

Country tourism has flourished in the last decade, especially in the highly popular region of Tuscany. However, most travelers still flock to the Chianti area, leaving many other parts of Tuscany wide open to discovery. Such is the gorgeous virgin territory of the Valdera Valley between stunning Volterra with its Etruscan origins and Pisa where everything has remained remarkably unspoiled. Affable host Sandro and his family bought a 100-acre farm property here and are restoring the ancient farmhouses piece by piece with guests' comfort foremost in mind. So far, eight neat apartments with one or two bedrooms and five guest bedrooms have been completed within three adjacent stone houses and are tastefully appointed with local antiques. Within one of the houses is the pleasant dining room with large arched windows where breakfast and dinners upon request are served, all prepared by Sandro's mother, who also conducts cooking lessons. Olive oil, wine, fruits, and vegetables all come directly from the farm. There is a beautiful borderless swimming pool and Sandro supplies guests with mountain bikes and a long list of interesting local itineraries. Easy day trips include Florence, Siena, San Gimignano, Lucca, Pisa and Volterra, famous for its alabaster artisans. *Directions:* Il Selvino is located off the main road 439 from Volterra (20 km) between Terricciola and La Sterza at Pieve a Pitti (marked on most maps).

IL SELVINO
Host: Alessandro Sgherri family
Localita: La Sterza, Via Pieve a Pitti 1
Terricciola (PI) 56030, Italy
Tel & fax: (0587) 670132, Cellphone: (338) 6209229
5 rooms, Double: €145, 8 apartments: €166–€207 daily
Minimum nights required: 3
Open: all year, Credit cards: MC, VS
Other languages: some English
Region: Tuscany, Michelin Map: 430
www.karenbrown.com/italy/ilselvino.html

Practically 70 percent of the families residing in the Alto Adige mountain region offer bed-and-breakfast accommodations so, unless it's Christmas or August, a bed is not hard to come by. This is a region with a distinct Austrian flavor where more German than Italian is spoken, and where more wurstel than pasta is likely to be served at the table. Signora Trompedeller welcomes international travelers to her typical Tyrolean-style home. The six simple guestrooms upstairs each have a private bath and are modestly decorated with basic light-wood furniture and down comforters—a decor common to the bed and breakfasts in this region. The small wood-paneled dining room boasts a splendid panoramic view over the mountain cliffs and green foothills. The house with adjacent barn for the cows is located several kilometers outside the quaint town of Tires on a road that comes to an end at a babbling brook surrounded by hushed woods with hiking trails. Depending on the season, guests can take advantage of the Val Gardena ski slopes or summer mountain climbing. *Directions:* From the Verona-Brennero autostrada, exit at Bolzano Nord and follow signs for Tiers. Go through the town and after 2 km make a hairpin left turn at the chapel and backtrack on a parallel road to the end.

VERALTENHOF
Host: Josef Trompedeller family
Oberstrasse 61
Tires (Tiers) (BZ) 39050, Italy
Tel & fax: (0471) 642102, Cellphone (348) 7694704
6 rooms, Double: €38–€48
Per person half board: €31–€35
Open: all year
Other languages: German
Region: Trentino-Alto Adige, Michelin Map: 429
www.karenbrown.com/italy/veraltenhof.html

Since 1830, the remote 12th-century castle and 4,000-acre farm of Titignano have belonged to the noble Corsini family who now offer travelers 15 guestrooms in the main house, a swimming pool, and three apartments in what was originally the farmer's quarters. They are pleasantly decorated with scattered country antiques. Management is in the hands of Monica and Francesca, delightful hostesses who take care of everything from looking after guests to cooking and serving. Meals are shared at a long table in one of the castle's graciously neglected rooms with an enormous gray-stone fireplace sporting the family coat of arms, and lofty ceilings made of the stamped terra-cotta blocks typical of Umbria. Off the dining hall are the spacious bedrooms, each with modernized pink travertine bathrooms and decorated eclectically with unrefined antiques and wrought-iron beds. They have a worn charm about them. Common areas include a living room with bright floral sofas around a fireplace, a game and TV room for children, and a large terrace with a breathtaking, sweeping view covering three regions. Bikes are available for touring the regional park of the River Tiber (part of the property). *Directions:* Leave the Roma-Florence A1 autostrada at Orvieto. Follow signs for Arezzo, turning on route 79 for Prodo. Follow the long winding road for 26 km past Prodo to Titignano. (30 km from Orvieto.)

FATTORIA TITIGNANO
Hosts: Monica Gori & Francesca Marchetti
Localita: Titignano 7
Titignano—Orvieto (TR) 05010, Italy
Tel: (0763) 308000 or 308022, Fax: (0763) 308002
15 rooms, Double: €94–€90, 3 apartments: €103 daily
Minimum nights required: 2
Open: all year, Credit cards: MC, VS
Other languages: some English, French
Region: Umbria, Michelin Map: 430
www.karenbrown.com/italy/titignano.html

In the midst of the bucolic countryside surrounding Todi sits the refined bed and breakfast of Poggio d'Asproli. Bruno Pagliari, a sculptor with a long family history in the hotel business, transferred his family from Naples to this 16th-century stone farmhouse and ex-convent several years ago and has succeeded in his aim of creating elegant but comfortable surroundings to make guests feel at home. Each of the romantic guestrooms is unique in style and decor. Rich fabrics draped at bedheads give a canopy effect with matching bedspreads and nice big bathrooms have travertine marble sinks. The home is filled to the brim with antiques and lovely artwork (some by Bruno's sister, Lilli), which blend in well with the stone walls, worn brick floors, and beamed ceilings. Breakfast and candlelit dinners are served either on the outside terrace or in the elegant dining room. At one end is a cozy sitting area with white sofas around an enormous fireplace. A swimming pool among the trees is a cool spot for relaxing. Daughter Claudia has now taken over the general management of the bed and breakfast. *Directions:* From Todi, follow signs for Orvieto and take a left at the sign for Izzalini. Before town, take the turning for Asproli and follow signs to the bed and breakfast.

POGGIO D'ASPROLI
Host: Claudia Pagliari
Localita: Asproli
Todi (PG) 06059, Italy
Tel & fax: (075) 8853385
8 rooms, Double: €109
Open: Mar 15 to Jan 3, Credit cards: all major
Other languages: good English
Region: Umbria, Michelin Map: 430
www.karenbrown.com/italy/asproli.html

Fortunate guests at the fascinating Tenuta di Canonica are assured of an unforgettable stay. Maria and Daniele, with son Michelangelo, have transformed a massive stone tower with foundation dating to the ancient Roman period and adjoining century-old house into a bed and breakfast of dreams. The spacious living room with stone fireplace and vaulted ceiling is reached down a few stairs from the entryway and looks out over the stunning valley down to Lake Corbara. Outstanding medieval architectural features such as stone walls, brick floors, and high, beamed ceilings have been enhanced by Provence-inspired colors. Stairs lead up to the library and bedrooms are divided between the three-story tower and house, respecting the epoch of each: bathrooms in the medieval quarters have gray stone tiles and travertine, while the others have white tile alternating with terra-cotta pieces. Each tastefully decorated, antique-filled room has some attractive feature, whether it be the more suite-like arrangements with sitting area or the smaller corner rooms with head-spinning views over hills and up to Todi. Common areas include a dining room and large swimming pool with 360-degree views. Cooking classes with a Cordon Bleu cook are also arranged. *Directions:* From Todi take the road for Orvieto, turning right at the sign for Prado/Titignano. After 2 km turn left for Cordigliano and follow the signpost for Tenuta di Canonica to the end of the road (1 km).

TENUTA DI CANONICA
Hosts: Maria & Daniele Fano
Localita: Canonica
Todi (PG) 06059, Italy
Tel: (075) 8947545, Cellphone: (335) 369492
Fax: (075) 8947581
11 rooms, Double: €125, 2 apartments
Open: all year, Credit cards: MC, VS
Other languages: good English
Region: Umbria, Michelin Map: 430
www.karenbrown.com/italy/canonicatodi.html

On the northern shores of Lake Bracciano, 45 kilometers from Rome, is the small town of Trevignano where ex-producer and music director Gianni's home is located a short drive up from town, taking advantage of the high viewpoint over the lake and surrounding countryside. The simpatico host's true passion is cooking and entertaining and guests are rewarded each day with a superbly prepared full meal based on traditional recipes whose ingredients come from his own organic vegetable garden and accompanied by select wines. Gianni also shares his vast knowledge of Italian cuisine by organizing lessons in his well-equipped kitchen. The six bedrooms on the upper two floors vary in size, from the smaller children's rooms to the master bedroom with Jacuzzi tub, terrace, and lovely lake views. True coziness and comfort is dedicated to the common areas, which include several living rooms with fireplace and grand piano, veranda dining room, garden, and swimming pool. There is one small apartment for weekly stays with double bedroom and living area with kitchenette for two to four persons. Enjoy the area's historical villages and Viterbo's thermal spas. *Directions:* From Rome's ring highway GRA take exit 5 for S.S.2 Cassia bis to km 35,100. After the Campagnano exit leave at the Trevignano exit and drive 11.3 km to Trevignano. Continue through town to km 1400 and turn right on Via Olivetello before the IP gas station. A detailed map is sent to you.

CASA PLAZZI
Host: Gianni Plazzi family
Via Olivetello 23
Trevignano, Romano (RM) 06069, Italy
Tel: (06) 9997597, Cellphone: (335) 6756290
Fax: (06) 99910196
6 rooms, Double: €94–€134, 1 apartment: €700 weekly
Open: all year
Other languages: some English
Region: Lazio, Michelin Map: 430
www.karenbrown.com/italy/plazzi.html

The Veneto region has so much to offer travelers in art, history, and culture, yet remains terribly weak when it comes to charming bed and breakfasts. This is mainly due to the very strict regulations particular to this region. The Ca'Masieri is a pleasant combination of both hotel and bed-and-breakfast-like accommodation in a country setting. The countryside property has been in the Zarantonello family for three generations and was transformed into a restaurant and inn after Signor Giovanni looked for a creative way to maintain the farm. He and his partner, Angelo, opened the restaurant first, creating an intimate ambiance within three stenciled dining rooms in the main villa. The restaurant gained considerable recognition and the next logical step was to offer a place to stay in the stone farmhouse right next door. These two buildings and the attached barn form a quadrangle, with a gated-in terraced swimming pool. The seven bedrooms are very comfortable with many amenities, though their modern decor contrasts with the country setting. The five new suites in the adjoining wing (former stables) are more in keeping with the general ambiance of the place. Signor Giovanni is also on Vicenza's tourism board and can suggest many itineraries in the area (villas of Palladio etc.). *Directions:* Exit from autostrada A4 at Montecchio and go towards Valdagno. After exactly 10 km enter the town of Trissino and follow signs for Masieri up to the Ca'Masieri.

CA'MASIERI
Hosts: Giovanni Zarantonello & Angelo Vassena
Localita: Masieri
Trissino (VI) 36070, Italy
Tel: (0445) 962100 or 490122, Fax: (0445) 490455
12 rooms, Double: €104–€170
Open: all year, Credit cards: all major
Other languages: good English
Region: Veneto, Michelin Map: 429
www.karenbrown.com/italy/camasieri.html

La Dogana means customs house in Italian, and the fascinating history of this 16th-century building—which until 1870 served as the Papal customs house for travelers through the Grand Duchy of Tuscany—boasts visits from luminary artists such as Michelangelo, Goethe, Byron, and Stendhal. The 100-acre property belongs to young hosts Emanuele and Paola and, aside from the main villa, includes a stone farmhouse and a building near the stables across the street. In these two "extra" buildings 25 apartment-suites have been created. The guest quarters vary widely in condition, but all feature a living area, kitchen, bathroom, and sleeping accommodations for two to six people. Each apartment is unique in decor, containing mixed antiques, prints, old sofas, and wrought-iron beds. Up on a hillside, guests have a lovely view over Lake Trasimeno whose encircling highway is audible even from here. In the summer months a dining room serving lunch and dinner is open. A small pool for children is on the premises or one can always take a dip in the lake. *Directions:* From Perugia, take N75 toward Florence, exiting at Tuoro. Turn left at the first intersection, continuing 3 km to La Dogana on the right side of the road.

LA DOGANA
Host: Marchese Emanuele de Ferrari
Via Dogana 4
Tuoro Sul Trasimeno (PG) 06069, Italy
Tel: (075) 8230158, Cellphone: (330) 280845
Fax: (075) 8230252
25 apartments: €240–€600 weekly (Jul & Aug)
Restaurant summer only, Open: all year
Other languages: good English
Region: Umbria, Michelin Map: 430
www.karenbrown.com/italy/ladogana.html

When the Marti family from Rome came across the abandoned castle of Montegualandro 18 years ago, it was love at first sight—only pure passion could have driven them to tackle such an overwhelming project as the entire restoration of the property following original plans. A winding dirt road (1.5 kilometers) leads up to the gates of the walled 9th-century castle. As you enter into the open circular courtyard, the main building and family residence lies to the left and immediately to the right is the long stone house, originally farmer's quarters, with small tower, stable, pottery kiln, dove house, and private chapel. Four apartments have been fashioned for guests, cleverly incorporating all original architectural features. All different, each has a living area with fireplace, kitchen, and bathroom and is characteristically furnished with country-style antiques. A walk up in the turreted walls gives a glimpse of the spectacular view out over olive groves to the lake. The Martis' daughter, Cristiana, takes special interest in guests' needs, suggesting easy day trips from the castle. Lovely Cortona is just 10 kilometers away. *Directions:* Montegualandro is marked on most maps. Leave the A1-Perugia highway at Tuoro. Take the road 75 bis towards Cortona and Arezzo. After 3 km, at km sign 44,700, take the road marked Fonte S. Angelo up to the castle or call from town.

CASTELLO DI MONTEGUALANDRO
Hosts: Franca & Claudio Marti
Via di Montegualandro 1
Tuoro Sul Trasimeno (PG) 06069, Italy
Tel & fax: (075) 8230267, Cellphone: (347) 2372070
4 apartments: €550–€660 weekly
Minimum nights required: 3
Open: all year
Other languages: good English
Region: Umbria, Michelin Map: 430
www.karenbrown.com/italy/castellodimontegualandro.html

The city of Turin, at one time the capital of Italy under the Savoia monarchy, is one of the country's leading industrial cities (home of Fiat), but is also home to a wealth of cultural events, museums (the Egyptian museum has the largest collection in Europe), and important monuments. Once you get past the rather dreary outskirts, the historic center is filled with monumental squares, baroque architecture, Medieval quarters, the Royal Palace, theatres, and art galleries. Natural hostess and interior decorator Maddalena Vitale, with her children all grown, found herself with a large centrally located apartment just right for a bed and breakfast. She happily receives international guests in her tastefully appointed home within three bedrooms, each with private bathroom (only one en suite). The apartment lends itself well to the enterprise since the guest wing is separate from the hostess's private quarters. Double bedrooms named for their color scheme (blue, green, and white), two with twin beds, are very personalized and individual as in a private home with family photos, antique furnishings, and paintings. Breakfast with homemade breads and cakes is served in the rooms. Maddalena is an excellent source of information on the city's current events, best restaurants, or day trips into the nearby Langhe wine country. A true home in the city. *Directions:* In the center of Turin, four blocks from the train station. (30 minutes from Turin airport.)

LA MADDALENA   *New*
Host: Maddalena Vitale Marrone
Via San Secondo 31
Turin 10128, Italy
Tel & fax: (011) 591267, Cellphone: (333) 2469532
3 rooms, Double: €120–€160
Other languages: good English, French
Region: Piedmont
www.karenbrown.com/italy/maddalena.html

The area of Lazio north of Rome known as "Tuscia" is rich in Etruscan history, small medieval villages, nature reserves, and three picturesque lakes. It is the homeland of the illustrious and powerful Farnese family whose palazzos and fortresses still stand as monuments of their glorious past. In the heart of this fascinating area not far from the coast is the ancient walled town of Tuscania, completely restored after the dramatic earthquake in 1978. Perla and her Argentine husband José brought back to life one of the buildings right in town, opening its doors as a cozy bed and breakfast and Michelin-star restaurant. A small reception area leads on one side to a lounge and wine bar (over 200 labels) and a courtyard. On the other side you find the cheerful, luminous restaurant with checked drapes and tablecloths, antique armoire, still-life paintings, large windows looking out over the tiled rooftops, and ubiquitous gallo (rooster) motif. Here José works his magic, serving innovative creations using seasonal local produce. (A 10% discount is given to our readers on meals.) Upstairs each very comfortable and appealing carpeted bedroom has its own color scheme in matching floral wallpaper, drapery, and bedspread. They have all amenities including air conditioning and are spacious, with high ceilings and marble bathrooms. Gracious hostess Perla guarantees guests' comfort and assists them in arranging local itineraries. *Directions:* In the center of Tuscania, well marked.

HOTEL AL GALLO
Hosts: Perla Blanzieri & José Pettiti
Via del Gallo 22
Tuscania (VT) 01017, Italy
Tel: (0761) 443388, Fax: (0761) 443628
13 rooms, Double: €90–€123
Restaurant closed Mon
Open: all year, Credit cards: all major
Other languages: good English
Region: Lazio, Michelin Map: 430
www.karenbrown.com/italy/algallo.html

Those who have fallen in love with the enchanting countryside of Tuscany but found its roads too well traveled should investigate the northern part of the Marches surrounding Urbino. The scenery is magnificent, the ancient towns perfectly preserved, and the ambiance authentic. The Benedetti-Blasi families, hard-working farmers, have dedicated themselves to balancing a productive farm with a bed and breakfast. The brother's side of the family tends to the fields, while Alberto, his wife Maria, and their two sons Andrea and Samuele see to the guests. Three simple terra-cotta-roofed gray houses make up the farm, and horses, cows, sheep, and even peacocks roam the grounds. The guestrooms, each with private bath, are spartan, and the decor uninspired, but the genuine familial warmth of the hospitality, the excellent home cooking, and the value compensate. Two small apartments are also available. In the rustic dining room with red-checked tablecloths or out on the porch overlooking the gently rolling, wooded countryside, guests indulge in Maria's spinach ravioli or hand-cut tagliatelle with mushroom sauce, fresh-baked flat bread, and local wine. This no-frills bed and breakfast is an economical choice for those who seek simplicity and authentic farm life. *Directions:* From Urbania head for Acqualagna and turn off right after town to Orsaiola (6 km of country road).

L'ORSAIOLA
Hosts: Benedetti & Blasi families
Localita: Orsaiola
Urbania (PS) 61049, Italy
Tel & fax: (0722) 318988, Cellphone: (339) 2230049
9 rooms, Double: €59
2 apartments: €525–€700 weekly (2 to 4 people)
Open: Mar to Dec
Other languages: very little English
Region: Marches, Michelin Map: 430
www.karenbrown.com/italy/lorsaiola.html

The Aiola opened its doors to guests six years ago when the Campellis restored the farmers' houses on the wine estate's vast property in Chianti. The family's villa with its ancient origins sits across the street from the guest quarters, almost completely hidden by enormous oak and cypress trees, where the bedrooms, one of which sleeps four persons, all have separate outside entrances. Original architectural features have been preserved and rooms are decorated with wrought-iron beds and antique or reproduction armoires. The vineyards come right up to the house and a wide, open view of the hills is offered to the other side. The barn next door includes common areas such as the breakfast room, where Federica's fresh-baked coffee cakes are served, and a living room. With Federica's mother, Signora Malagodi, being the President of the Wine Tourism Association, visits to the cellar and the villa, and wine tasting begin right here at the Aiola. Federica and Enrico aim to make each guest feel special, dedicating much time to suggesting itineraries with maps and making reservations at restaurants, museums, and local concerts. At 12 kilometers from Siena and an easy distance from the highlights of the region, the Aiola serves as an excellent touring base. Total silence reigns here, with only the buzz of cicadas breaking it. *Directions:* From Siena follow route 102 just past Vagliagli—the Aiola property (well marked) is on this same road.

CASALI DELLA AIOLA
Hosts: Federica & Enrico Campelli
Vagliagli (SI) 53010, Italy
Tel: (0577) 322797, Fax: (0577) 322509
8 rooms, Double: €88–€134
Open: all year, Credit cards: all major
Other languages: good English
Region: Tuscany, Michelin Map: 430
www.karenbrown.com/italy/laaiola.html

Varenna is a quaint little village sitting halfway up Lake Como's eastern edge. It is situated at the point where the ferryboats for cars cross over to the other side of the lake to Menaggio. In the main piazza lakeside is the generations-old family-run Olivedo hotel with its pale-yellow façade where Signora Laura welcomes her guests. Time seems to have stood still within its old-fashioned interior. The reception area and side bar are dressed with faded floral wallpaper, scattered antiques, and a large grandfather clock chiming the hour. Off to the other side of the reception area is a dining room/restaurant with simple frescoes, serving all meals. A curved stairway takes guests up to the bedrooms, most with en-suite bathroom and lake views. These are decorated simply with grandmother's furniture and old prints. There is no need to worry about noise except on Saturday nights since traffic is not allowed in the piazza. Bathrooms are being progressively renewed and added. Olivedo serves as a good, economical base from which to explore beautiful Lake Como including its many gardens (Villa Serbelloni, Melzi, and Carlotta). *Directions:* From the Como branch of the lake, head north on either side of lake and take the ferry over from either Bellagio or Menaggio.

OLIVEDO
Host: Colombo family
Piazza Martiri 4, Varenna (LC) 23829, Italy
Tel & fax: (0341) 830115
14 rooms, Double: €86–€116
Per person half board: €70–€80
Minimum nights required: 2
Closed: mid-Nov to mid-Dec
Other languages: good English
Region: Lombardy, Michelin Map: 428
www.karenbrown.com/italy/olivedo.html

It is a pleasure to be able to include such a perfectly efficient, family-run hotel as the Due Fanali, located in a lovely square next to the 12th-century San Simeon church with its original Tintoretto painting. The hotel is housed in a 12th-century palazzo, once part of the church complex. The Feron family had the building lovingly restored seven years ago to include the sixteen bedrooms (some with smaller "French" double) on the top three floors. A small elevator has been added for the convenience of guests. Extra care has been taken in the selection of appropriate antiques for the guestrooms, reception area, and breakfast room. The soft ambiance is that of an elegant yet warm home, accentuated by lovely Oriental carpets and rich-cream draperies. Breakfast is taken either out in the "garden" in front of the hotel or up in the delightful third-floor veranda, under the open terrace, with its superb view over the square to the Grand Canal. As an alternative to the hotel, there are four independent apartments near San Marco Square, divinely decorated and including bedroom, living room with view, kitchenette, and bathroom with hydromassage tub. Take all these esthetic elements accompanied by the exceptional hospitality offered by Signora Marina and her daughter, Stefania, and you have a true winner of a hotel. *Directions:* The hotel is a five-minute walk from the train station or you can take the No. 1 waterbus to the Riva di Biasio stop.

❄ ⚓ 🍴 🛎 💳 ☎ 🐕 👫 🏃 🍷 🚭 🏃 🚿 🍇 🎋

HOTEL AI DUE FANALI
Host: Marina Feron family
Santa Croce 946
Venice 30135, Italy
Tel: (041) 718344, Fax: (041) 718490
16 rooms, Double: €160–€207
4 apartments: €197–€380 daily
Closed: Jan, Credit cards: all major
Other languages: good English
Region: Veneto, Michelin Map: 429
www.karenbrown.com/italy/fanali.html

Your attractive young host, Giuliano Dall'Agnola, managed a hotel on the Lido in Venice for ten years before deciding to open his own in an historic 5th-century building. The building needed total renovation, but Giuliano was wise in his choice of location—it's perfect—tucked onto a tiny side street just steps from Piazza San Marco. Don't be put off by the exterior: it is an unimpressive gray building with a nondescript door. The entry hall too is quite simple, with a check-in counter and a staircase leading to the upper floors. But here the surprise awaits: the rooms, decorated by Marcella, are amazingly attractive and offer great quality for such a well-priced hotel in the heart of Venice. All the walls are covered in fabric and enhanced by color-coordinated draperies and bedspreads, while Venetian-style furnishings including painted headboards and Murano glass chandeliers complete the appealing ambiance. The amenities too far outshine what one would expect from a budget hotel. The soundproof rooms are air-conditioned, have direct-dial phones, mini bars, televisions, and well-equipped, modern bathrooms. All of the rooms are sweet, some with views overlooking a small square. What makes this intimate hotel so special is the care of its owners who pamper guests like friends in their home. *Directions:* San Zaccaria vaporetto stop on all vaporetto boat lines, including the Alilaguna boats from the airport. The hotel is just 50 meters from the stop.

LOCANDA AL LEON
Hosts: Marcella & Giuliano Dall'Agnola
Castello, Campo St Filippo e Giacomo
Venice 30122, Italy
Tel: (041) 2770393, Fax: (041) 5210348
9 rooms, Double: €90–€180
Open: all year, Credit cards: MC, VS
Other languages: good English
Region: Veneto, Michelin Map: 429
www.karenbrown.com/italy/alleon.html

With admirable determination and family pride, Alessandro and Debora took on the task of renovating and running this hotel property, which has been part of the family for three generations. They deserve great credit since they are more concerned with providing warm hospitality and attention to guests' needs than with keeping up with Venice's inflated hotel rates. The spacious and luminous reception area with white travertine floors is a welcome oasis amid the city's more cramped hotels, bustling squares, and crowded narrow streets. Although only a three-minute walk from the Guggenheim collection and Accademia, it has the feeling of being away from the mainstream traffic. The front rooms have water views (higher rate) and all rooms maintain an original flavor with paintings and personal family objects, parquet floors and matching wood furniture, blue-colored armchairs, new bathrooms, and air conditioning. Four bedrooms have private terraces for a higher rate and other guests enjoy the delightful rooftop terrace. A full buffet breakfast and bar service and light meals at La Piscina are offered either in the breakfast room with country accents or out on the large front dock terrace where you can watch the boats going by. Reserve well in advance. Comfortable suites and apartments are available in a residential quarter just across the bridge. *Directions:* Take the No. 51 waterbus to Zattere, then follow the quay to the right to the hotel terrace.

❄ ⚓ ☕ 💳 ☎ 🧍 🍴 ⚓ 🍷

PENSIONE LA CALCINA
Hosts: Debora & Alessandro Szemere
Dorsoduro 780
Venice 30123, Italy
Tel: (041) 5206466, Fax: (041) 5227045
32 rooms, Double: €130–€182
2 apartments (or suite): €1,270–€1,673 weekly
Open: all year, Credit cards: all major
Other languages: German
Region: Veneto, Michelin Map: 429
www.karenbrown.com/italy/pensionelacalcina.html

The newly renovated Locanda San Barnaba stands out among the many choices of three-star establishments in Venice. The first outstanding feature is its location in a quiet neighborhood just a half-block walk from the vaporetto stop Ca'Rezzonico on the opposite side of the Grand Canal from St. Mark's (not something to be overlooked when lugging baggage through narrow streets and over bridges in Venice). The intimate hotel in its 16th-century context has the feeling of the private home that it once was—it belonged to the grandfather of hostess Silvia—with each of its 13 guestrooms retaining its individual character. The first floor upstairs boasts a large frescoed former ballroom with stained-glass windows, very different in style from the air-conditioned bedrooms, which remain rather basic and are appointed in either pink, red, or blue hues with antique furnishings. The superior double rooms, at a slightly higher rate, have the added touch of a frescoed ceiling. A nice buffet breakfast is served in the beamed dining room or in the small walled-in courtyard garden just off the reception area, a rarity in Venice. Silvia and her amiable staff are always on hand to assist travelers with any needs. *Directions:* Take waterbus No. 1 to the Ca'Rezzonico stop. Directly in front is the Calle del Traghetto where the hotel is located on the left-hand side.

❄ ⚓ ☕ 🧺 [CREDIT] ☎ 🏌 🚭 ⚓ 🍴

LOCANDA SAN BARNABA
Host: Silvia Okolicsanyi
Calle del Traghetto 2785-2786, Dorsoduro
Venice 30124, Italy
Tel: (041) 2411233, Fax: (041) 2413812
13 rooms, Double: €130–€230
Open: all year, Credit cards: all major
Other languages: good English
Region: Veneto, Michelin Map: 429
www.karenbrown.com/italy/barnaba.html

Around the corner from the Santa Maria del Giglio square, sitting on a small private canal's edge is the small and intimate San Moise hotel, named after the nearby church. Hospitality is a tradition in the Donzello family who own three other hotels in Venice, and hostess and owner Signora Irvin obviously takes pride in her work as seen in the attention to detail of her nicely renovated accommodation. Upon entering the pale-yellow 15th-century building, you find the reception desk and the stairway up to the guestrooms immediately on the right. To the left is the very small but cozy combination lounge and breakfast room decorated with elegant antiques, Murano glass chandeliers, and walls covered with soft-pink flocked fabric. Bedrooms on the second and third floors are in the same vein with variations in the color scheme, some having the advantage of a partial canal view without the usual noise. Rooms are fully equipped with all amenities including air conditioning and satellite TV and you can even leave your gondola at the private dock! *Directions:* Take the No. 1 waterbus to stop 15, San Marco, walk straight up to Calle 22 Marzo and turn left. Pass the church on the left and turn right at the sign for the hotel.

HOTEL SAN MOISE
Host: Irvin Donzello
San Marco 2058
Venice 30124, Italy
Tel: (041) 5203755, Fax: (041) 5210670
16 rooms, Double: €100–€310
Minimum nights required: 2
Open: all year, Credit cards: all major
Other languages: fluent English, German
Region: Veneto, Michelin Map: 429
www.karenbrown.com/italy/moise.html

With just eleven rooms, including three junior suites, paired up throughout the six-floor building (luckily with an elevator), the intimate Santo Stefano was actually the watchtower to an ancient convent. The compact hotel, most recently a private home, is right in the middle of one of Venice's largest squares, leading to St. Mark's on one side and to the bridge for the Accademia on the other. Being close to the busy center, you can observe the Venetians going about their daily business. The hotel is owned by brothers Roberto and Marcello of the Hotel Celio in Rome, who have added fresh decorating touches to bedrooms and reception area. Just beyond is a miniature breakfast room, looking out to an ancient well, for days when the weather does not permit eating out in the front piazza. Touches of elegance in Venetian style follow through in rooms appointed with Barovier & Toso chandeliers, coordinated draperies and bedspreads, and painted antiques with a floral motif. Many amenities are offered including air conditioning. Renovation of all bathrooms included the installation of Jacuzzi and steam baths. Roberto is an experienced and amiable host with a definite aim to please guests. *Directions:* Take waterbus No. 82 to the San Samuele stop or No. 1 to the Accademia stop. Pass over the bridge and go straight into Campo Santo Stefano.

HOTEL SANTO STEFANO
Host: Roberto Quatrini
San Marco 2957
Venice 30124, Italy
Tel: (041) 5200166, Fax: (041) 5224460
11 rooms, Double: €170–€350
Open: all year, Credit cards: all major
Other languages: good English
Region: Veneto, Michelin Map: 429
www.karenbrown.com/italy/hotelsantostefano.html

Just 20 kilometers from the Swiss border, halfway along the shore of Lake Maggiore, at the point where the road curves back down to Verbania, is a farmhouse situated high above the lake (700 meters). It commands a 360-degree view that includes the Alps and Lakes Mergozzo, Monate, Varese, and Maggiore with its miniature Borromeo Islands (accessible by ferryboat). A 5-kilometer long road with many hairpin turns winds its way up to the turn-of-the-last-century house with tower. Energetic and friendly hostess Iside Minotti and her family run the inn and rustic restaurant, which is a busy spot and can get noisy in the summer when locals come up to dine or celebrate an event and take advantage of the cooler air and the spectacular view. Menu ingredients come directly from the vegetable garden and orchards to the kitchen, where sumptuous local specialties are prepared. The 25-acre farm includes riding stables, and the bed and breakfast can also arrange helicopter rides from the property for a breathtakingly scenic tour over the lake, boat excursions, and mountain bike rentals. Nine very basic no-frills bedrooms come in various combinations of twins, triples, and quads, each with a snug shower room. *Directions:* On the outskirts of Verbania, at a major road junction with traffic lights (Pallanza), take Via Azari (also signposted Trobaso) left for 1 km. Go sharp left at the signpost for Monterosso and up 5 km of winding road (I counted 43 hairpin bends).

IL MONTEROSSO
Host: Iside Minotti
Cima Monterosso-C.P. 13
Verbania (NO) 28922, Italy
Tel: (0323) 556510 or 551578, Cellphone: (335) 6442859
Fax: (0323) 519706
9 rooms, Double: €52–€62, Per person half board: €42
Open: all year, Credit cards: MC, VS
Other languages: some English
Region: Piedmont, Michelin Map: 428
www.karenbrown.com/italy/ilmonterosso.html

For years Andrea and Silvia have literally opened their entire home to guests, welcoming and rewelcoming "friends of La Volpaia," their bed and breakfast. International guests gather together in the evenings out on the patio or in the converted barn for one of Silvia's delightful meals based on fresh vegetables and meats enhanced with their own extra-virgin olive oil. Conversation is never lacking with meals accompanied by La Volpaia's own Chianti (all beverages are included in the half-board rate). Andrea, a native Roman architect and sculptor, bought the wine estate with its 16th-century farmhouse 19 years ago and his pieces in olive wood are displayed in and about the property. The five cozy bedrooms are appointed with antiques, as is the large living room with fireplace. Beyond the patio where meals are served is the spectacular swimming pool with its heavenly views of what can only be described as a truly classic Tuscan landscape. Horses, personally trained by the hosts, are available for excursions into the surrounding countryside (experienced riders only). Guests are made to feel immediately right at home in this informal setting and so it is no wonder that many become "regulars" to this idyllic spot so close to the highlights of Tuscany. *Directions:* From the town of Vico d'Elsa follow Via della Villa (on the right) for 2 km, turning left at the wooden signpost for La Volpaia.

LA VOLPAIA
Hosts: Silvia & Andrea Taliaco
Strada di Vico 5-9, Vico d'Elsa (FI) 50050, Italy
Tel: (055) 8073063, Cellphone: (368) 248287
Fax: (055) 8073170
5 rooms, Double: €216*
*Includes breakfast & dinner
Minimum nights required: 3
Open: all year, Other languages: good English
Region: Tuscany, Michelin Map: 430
www.karenbrown.com/italy/lavolpaia.html

Situated on Monte Faito between the Amalfi coast and Sorrento, Villa Giusso, a unique bed and breakfast, was a 15th-century monastery for cloistered monks. A long, very narrow road takes you up to the isolated, stone-walled property whose entrance is marked by an arched gateway with watchtower leading into a park. From there you have an enthralling view over Sorrento, the gulf, and Naples. The monastery itself is surrounded by a high stone wall within which is found a grass courtyard and ancient well still in use. The Giusso family has owned this beloved property for the past 200 years and siblings Onorina, Giovanna, Micaela, and Tullio's strong intention is to continue the restoration process while preserving its monastic features. A long corridor leads to a suite with two bedrooms and a bathroom and three double bedrooms, appointed with worn period furniture and huge paintings. Breakfast with local fresh ricotta, figs in season, and homemade cakes is served in the original kitchen completely tiled with 17th-century Vietri ceramics. Though not for everyone, Villa Giusso is fascinating and offers the visitor a unique slice of Italian history. Almost like staying in a museum. *Directions:* Exit at Castellammare from the A3, following signs for Sorrento. Drive to Seiano and just after Moon Valley Hotel take a left at the sign for Monte Faito. Drive to the Arola sign (4.6 km) and go first right up the narrow dirt road to the monastery.

VILLA GIUSSO
Host: Giusso Rispoli family
Localita: Arola, Via Camaldoli 51
Vico Equense (NA) 80069, Italy
Tel: (081) 8024392 or 403797, Fax: (081) 403797
5 rooms, Double: €80–€95
Minimum nights required: 3
Open: Apr to Oct 30
Other languages: good English
Region: Campania, Michelin Map: 431
www.karenbrown.com/italy/giusso.html

Villa Verucchio is a small commercial area just inland from the famous beaches of Rimini, the summer playground of young Italians attracted by its nightlife and budget rates. The Tenuta Amalia is a vast property owned by the Savazzi family, divided up into several different businesses, each run individually. Case Rosse is the red farmhouse transformed into a pleasant little bed and breakfast and there are also three different restaurants, vineyards, and a 27-hole golf course created around the family's 18th-century villa. Although it is a bit confusing at first, the bed and breakfast is right on the road leading to the golf club entrance. Lucia Gatei welcomes guests to the rustic farmhouse, which offers four double bedrooms upstairs and two on the ground floor. Each is appointed individually with country antiques and yellow bedspreads. A separate three-bedroom house nearby offers accommodation for six persons. Breakfast is served either out on the covered porch or in the beamed breakfast room overlooking a small garden and there is a cozy living room with large stone fireplace. From here you have easy access to the beautiful countryside bordering the Marches with such highlights as the independent state of San Marino, San Leo, Santarcangelo, and Urbino. *Directions:* From Rimini take the S.S.258 for 12 km to Villa Verucchio and watch for a sign on the right to the Amalia.

TENUTA AMALIA/AGRITURISMO LE CASE ROSSE
Host: Lucia Gatei
Via Tenuta Amalia 141
Villa Verucchio (RN) 47040, Italy
Tel: (0541) 678123, Fax: (0541) 678876
6 rooms, Double: €62–€72
1 house: €500–€620 weekly
Open: all year, Credit cards: all major
Other languages: very little English
Region: Emilia-Romangna, Michelin Map: 429
www.karenbrown.com/italy/amalia.html

On the northern outskirts of the beautiful city of Treviso is a busy farm that was once a convent. The long building has been made into several residences, one belonging to the two Milani brothers, where a restaurant and six bedrooms have been fashioned for guests. All of the bedrooms have private baths, and their decor is very much in keeping with the simple country style of the farm. Typical Venetian antiques enhance the rooms, which also feature homey touches such as white lace curtains and soft floral armchairs. Guests can observe wine production on the farm and are also welcome to take horses out on excursions, or take riding lessons if desired. The popular restaurant prides itself on serving local specialties prepared with the farm's fresh produce and game. The restaurant with its large, open central hearth is a welcoming gathering spot, decorated with lots of pictures, brass pots, pink tablecloths, and fresh flowers. Although the immediate surrounding flat countryside is not the most inspiring, this a great base for visiting Venice, Padua, Vianza, and Verona. *Directions:* From Venice (34 km away), take route N13 through Treviso, and on toward Villorba, turning left at the sign for Podere del Convento Alternatively, exit at Treviso Nord from the A27.

PODERE DEL CONVENTO
Host: Renzo Milani
Via IV Novembre 16
Villorba (TV) 31050, Italy
Tel: (0422) 920044, Fax: (0422) 444783
6 rooms, Double: €64
Closed: Aug, Credit cards: AX, VS
Other languages: none
Region: Veneto, Michelin Map: 429
www.karenbrown.com/italy/podere.html

Viterbo, along with the surrounding area called Tuscia, is rich in Etruscan history and offers a variety of attractions including ancient villages, thermal baths, and small lakes, all within easy reach of Rome. Cordial hostess Giovanna offers guest accommodation within three rooms in a private section of the family's large 14th-century home. This was originally a retreat for the monks of the nearby monastery, which lends its name to the street where this bed and breakfast is located: Santa Maria di Gradi. Once a countryside estate, Citerno is now surrounded by the city and neighboring properties, though it does maintain a large front garden. The well-decorated wallpapered rooms have antique furnishings, wood floors, and new bathrooms, with one room having an adjoining room for two extra persons. These rooms have an independent entrance, which leads directly into the sitting/breakfast room divided by a large brick arch. Giovanna's sister has a delightful restaurant, Il Richiastro, right in the medieval section of Viterbo, which features old recipes from other eras, serving homemade pastas and hearty soups in a casual setting. (Open from Thursday to Sunday lunch only and closed in July and August.) *Directions:* On the west side of the ancient walls encircling the city of Viterbo is the Porta Romana. Via S. Maria di Gradi begins at this gate, leading to the city heading directly east. After .5 km turn into the driveway at number 70.

CITERNO
Host: Giovanna Scappucci
Via S. Maria di Gradi 70
Viterbo 01100, Italy
Tel: (0761) 220500, Cellphone: (348) 6961731
Fax: (0761) 290149
3 rooms, Double: €62–€72
Closed: Jul & Aug
Other languages: some English
Region: Lazio, Michelin Map: 430
www.karenbrown.com/italy/citerno.html

Ninni Bacchi has done wonders in transforming her family's 300-acre tobacco and grain farm (just on the outskirts of the city) into a very comfortable bed and breakfast in an area that was once the heart of the Etruscan civilization. The Rinaldone is run more like a hotel than a bed and breakfast—arriving guests are warmly received in the luminous, open living room furnished with antiques surrounding a grand fireplace. On hand for guests at reception is cordial manager Farid. Downstairs is the large, arcaded restaurant dating back to the 15th century, where guests can enjoy the typical cuisine of the Lazio region or dine outdoors by the pool. The five bedrooms off the courtyard in the main house have the most character with architectural features intact, while the other five rooms and ten suites are lined up in two cottage-like wings, and are more spacious and modern in decor. A nice job has been done with the landscaping, pleasingly distracting the eye from the rather bland, flat countryside and encroaching commercial area hereabouts. Tennis, biking, and horse riding, plus the nearby thermal spa are some of the activities available as well as visits to ancient Viterbo and the gardens of Villa Lanti. Orvieto is 38 km away. *Directions:* From Rome (120 km away) follow signs for Viterbo. Take the Cassia road north of Viterbo for 3 km toward Montefiascone, turning right at the Rinaldone sign.

COUNTRY HOTEL RINALDONE
Host: Ninni Bacchi
Strada Rinaldone, 9-S.S. Cassia km 86
Viterbo 01100, Italy
Tel: (0761) 352137, Fax: (0761) 353116
20 rooms, Double: €95–€105
Minimum nights required: 2
Open: Apr to Dec, Credit cards: MC, VS
Other languages: some English
Region: Lazio, Michelin Map: 430
www.karenbrown.com/italy/residencerinaldone.html

The northern part of the Lazio region holds many intriguing treasures to explore. Besides being less than an hour from Rome, it is the center of Etruscan history, with lakes, nearby seaside, thermal baths, and lovely gardens. Just down the street from the delightful Renaissance gardens of Villa Lante in Bagnaia is the gracious Villa Farinella, a very pleasant bed and breakfast within the 18th-century home of Maurizio and his family. Rita, his mother, lives in a restored farmhouse on the property and has passed her grandfather's ancient home down to her son. In order to revive the home to its original splendor, the bed and breakfast solution was a perfect one. The first floor is entirely dedicated to guests, with four cozy bedrooms entering into one of two spacious living/dining rooms appointed with original antiques and elegant chandeliers. Each quaint bedroom with new bathroom has its own floral theme, which is followed through in color scheme, wallpaper, bedspreads, and curtains. One particularly large room has frescoed vaulted ceilings. On the ground floor, for longer stays, a two-bedroom apartment with kitchen opens out to the garden. You will be delighted with the warm hospitality, historic surroundings, and very reasonable rate. *Directions:* From Viterbo drive towards Bagnaia (directly east) on Viale Trieste to the suburb of La Quercia. Just after the AGIP station turn left on Via Capodistria past houses to the end of the lane.

VILLA FARINELLA
Hosts: Maurizio Makovec & family
Localita: La Quercia, Via Capodistria 14
Viterbo 01100, Italy
Tel & fax: (0761) 304784 or 344253
Cellphone: (339) 3655617
4 rooms, Double: €70–€80, 1 apartment: €500–€700 weekly
Open: all year
Other languages: French, good English
Region: Lazio, Michelin Map: 430
www.karenbrown.com/italy/farinella.html

Key Map

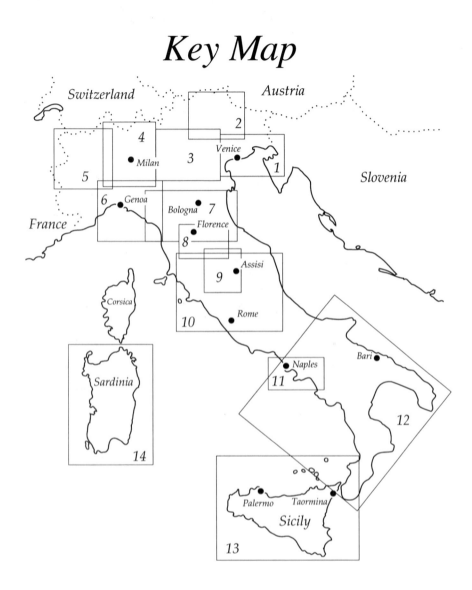

Map 1

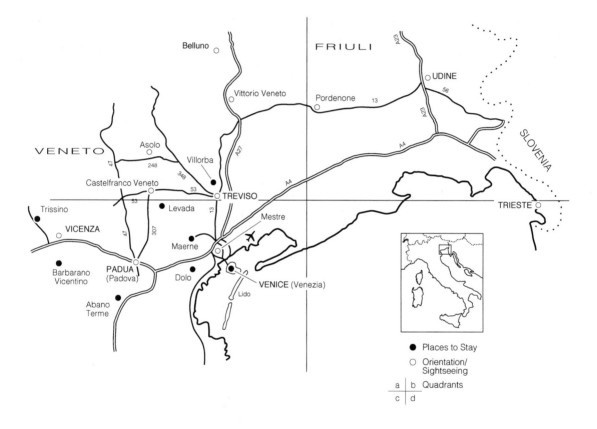

Belluno

Vittorio Veneto

FRIULI

UDINE

Pordenone 13

A23

56

A23

SLOVENIA

VENETO

Asolo

248

47

348

Villorba

A27

A4

A4

Castelfranco Veneto

53

53

Levada

13

TREVISO

Mestre

Trissino

VICENZA

47

307

Maerne

Barbarano
Vicentino

PADUA
(Padova)

Dolo

VENICE (Venezia)

Lido

Abano
Terme

TRIESTE

● Places to Stay
○ Orientation/
   Sightseeing

| a | b | Quadrants |
| c | d | |

Map 2

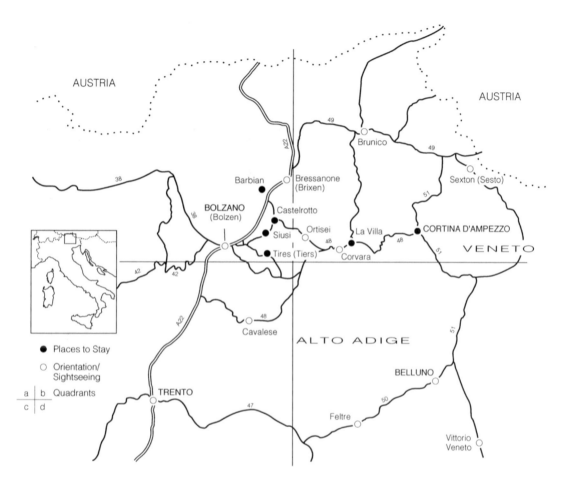

AUSTRIA

AUSTRIA

49

Brunico

49

38

Barbian

Bressanone
(Brixen)

Sexton (Sesto)

51

BOLZANO
(Bolzen)

Castelrotto

38

Ortisei

La Villa

CORTINA D'AMPEZZO

Siusi

48

48

VENETO

Tires (Tiers)

Corvara

51

A22

42

48

Cavalese

ALTO ADIGE

51

BELLUNO

● Places to Stay

○ Orientation/
   Sightseeing

| a | b | Quadrants
|---|---|
| c | d |

A22

TRENTO

47

50

Vittorio
Veneto

Feltre

305

Map 3

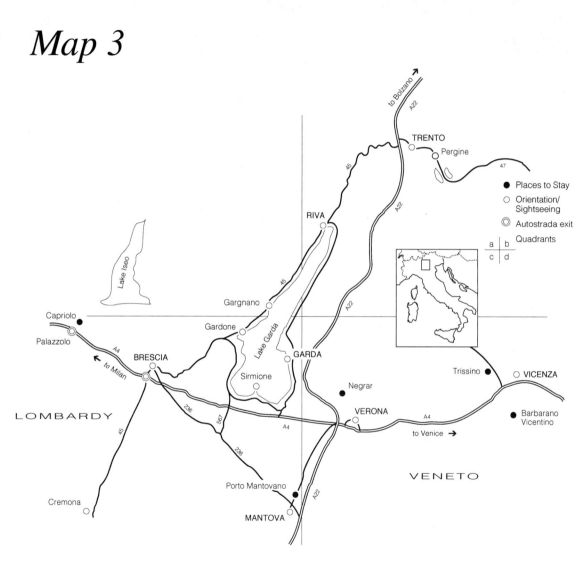

to Bolzano
A22

TRENTO ○
Pergine ○

47

● Places to Stay
○ Orientation/
   Sightseeing
◎ Autostrada exit
   Quadrants

a	b
c	d

45

A22

RIVA ○

A22

Lake Iseo

45

Gargnano ○

Gardone ○

Capriolo ●
Palazzolo ◎

A4
to Milan

Lake Garda

GARDA ○

Trissino ●   ○ VICENZA

BRESCIA ○

Sirmione ○

Negrar ●

LOMBARDY

236

567

VERONA ○

A4   to Venice →

Barbarano
Vicentino ●

45

236

A4

VENETO

Cremona ○

Porto Mantovano ●

A22

MANTOVA

Map 4

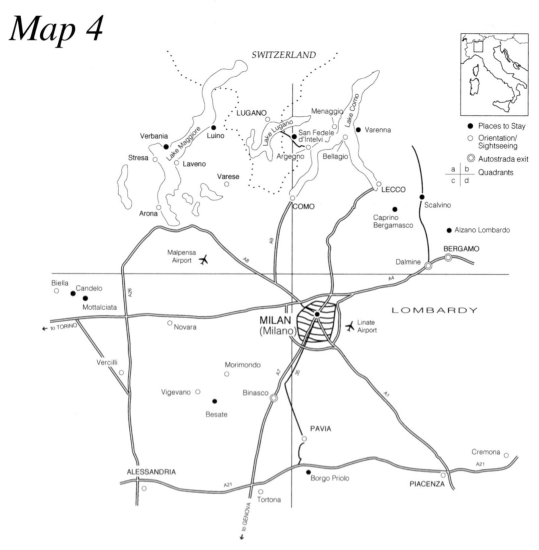

SWITZERLAND

LUGANO

Menaggio

Lake Como

Verbania

Luino

Lake Lugano

San Fedele
d'Intelvi

Varenna

Stresa

Laveno

Argegno

Bellagio

Lake Maggiore

Varese

LECCO

Scalvino

Arona

COMO

Caprino
Bergamasco

Alzano Lombardo

● Places to Stay

○ Orientation/
Sightseeing

◎ Autostrada exit

a	b
c	d

Quadrants

Malpensa
Airport ✈

A8

A9

BERGAMO

Dalmine

Biella

Candelo

Mottalciata

A26

A4

LOMBARDY

← to TORINO

Novara

MILAN
(Milano)

✈ Linate
Airport

Vercilli

Morimondo

A7

35

Vigevano

Binasco

A1

Besate

PAVIA

Cremona

ALESSANDRIA

A21

Borgo Priolo

PIACENZA

A21

Tortona

↓ to GENOVA

307

Map 5

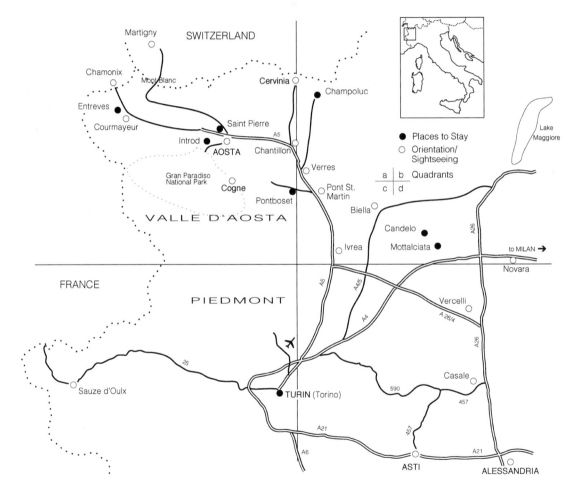

Martigny

SWITZERLAND

Chamonix

Mont Blanc

Cervinia

Champoluc

Entreves

Courmayeur

Saint Pierre

Introd

AOSTA

Chantillon

A5

Gran Paradiso
National Park

Cogne

Pontboset

Verres

Pont St.
Martin

Biella

VALLE D'AOSTA

Candelo

Mottalciata

Ivrea

FRANCE

PIEDMONT

A5

A4/5

A4

Vercelli

A 26/4

A26

Novara

to MILAN →

Lake
Maggiore

● Places to Stay

○ Orientation/
Sightseeing

a	b
c	d

Quadrants

25

Sauze d'Oulx

TURIN (Torino)

590

Casale

457

A21

A6

A21

A26

ASTI

ALESSANDRIA

Map 6

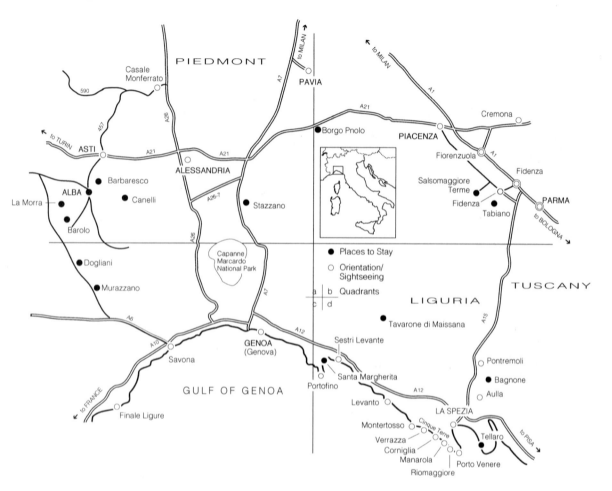

PIEDMONT

to MILAN

Casale Monferrato

590

457

A26

to TURIN

ASTI

A21

A21

ALESSANDRIA

Barbaresco

ALBA

La Morra

Canelli

Barolo

A26-7

Stazzano

A26

Capanne Marcardo National Park

Dogliani

Murazzano

A7

A6

A10

Savona

GENOA (Genova)

A12

Sestri Levante

Portofino

Santa Margherita

GULF OF GENOA

to FRANCE

Finale Ligure

Levante

Montertosso

Verrazza

Corniglia

Manarola

Riomaggiore

Cinque Terre

LIGURIA

Tavarone di Maissana

A12

PAVIA

A7

A21

Borgo Pnolo

PIACENZA

A1

Cremona

Fiorenzuola

A1

Fidenza

Salsomaggiore Terme

Fidenza

Tabiano

PARMA

to BOLOGNA

● Places to Stay

○ Orientation/ Sightseeing

| a | b |
| c | d |

Quadrants

TUSCANY

A15

Pontremoli

Bagnone

Aulla

LA SPEZIA

Tellaro

Porto Venere

to PISA

309

Map 7

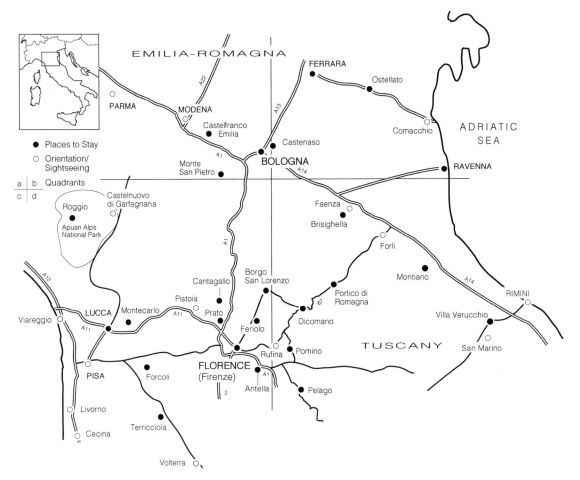

EMILIA-ROMAGNA

FERRARA

Ostellato

Comacchio

ADRIATIC
SEA

PARMA

MODENA

Castelfranco
Emilia

Castenaso

BOLOGNA

RAVENNA

● Places to Stay

○ Orientation/
   Sightseeing

a	b
c	d

Quadrants

Monte
San Pietro

Castelnuovo
di Garfagnana

Faenza

Brisighella

Roggio

Apuan Alps
National Park

Forlì

Montiano

RIMINI

Cantagallo

Borgo
San Lorenzo

Pistoia

Portico di
Romagna

Villa Verucchio

Lucca

Montecarlo

Prato

Viareggio

Feriolo

Dicomano

TUSCANY

San Marino

Pomino

Rufina

PISA

Forcoli

FLORENCE
(Firenze)

Antella

Pelago

Livorno

Terricciola

Cecina

Volterra

310

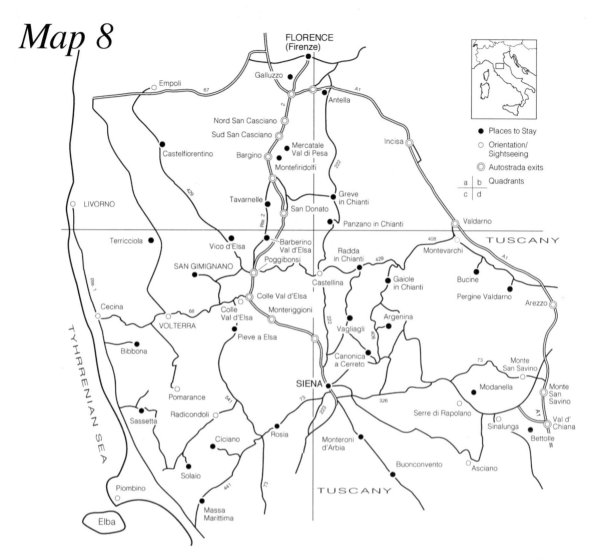

Map 8

FLORENCE
(Firenze)

Empoli
67
Galluzzo
Antella
2
Nord San Casciano
Sud San Casciano
Incisa
Castelfiorentino
Mercatale
Val di Pesa
222
Bargino
Montefiridolfi
439
Greve
in Chianti
Tavarnelle
San Donato
LIVORNO
Panzano in Chianti
Valdarno
Terricciola
Vico d'Elsa
Barberino
Val d'Elsa
TUSCANY
408
Poggibonsi
Montevarchi
A1
Radda
in Chianti
SAN GIMIGNANO
429
Bucine
SS 1
Castellina
Gaiole
in Chianti
Colle Val d'Elsa
Pergine Valdarno
Cecina
68
Colle
Val d'Elsa
Monteriggioni
Arezzo
VOLTERRA
222
Pieve a Elsa
Argenina
Bibbona
Vagliagli
408
73
Monte
San Savino
Pomarance
Canonica
a Cerreto
SS 1
Modanella
Monte
San
Savino
Sassetta
Radicondoli
SIENA
Serre di Rapolano
A1
Solaio
541
73
326
Sinalunga
Val d'
Chiana
Ciciano
Rosia
223
Bettolle
Monteroni
d'Arbia
Piombino
Buonconvento
Asciano
Elba
441
f2
Massa
Marittima
TUSCANY

TYHRRENIAN SEA

● Places to Stay
○ Orientation/
   Sightseeing
◎ Autostrada exits
| a | b |
| c | d |
Quadrants

Map 9

← to Florence

TUSCANY

Caprese
Michelangelo

○ URBINO

73

Urbania

Sansepolcro

○ Fossombrone

3

○ AREZZO

Citta del Castello

GUBBIO

Monte
Savino

73

326

SIENA

S. Caterina
(di Cortona)

CORTONA

Umbertide

3

UMBRIA

Lisciano Niccone

Mengara

Val
di Chiana

15

Tuoro Sul Trasimeno

3

Lucignano
d'Asso

Ponte Pattoli

Pianello

San Quirico

Lake
Trasimeno

15

PERUGIA —

ASSISI

Montalcino

Pienza

Panicale

Castel
del Piano
Umbro

3

Spello

Montepulciano

Chiusi

Tavernelle di
Panicale

Macciano

Paciano

220

Bettona

Foligno

Sarteano

Citta della
Pieve

Deruta

Radicofani

Monteleone

Montecastello
di Vibio

Trevi

San Casciano
dei Bagni

Fabro

San
Venanzo

Bovara di Trevi

Ficulle

Ospedaletto

Loreto

Poreta

Allerona

Proceno

2

Orvieto
exit

TODI

SPOLETO

Acquapendente

ORVIETO

Titignano

Grotte
di Castro

Bolsena

Baschi

Lake Corbara

3

TERNI

Lake
Bolsena

to Rome ↓

Amelia

● Places to Stay

○ Orientation/
Sightseeing

◎ Autostrada exits

a	b	Quadrants
c	d	

Narni

Stroncone

Orte

Orte exit

312

Map 10

PESARO

A14

Conero
National Park

Scapezzano
di Senigallia

MARCHES

ANCONA

Gagliole · Jesi · Portonovo

Massignano · Sirolo

Fabriano · Osimo · LORETO

UMBRIA

ASSISI

Castelraimondo · Macerarta · Recanati

Porto S. Giorgio

Fermo · Marina Palmense

Montefiore dell'Aso

PERUGIA

Grottammare

TUSCANY

SIENA

Rosia

Ciciano

Sinalunga

Montalcino

S. Angelo in Colle

Poggi del Sasso

Campagnatico

Caldana

GROSSETO

Scansano

Montemerano

Saturnia

Orbetello

TODI

Trevi

Bovara di Trevi

Poreta

SPOLETO

Ascoli
Piceno

Teramo

Orvieto

Civitella
d'Agliano

Orte

Terni

RIETI

A24

Pescara

Roccatederighi

73

223

E1

7A

Capalbio

Porto Ercole

Otricoli

Tuscania

Calvi dell' Umbria

Montasola

Loreto Aprutino

L'Aquila

Pianella

Chieti

A1

VITERBO

Tarquinia

Trevignano

Selci

Casperia

Poggio Nativo

313

3

A7

3

3

ABRUZZO

Lake
Bracciano

CIVITAVECCHIA

Bracciano

Ladispoli

Leonardo da Vinci Airport

ROME
(Roma)

LAZIO

A1

A24

A25

E1/A2

E1

FIUMICINO

OSTIA

Frascati

148

ADRIATIC
SEA

● Places to Stay

○ Orientation/
    Sightseeing

a | b   Quadrants
c | d

TYHRRENIAN SEA

Map 11

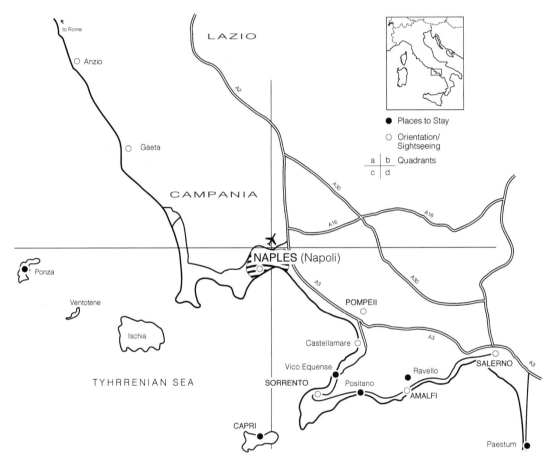

to Rome

LAZIO

○ Anzio

○ Gaeta

CAMPANIA

A2

A30

A16

A16

● Places to Stay

○ Orientation/
Sightseeing

| a | b | Quadrants |
| c | d | |

NAPLES (Napoli)

A3

POMPEII
○

A30

A16

Ponza ●

Ventotene

Ischia

TYHRRENIAN SEA

Castellamare ○

A3

SALERNO ○

A3

Vico Equense
●

Ravello
●

SORRENTO

Positano
○

AMALFI
●

CAPRI
●

Paestum ●

Map 12

Map 13

Sicily

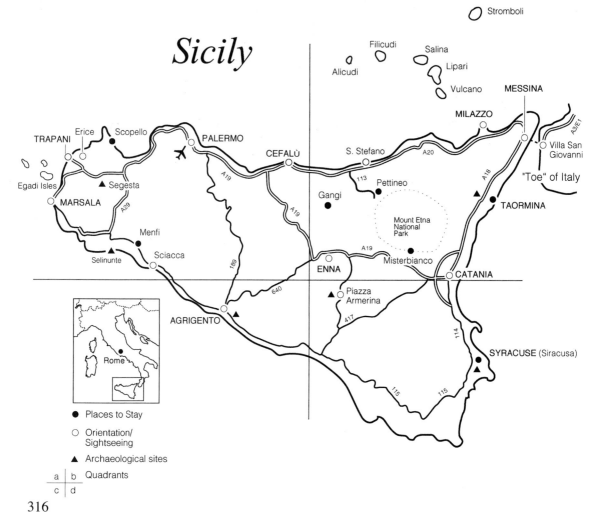

Stromboli

Filicudi

Salina

Alicudi

Lipari

Vulcano

MESSINA

MILAZZO

Erice   Scopello

TRAPANI

PALERMO

CEFALÙ

S. Stefano   A20

Villa San
Giovanni

Egadi Isles

▲ Segesta

113   Pettineo

"Toe" of Italy

MARSALA

A19   A19

Gangi

A18   TAORMINA

A29

Mount Etna
National
Park

Menfi

A19

▲ Selinunte   Sciacca

ENNA   Misterbianco

CATANIA

189   640

▲ Piazza
Armerina

AGRIGENTO   ▲

417   114

Rome

115   SYRACUSE (Siracusa)
▲

115   115

● Places to Stay

○ Orientation/
  Sightseeing

▲ Archaeological sites

a	b
c	d

Quadrants

316

Map 14

Sardinia

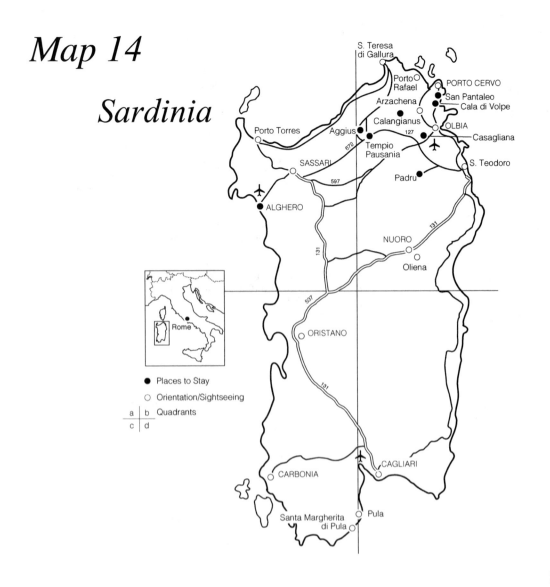

S. Teresa
di Gallura

Porto
Rafael

PORTO CERVO

San Pantaleo

Arzachena

Cala di Volpe

Calangianus

Porto Torres

Aggius

OLBIA

127

Casagliana

Tempio
Pausania

572

SASSARI

597

Padru

S. Teodoro

ALGHERO

131

NUORO

Oliena

131

537

ORISTANO

131

CAGLIARI

Rome

CARBONIA

● Places to Stay

○ Orientation/Sightseeing

a	b
c	d

Quadrants

Santa Margherita
di Pula

Pula

317

Index

auto ☎ europe.

Karen Brown's

Preferred Provider of

Car Rental Services in Europe

International Car Rental Services

Chauffeur & Transfer Services

Prestige & Sports Cars

800-223-5555

Be sure to identify yourself as a Karen Brown Traveler
For special offers and discounts use your

Karen Brown ID number 99006187

Make reservations online via our website, *www.karenbrown.com*
Click "Auto Rentals" on our home page or call 800-223-5555

destination ∂ europe

Karen Brown's

Preferred Provider of

Discount Air Travel to Europe

Coach- and Business-Class Tickets

Regularly Scheduled Flights on Major International Carriers
Service to 200 Gateway Destination Cities

Additional 5% off Published Fares in 2003
for Karen Brown Travelers

800-223-5555

Be sure to identify yourself as a Karen Brown Traveler
For special offers and discounts use your

Karen Brown ID number 99006187

Make reservations online via our website, *www.karenbrown.com*
Click "Discount Airfares" on our home page or call 800-223-5555

Any of the accommodations in this guide can be reserved through author Nicole Franchini's travel service for independent travelers, **Hidden Treasures of Italy.**

Together with your accommodation reservations, **Hidden Treasures** can also provide additional services such as:

~ *Individual itinerary recommendations (trains / car rentals / chauffeured transfers)*   ~ *Ground transportation arrangements*   ~ *Private guides / museum and concert tickets*   ~ *Special interest activities (food and wine tours / cooking classes / golf programs / organized dinners in private historical villas / private garden visits / chartered sailing itineraries to islands / and many others).*

Hidden Treasures *also represents a unique "Limited Collection" of personally selected villas available for unforgettable vacations, special events, family reunions, weddings, or other personalized programs.*

Service fees apply.

HIDDEN TREASURES OF ITALY, INC.
665 West Sheridan Road
Chicago, IL 60613
U.S. Toll Free Tel: (888) 419-6700

U.S. Tel: (773) 871-0500
Fax: (773) 871-2970
e-mail: info@htitaly.com
Web Site: www.htitaly.com

Hidden Treasures of Italy

also Specializes in Complete On-Site Wedding / Honeymoon Planning.

Personalized consultation and arrangements for civil or religious wedding ceremonies and reception in the city of your choice. Complete local organization of all legal, administrative, and logistical details to help make your wedding in Italy truly memorable and hassle-free.

From a private romantic ceremony for two, to a complete traditional wedding package in any of the most enchanting historical sites Italy has to offer.

__Hidden Treasures__ can also assist in organizing customized trips for groups of friends, extended family, or business associates.

Whether for a once in a lifetime family occasion, or as a special incentive for your best employees, __Hidden Treasures__ provides the highest expression of quality, service, and hospitality in the most charming locations throughout all of Italy.

HIDDEN TREASURES OF ITALY

www.btitaly.com

Enhance your Guides—Visit us Online

www.karenbrown.com

- Hotel specials
- Color photos of hotels and B&Bs
- 20% online discount for book purchases
- Discount airfare, both business and coach class
- Direct links to individual property websites and e-mails
- Up-to-the-minute phone, fax, and e-mail information
- Rental cars, travel planning, trip insurance, itineraries, maps, and more

Become a Member of the Karen Brown Club

- Additional specials and offers from our travel partners
- Exclusive access to "new discoveries" from our current research
- An additional 20% savings on purchases from our online store

A complete listing of member benefits can be found on our website

Don't delay, join online today!

www.karenbrown.com

Travel Your Dreams • Order Your Karen Brown Guides Today

Please ask in your local bookstore for Karen Brown's Guides. If the books you want are unavailable, you may order directly from the publisher. Books will be shipped immediately.

_____ *Austria: Charming Inns & Itineraries* $19.95

_____ *California: Charming Inns & Itineraries* $19.95

_____ *England: Charming Bed & Breakfasts* $18.95

_____ *England, Wales & Scotland: Charming Hotels & Itineraries* $19.95

_____ *France: Charming Bed & Breakfasts* $18.95

_____ *France: Charming Inns & Itineraries* $19.95

_____ *Germany: Charming Inns & Itineraries* $19.95

_____ *Ireland: Charming Inns & Itineraries* $19.95

_____ *Italy: Charming Bed & Breakfasts* $18.95

_____ *Italy: Charming Inns & Itineraries* $19.95

_____ *Mexico: Charming Inns & Itineraries* $19.95

_____ *Mid-Atlantic: Charming Inns & Itineraries* $19.95

_____ *New England: Charming Inns & Itineraries* $19.95

_____ *Pacific Northwest: Charming Inns & Itineraries* $19.95

_____ *Portugal: Charming Inns & Itineraries* $19.95

_____ *Spain: Charming Inns & Itineraries* $19.95

_____ *Switzerland: Charming Inns & Itineraries* $19.95

Name _____ Street _____

Town _____ State_____ Zip _____ Tel _____

Credit Card (MasterCard or Visa) _____ Expires: _____

For orders in the USA, add $5 for the first book and $2 for each additional book for shipment. Overseas shipping (airmail) is $10 for 1 to 2 books, $20 for 3 to 4 books etc. CA residents add 8.25% sales tax. Fax or mail form with check or credit card information to:

KAREN BROWN'S GUIDES
Post Office Box 70 • San Mateo • California • 94401 • USA
tel: (650) 342-9117, fax: (650) 342-9153, e-mail: karen@karenbrown.com, www.karenbrown.com

Seal Cove Inn

Located in the San Francisco Bay Area

Karen Brown Herbert (best known as author of Karen Brown's Guides) and her husband, Rick, have put 23 years of experience into reality and opened their own superb hideaway, Seal Cove Inn. Spectacularly set amongst wildflowers and bordered by towering cypress trees, Seal Cove Inn looks out to the distant ocean over acres of county park: an oasis where you can enjoy secluded beaches, explore tide-pools, watch frolicking seals, and follow the tree-lined path that traces the windswept ocean bluffs. Country antiques, original watercolors, flower-laden cradles, rich fabrics, and the gentle ticking of grandfather clocks create the perfect ambiance for a foggy day in front of the crackling log fire. Each bedroom is its own haven with a cozy sitting area before a wood-burning fireplace and doors opening onto a private balcony or patio with views to the park and ocean. Moss Beach is a 35-minute drive south of San Francisco, 6 miles north of the picturesque town of Half Moon Bay, and a few minutes from Princeton harbor with its colorful fishing boats and restaurants. Seal Cove Inn makes a perfect base for whale watching, salmon-fishing excursions, day trips to San Francisco, exploring the coast, or, best of all, just a romantic interlude by the sea, time to relax and be pampered. Karen and Rick look forward to the pleasure of welcoming you to their coastal hideaway.

*Seal Cove Inn • 221 Cypress Avenue • Moss Beach • California • 94038 • USA
tel: (650) 728-4114, fax: (650) 728-4116, website: www.sealcoveinn.com*

NICOLE FRANCHINI, author of *Italy: Charming Bed & Breakfasts,* was born in Chicago and raised in a bilingual family, her father being Italian. She received a B.A. degree in languages from William Smith College and the Sorbonne, Paris, and has been residing in Italy for the past 17 years. Currently living in the countryside of Sabina near Rome with husband, Carlo, and daughters, Livia and Sabina, she runs her own travel consulting business, Hidden Treasures of Italy, which organizes personalized group and individual itineraries.

ELISABETTA FRANCHINI, the talented artist responsible for the illustrations in *Italy: Charming Bed & Breakfasts*, lives in her hometown of Chicago with her husband, Chris, and their two young children, where she paints predominantly European landscapes and architectural scenes. On her annual trip to Italy she enjoys accompanying her sister, Nicole, on her travel research. A Smith College graduate in Art History and French Literature, Elisabetta has exhibited extensively in the Chicago area for the past 20 years, and has had extremely well-received shows in Miami, New York, and San Francisco.

JANN POLLARD, the artist responsible for the beautiful painting on the cover of this guide, has studied art since childhood, and is well known for her outstanding impressionistic-style watercolors, which she has exhibited in numerous juried shows, winning many awards. Jann travels frequently to Europe (using Karen Brown's Guides) where she loves to paint historical buildings. Jann's original paintings are represented through The Gallery, Burlingame, CA, 650-347-9392 or *www.thegalleryart.net.* Fine-art giclée prints of the cover paintings are also available at *www.karenbrown.com.*

Icons Key

This year we have introduced the icons listed below in the guidebooks and on our website (*www.karenbrown.com*). These allow us to provide additional information about our recommended properties. When using our website to supplement the guides, placing the cursor over an icon will in many cases give you further details.

Air conditioning in rooms

Breakfast included in room rate

Children welcome

Cooking classes offered

Credit cards accepted

Dinner served upon request

Direct-dial telephone in room

Dogs by special request

Elevator

Exercise room

Mini-refrigerator in room

Non-smoking rooms

Parking available

Restaurant

Swimming pool

Tennis

Television

Wedding facilities

Wheelchair friendly

Golf course nearby

Hiking trails nearby

Horseback riding nearby

Skiing nearby

Water sports nearby

Wineries nearby